This is a detailed account of the theatrical fortunes of *A Midsummer Night's Dream* on the British stage, from the 1590s to the 1990s. The substantial, illustrated introduction traces the rise of the play from theatrical neglect in the eighteenth century through the spectacular productions of the nineteenth century to its current high status.

The authoritative New Cambridge Shakespeare text of the play is accompanied by detailed notes on actors' interpretations, settings and textual alterations. The author considers the cultural changes which have affected the play's popularity, 'Athenian' and 'Elizabethan' stagings, as well as the conceptions of individual directors from David Garrick and George Colman, via Madame Vestris and Beerbohm Tree, Granville Barker and W. Bridges Adams to Peter Brook, Robert Lepage and Adrian Noble. An appendix lists the musical contributions, especially Mendelssohn's, to particular productions.

The book shows theatre history as cultural history. It will be invaluable to students of Shakespeare in performance and to those intrigued by the changing reputation of Shakespeare.

SHAKESPEARE IN PRODUCTION

A MIDSUMMER NIGHT'S DREAM

SHAKESPEARE IN PRODUCTION

SERIES EDITORS: J.S. BRATTON AND JULIE HANKEY

This series offers students and researchers from A level Theatre Arts to postgraduate dissertation the fullest possible stage histories of individual Shakespearean texts.

In each volume a substantial introduction presents a conceptual overview of the play, marking out the major stages of its representation and reception. In this context, no single approach to the play can be described as more 'authentic' than any other. The extrapolations of Tate, the interpretations of Dryden, the upholstering of Charles Kean and the strippings-down of Marowitz are all treated as ways of reading and rewriting Shakespeare's text and understood in terms of contemporary audiences, tastes and sensibilities.

The commentary, presented alongside the New Cambridge edition of the text itself, offers detailed, line-by-line evidence for the overview presented in the introduction, making the volume a flexible tool for further research. The editors have selected interesting and vivid evocations of settings, acting and stage presentation and range widely in time and space.

The plays of Shakespeare are a particularly rich field for such treatment, having formed a central part of British theatrical culture for four hundred years. Major stage productions outside Britain are also included, as are adaptions, film and video versions.

ALSO PUBLISHED:

Antony and Cleopatra, edited by Richard Madelaine
Hamlet, edited by Robert Hapgood
Much Ado About Nothing, edited by John Cox

A MIDSUMMER NIGHT'S DREAM

EDITED BY

TREVOR R. GRIFFITHS

Professor, School of Literary and Media Studies,
University of North London

✛

🛡 **CAMBRIDGE**
UNIVERSITY PRESS

PUBLISHED BY THE PRESS SYNDICATE OF THE UNIVERSITY OF CAMBRIDGE
The Pitt Building, Trumpington Street, Cambridge, United Kingdom

CAMBRIDGE UNIVERSITY PRESS
The Edinburgh Building, Cambridge CB2 2RU, UK   http://www.cup.cam.ac.uk
40 West 20th Street, New York, NY 10011-4211, USA   http://www.cup.org
10 Stamford Road, Oakleigh, Melbourne 3166, Australia
Ruiz de Alarcón 13, 28014 Madrid, Spain

First published in 1996
Reprinted 2000

Printed in the United Kingdom at the University Press, Cambridge

A catalogue record for this book is available from the British Library

Library of Congress cataloguing in publication data
A midsummer night's dream / edited by Trevor R. Griffiths.
p.   cm. – (Shakespeare in production)
Includes bibliographical references and index.
ISBN 0 521 44560 4 (hardback)
ISBN 0 521 57565 6 (paperback)
1. Shakespeare, William, 1564–1616. Midsummer night's dream.
2. Shakespeare, William, 1564–1616. Midsummer night's dream – Criticism, Textual.
3. Shakespeare, William, 1564–1616 – Film and video adaptions.
4. Shakespeare, William, 1564–1616 – Stage history. 1. Griffiths, Trevor R. II. Series.
PR2827. M53 1996
822.3 3 – DC20   95-4647   CIP

ISBN 0 521 44560 4 hardback
ISBN 0 521 57565 6 paperback

TAG

CONTENTS

ILLUSTRATIONS

CREDITS
1–4 Theatre Museum, Victoria and Albert Museum
5–10 The Shakespeare Centre Library, Stratford-upon-Avon
(8 and 9 Joe Cocks Studio Collection; 10 Tom Holte Collection)
11 © Robert Barber
12 and 13 © Donald Cooper Photostage

SERIES EDITORS' PREFACE

It is no longer necessary to stress that the text of a play is only its starting-point, and that only in production is its potential realised and capable of being appreciated fully. Since the coming-of-age of Theatre Studies as an academic discipline, we now understand that even Shakespeare is only one collaborator in the creation and infinite recreation of his play upon the stage. And just as we now agree that no play is complete until it is produced, so we have become interested in the way in which plays often produced – and pre-eminently the plays of the national Bard, William Shakespeare – acquire a life history of their own, after they leave the hands of their first maker.

Since the eighteenth century Shakespeare has become a cultural construct: sometimes the guarantor of nationhood, heritage and the status quo, sometimes seized and transformed to be its critic and antidote. This latter role has been particularly evident in countries where Shakespeare has to be translated. The irony is that while his status as national icon grows in the English-speaking world, his language is both lost and renewed, so that for good or ill, Shakespeare can be made to seem more urgently 'relevant' than in England or America, and may become the one dissenting voice that the censors mistake as harmless.

'Shakespeare in Production' gives the reader, the student and the scholar a comprehensive dossier of materials – eye-witness accounts, contemporary criticism, promptbook marginalia, stage business, cuts, additions and rewritings – from which to construct an understanding of the many meanings that the plays have carried down the ages and across the world. These materials are organised alongside the New Cambridge Shakespeare text of the play, line by line and scene by scene, while a substantial introduction in each volume offers a guide to their interpretation. One may trace an argument about, for example, the many ways of playing Queen Gertrude, or the political transmutations of the text of *Henry V*; or take a scene, an act or a whole play, and work out how it has succeeded or failed in presentation over four hundred years.

For, despite our insistence that the plays are endlessly made and remade by history, Shakespeare is not a blank, scribbled upon by the age. Theatre history charts changes, but also registers something in spite of those changes. Some productions work and others do not. Two interpretations may be entirely different, and yet both will bring the play to life. Why? Without setting out to give absolute answers, the history of a play in the theatre can often show where the energy and shape of it lie, what has made it tick, through many permutations. In this way theatre history can find common ground with literary criticism. Both will find suggestive directions in the introductions to these volumes, while the commentaries provide raw material for readers to recreate the living experience of theatre, and become their own eye-witnesses.   *J. S. Bratton*

Julie Hankey

This series was originated by Jeremy Treglown and published by Junction Books, and later by Bristol Classical Press, as 'Plays in Performance'. Four titles were published; all are now out of print.

ACKNOWLEDGMENTS

I am very grateful to the University of Warwick American Exchange Scheme which funded my initial research in the USA, to the University of Strathclyde and the Polytechnic of North London for supporting later stages of my research, and to the University of North London for sabbatical leave in the final stages of the project. I am also very grateful to the UGC for support from its Humanities research funds and to the Una Ellis-Fermor Memorial Fund for its support.

My research has been made much easier by the friendly advice and assistance of the staffs of the British Library, the Theatre Museum, the Folger Shakespeare Library, the Shakespeare Centre Library, the Harvard Theatre Collection, the Royal National Theatre, the New York Public Library, the Old Vic, the Vic–Wells Association, the Huntington Library, the Birmingham, Brixton, Lambeth, Finsbury, Marylebone, Shoreditch and Westminster Public Libraries, as well as those of the Universities of Edinburgh, North London, Strathclyde and Warwick.

It is a particular pleasure to record my thanks for the helpful advice and wise counsel I received at various stages from M. H. Black, Christopher Calthrop, Nevill Coghill, Donald Cooper, Eileen Cottis, G. K. Hunter, J. G. McManaway, David Mayer, A. H. Scouten, Charles Shattuck, Sue Smith, George Speaight, Peter Thomson, Stanley Wells, Ruth Widmann, Carole Woddis, Martin Wright, and my series editors, J. S. Bratton and Julie Hankey, who have been both supportive and patient.

I owe personal debts to those colleague and students who have debated some of the issues raised here and to those whose practical support has helped me to pursue this project, particularly Stephanie King, Roo Shaw, Melanie Honer, Sue and Bob Watts, Carina Petter, Geoffrey and Barbara Griffiths, Malcolm Johnson, Bel Harris, Mark and Marie Stewart and Maggie Rae. My biggest debt remains, as always, to Kathy Rooney.

I would also like to thank Jim Ellis and J. W. Donohue who invited me to read a paper on Frederic Reynolds's *Dream* at the Amherst conference in 1974 and the editors of *Theatre Notebook* and *Shakespeare Quarterly* who published earlier versions of my work on Barker and Vestris (although, due to the vagaries of transatlantic mail, the *Shakespeare Quarterly* essay appeared with the biography of the dramatist Trevor Griffiths, it was written by me).

I am also grateful to the copyright owners for permission to reproduce the illustrations.

EDITOR'S NOTE

I have silently corrected obvious misprints in newspaper articles, and I have also silently regularised initial upper case letters in quotations that run on within my own sentences.

The playtext used is *A Midsummer Night's Dream*, ed. R. A. Foakes, 1984 (New Cambridge Shakespeare).

PRODUCTIONS

The following is a selective chronological list of productions of *A Midsummer Night's Dream* in English. 'M' under music stands for Mendelssohn, 'M*' for the Mendelssohn overture; 'adapt.' under style stands for adaptation, 'A' for Athenian and 'E' for Elizabethan. These categories, like the very brief description of other productions, are intended only as an aid to comprehension and conceal many individual differences picked out in both commentary and introduction. Readers are referred to the separate list of music for a fuller account of the music in each production. Most nineteenth-century productions included music by other composers and/or a further selection from Mendelssohn as well his overture and incidental music to the *Dream*.

date	company/adapter/director	venue	music	style
pre-1600	Chamberlain's Men	The Theatre?		
1662	King's	Vere Street		
1692	*The Fairy Queen*	Dorset Garden	Purcell	opera
1716	*Pyramus and Thisbe*	Lincoln's Inn Fields	Leveridge	parody
1745	*Pyramus and Thisbe* (Lampe)	Covent Garden	Lampe	parody
1755	*The Fairies* (Garrick/Smith)	Drury Lane	Smith	opera
1763	Colman/Garrick	Drury Lane	Smith	child fairies
1763	*A Fairy Tale* (Colman)	Drury Lane	Smith	child fairies
1816	Frederic Reynolds	Covent Garden	misc.	adapt.
1833	Reynolds, ed. Alfred Bunn	Drury Lane	M*, misc.	adapt.
1840	Madame Vestris	Covent Garden	M*, misc.	A
1853–61	Samuel Phelps	Sadler's Wells	M	A
1856–9	Charles Kean	Princess's	M	A
1870	John Ryder (Phelps as Bottom)	Queen's	M	A
1875	Phelps	Gaiety	M	A
1880	Edward Saker	Sadler's Wells	M	A/children
1889–1916	F. R. Benson	touring	M	A

date	company/adapter/director	venue	music	style
1895	Augustin Daly	Daly's	M	A
1900, 11	Beerbohm Tree	Her/His Majesty's	M	A
1905	Oscar Asche	Adelphi	M	A
1914	Granville Barker	Savoy	Sharp	eclectic
1914	Patrick Kirwan	Stratford	Elizabethan	
1914–18	Ben Greet	Old Vic	M	A
1918	George Foss	Old Vic	M	A
1919–34	Bridges Adams	Stratford		
	1919, 23, 24, 26, 28, 31		M	A
	1921		Purcell	A
	1932, 34		Elizabethan	
1920	Russell Thorndike/ Charles Warburton	Old Vic	M	A
1920	J. B. Fagan	Court	Greenwood	A
1921, 23, 24	Robert Atkins	Old Vic	M	A
1923	Donald Calthrop	Kingsway	arr. Lee	eclectic
1924	Basil Dean	Drury Lane	M	A
1926	Andrew Leigh	Old Vic	M	A
1929, 31	Harcourt Williams	Old Vic	Sharp	E
1935	Max Reinhardt	Film	M	E/A
1937	E. Martin Browne	Stratford	Elizabethan	
1937–8	Tyrone Guthrie	Old Vic	M	A
1938	Andrew Leigh	Stratford	Bernard	E
1941	Donald Wolfit	Strand	M	A
1942	Ben Iden Payne	Stratford	M	E
1942	Robert Atkins	Westminster	M	A
1943	Baliol Holloway	Stratford	M	E
1944	Robert Atkins	Stratford	M	E
1945	Nevill Coghill	Haymarket	Bridgewater	E
1949	Robert Atkins	St Martin's	M	A
1949	Michael Benthall	Stratford	M	A/eclectic
1951	Tyrone Guthrie	Old Vic		eclectic
1954	George Devine	Stratford	Gerhard	eclectic
1954	Michael Benthall	Old Vic tour	M	A
1957	Michael Benthall	Old Vic	M	A

date	company/adapter/director	venue	music	style
1959, 62–3	Peter Hall	Stratford/ Aldwych	Leppard	E
1960	Michael Langham	Old Vic	Thea Musgrave	A/E
1962	Tony Richardson	Royal Court	John Addison	A
1967	Frank Dunlop	Saville	Dankworth	modern dress
1970–3	Peter Brook	Stratford/tour	Peaslee/M	white box
1977	John Barton	Stratford/ Aldwych	Woolfenden	E
1981–2	Ron Daniels	Stratford/ Barbican	Oliver	Victorian toy theatre
1982–3	Bill Bryden	Cottesloe/ Lyttelton	Tams	Edwardian
1986–7	Bill Alexander	Stratford/ Barbican	Sams	Hippolyta's dream
1989–90	John Caird	Stratford/ Barbican	Sekacz/M	St Trinian's
1990	Kenneth Branagh	Renaissance Co, tour	Patrick Doyle	eclectic
1992	Robert Lepage	Olivier	Lee/Salem	mud
1994	Adrian Noble	Stratford	Sekacz	eclectic

ABBREVIATIONS

BSL: Department of Language and Literature, Birmingham Central Library (The Birmingham Shakespeare Library)

F: *Mr William Shakespeares Comedies, Histories, & Tragedies*, 1623 (First Folio)

F2: *Mr William Shakespeares Comedies, Histories, and Tragedies*, 1632 (Second Folio)

F3: *Mr William Shakespeares Comedies, Histories, & Tragedies*, 1663 (Third Folio)

Foakes: *A Midsummer Night's Dream*, ed. R. A. Foakes, 1984 (New Cambridge Shakespeare)

FSL: The Folger Shakespeare Library

Guardian: *The Manchester Guardian* to 1959, thereafter the *Guardian*

HTC: The Harvard Theatre Collection

ILN: *Illustrated London News*

LTR: Ian Herbert, ed. *The London Theatre Record*, 1981–

PMLA: *Publications of the Modern Language Association of America*

Q1: *A Midsommer night's dreame*, Thomas Fisher, 1600 (first quarto)

Q2: *A Midsommer night's dreame*, James Roberts, 1600 (in fact William Jaggard, 1619, second quarto)

Qq: Both quartos

RSC: Royal Shakespeare Company

SCL: The Shakespeare Centre Library

SD: stage direction

SQ: *Shakespeare Quarterly*

SS: *Shakespeare Survey*

TLS: *Times Literary Supplement*

TM: The Theatre Museum, London

TN: *Theatre Notebook*

VW: The Vic–Wells Association Library

INTRODUCTION

A Midsummer Night's Dream, now safely ensconced as one of the three Shakespeare plays to be studied in schools as part of the English National Curriculum, has come to be regarded as 'one of the best loved and most performed of Shakespeare's plays'.[1] However, this represents a major turn around in the play's fortunes, since for some two hundred years it scarcely enjoyed any kind of theatrical life at all, languishing in almost total eclipse in the late seventeenth and eighteenth centuries.

The theatrical fortunes of *A Midsummer Night's Dream* have been as varied and as unusual as the elements that make up the play. En route to its current status, it has enjoyed (or suffered) the full spectrum of the possible stage fates of Shakespearean comedy from fragmentation to encrustation via operatisation and over-fantastication. Its theatrical effectiveness has often been called into question, its apparent lack of dramatic conflict has been much canvassed and its ample Shakespearean justification for music and dancing has often been treated as a licence for broadly spectacular treatments that have created a kind of superior Shakespearean pantomime for holiday seasons. This introduction traces the play's stage history, examining the various metamorphoses, tribulations and triumphs which have characterised its journey and attempting to show some of the causes, intrinsic and extrinsic, for various stages in that journey.[2]

We do not know when or where *A Midsummer Night's Dream* was first staged and its subsequent stage career was very limited until the nineteenth century: there are only two known performances of the play under its own name between 1660 and the 1816 production of a comic-operatic adaptation by the journeyman dramatist Frederic Reynolds. In the eighteenth century,

---

1 Programme note for David Giles's production, Edinburgh Festival, 1978.
2 My discussions are based on extensive research in Great Britain and the USA in which I have consulted promptbooks, playbills, programmes, contemporary reviews, memoirs, photographs, scene designs and other records of productions. Lack of space prevents the reproduction of a considerable amount of detailed information about casts, lengths of runs, technical staff, etc., which underpins my discussion. Such information for 1660–1800 is to be found in Avery, *London Stage*, for the nineteenth century in Griffiths, *'Dream and Tempest'* (PhD), for the early twentieth century in Wearing, *London Stage* and for Stratford in Mullin, *Theatre at Stratford*.

the play's very limited claims to theatrical attention rested on the shallow foundation of a series of adaptations which, from differing viewpoints, dealt with the particular challenges of the play by assimilating it, by Procrustean methods, into the operatic mode which was the dominant form for dealing with the supernatural in the eighteenth-century theatre. Salvation from this predicament came in the nineteenth century with another form of assimilation, pioneered by Madame Vestris in 1840. The practices of Romantic ballet coupled with Mendelssohn's overture (and later his incidental music) facilitated the presentation of the supernatural through music, dance and increasingly sophisticated theatrical technology, allowing the play to be staged successfully as a quasi-archaeological Athenian musical woodland extravaganza. Although this mixture proved to be brilliantly successful in some ways, it became both an artistic straitjacket and an economic liability as twentieth-century theatres grappled with rising labour costs which reduced the size of mortal and fairy courts as well as theatre orchestras.[3]

Granville Barker's 1914 production, with its unrealistic wood, non-Athenian setting and use of English folk music, offered a radical challenge to the nineteenth-century consensus, leading to an unsettling of conventional assumptions and a wider variety of approaches, although the remarkably resilient Mendelssohnian tradition provides a framework that still continues to be a target for parody in the last decade of the twentieth century. The discovery of the Swan drawing, and the work of William Poel at the turn of the century, also gave an impetus towards the use of Elizabethan settings and costuming, which has been a significant feature of many productions from the 1920s onwards. Peter Brook's extraordinary 1970 staging convincingly challenged many new orthodoxies, reassessing the play in terms of its theatricality (and metatheatricality), initiating lines of development that are still being explored today.

The structure of *A Midsummer Night's Dream* poses specific challenges of its own: as successive adapters showed in the late seventeenth and eighteenth centuries, it is possible to stage elements of the Mechanicals and the fairy plots separately, while Benjamin Britten's twentieth-century opera managed to dispense with the first act entirely. There are limits to the play's apparent tractability, since George Colman and David Garrick's eighteenth-century removal of Act Five was not successful; but the Athenian court characters, the fairies and the Mechanicals do maintain remarkably independent existences for much of the action. So, *A Midsummer Night's Dream* offers a par-

---

3 See Hughes, 'Lyceum', p. 11 on this point.

ticularly complex set of theatrical challenges associated with its unconventional approach to plot, its groupings of characters and the sustained involvement of supernatural characters in the action. The key elements in the play which have made it such a theatrical challenge are the combination of three disparate groups of characters held together less by the subordination of one plot to another or some characters to a central protagonist, than by principles of symmetry and analogy between situations and motifs. The sustaining link comes through the treatment of the relationship between the rational and the irrational, the conscious and the subconscious, the natural and the supernatural, the 'real' and the 'unreal', mediated particularly through the physical manifestation of many of these elements in the forms of the fairies and in the Mechanicals' attempts to grapple with the nature of theatre.[4]

A Midsummer Night's Dream is a powerful proof of Coleridge's suggestion that comedies tend to create their effects like a wreath of flowers, concentrating less on one central character than do tragedies, but in the *Dream* this phenomenon is carried to an extreme which may have been responsible for some of the difficulties faced by the theatre in finding suitable approaches to respond to its challenges. Its quadripartite (or tripartite if one does not separate out the four young lovers from the other human court characters) structure has lent itself to centrifugal rather than centripetal interpretation. Actors and directors have always had to resolve major strategic questions of focus when attempting to stage the play.[5] In this context it is noteworthy that such major actors as Betterton, Edmund Kean, Macready, Henry Irving and Olivier did not stage or appear in the play and that actor–managers who did stage it had a difficult choice as to their own part: Madame Vestris played Oberon, Charles Kean did not appear in his production, Samuel Phelps and Beerbohm Tree both played Bottom, while F. R. Benson tried both Lysander and, as he got older, Theseus.

The interweaving of strands in *A Midsummer Night's Dream* also militates against attempts to create a single character-centred reading of the kind that has contributed to the sustained theatrical success of the tragedies or even *Twelfth Night* and *As You Like It*. In *Othello*, for example, the focus is clearly on Othello and Iago who speak some two-thirds of the lines in

---

4 For contemporary critical responses, see Bloom, *Dream*, Calderwood, *Dream*, Price, *Dream*, and their bibliographies.

5 I have used the term director anachronistically throughout this work to describe the main person responsible for staging the play, since producer now tends to carry the connotation of the person responsible for economic rather than aesthetic decisions.

the play, and in *As You Like It* Rosalind has just under 20 per cent of the lines. However, in *A Midsummer Night's Dream* there are five characters each with between 200 and 230 lines, giving them about 50 per cent of the play's lines; Oberon has the most lines, followed by Helena, Theseus, Bottom and Puck, and, rounding up the percentages, the fairies speak some 29 per cent of the lines, the lovers about 35 per cent, the Mechanicals roughly 21 per cent, and the other court characters about 16 per cent. Line counts and percentages can be misleading, since, for example, the groups do have different numbers of characters within them, and three of the Mechanicals have very few lines each.[6] It would, therefore, be unrealistic to suggest that these figures show exactly where some putatively authentic Shakespearean focus might have lain, without reference to the other elements which contribute to the performance text but which remain unrecorded in the dramatic text. However, because of the range of possible focusses and the relatively small amount of time spent on each character, historically it has proved difficult to achieve a satisfactory balance between the competing areas and it is not surprising that productions have often turned to external factors to provide that apparently missing focus or skeleton. In practice this has often been achieved by making room for more business, music and spectacle elsewhere, and identifying one area (usually the lovers) as the place to make changes which will reduce it to a subordinate position. The characteristic reviewers' complaints are that the play is unstageable or that a production gave undue weight to either the low comedy, often accompanied by gags and improvisation, of the Mechanicals, or the music and spectacle that have come to be associated with the fairies.

As Granville Barker acknowledged in one of his prefaces to *A Midsummer Night's Dream*, 'the fairies are the producer's test'.[7] The nature of that test has obviously varied over the centuries but has always related to the difficulty in finding appropriate theatrical conventions for dealing with the actual presence of supernatural characters on the stage, a problem related to the intelectual climate of each period and the nature of its belief in fairies and magic. Moreover, Shakespeare's fairies are not themselves straightforward and unitary, deriving from a single tradition, whether literary or popular. Instead

6 A 1986 adaptation by the touring company Cheek by Jowl removed the three least vocal Mechanicals, leaving Miss Quince, Miss Flute and the Reverend Bottom to stage the play as best they could.
7 From the Preface to Barker's acting edition, reprinted in Granville-Barker, *Prefaces*, VI, p. 35. Granville Barker adopted the hyphenated form of his name after the First World War.

they are drawn from many different traditions: Oberon (who comes from medieval Romance) and Titania (whose name comes from Ovid) have many attributes of classical gods in their relationship with mortals. Titania's fairy train are named after familiar flora and fauna, Puck belongs to a class of spirits associated with domestic mishaps and yet his role in respect of the lovers is close to that of Cupid. Then there is the vexed question of size: on the basis of the tasks they are asked to perform by both Titania and Bottom, the members of Titania's train appear to be diminutive and yet it is not impossible that they were originally played by the actors who played the lesser Mechanicals, rather than the children that later generations have tended to assign to the roles. In view of the play's stress on relativity of perception, the sometimes conflicting evidence of different senses, the creation of concord out of discord, and the metatheatrical elements associated not only with the Mechanicals but Theseus' 5.1 references to Bottom recovering to be an ass and to fairy time, it seems entirely possible that Shakespeare, who was after all a practical man of the theatre, was deliberately exploiting the clear physical impossibility of any theatrical representation offering truly diminutive fairies. He thus set a test which the increasingly routinely mimetic theatre that followed would find very difficult to meet.[8]

From 1840 there has been a steady tradition of staging *A Midsummer Night's Dream* in London, and it has been a staple of the Stratford-upon-Avon Festival since its early days in the late nineteenth century. I have concentrated on this unrivalled continuous tradition, drawing on productions elsewhere only if they offer significant insights into the play which have not been explored in London or Stratford. Because one of the major threads of interest has been the relationship between the text of the play and the ways in which it has been interpreted in the theatre, I have not considered productions in translation: the issues for a German production dealing with the early nineteenth-century Schlegel–Tieck translations, for example, are very different from those of an English director dealing with the language of the late sixteenth century. Similarly, whatever conclusions we reach about the first stagings of *A Midsummer Night's Dream*, the so-called pastoral tradition of staging the play outdoors in open-air theatres, whether purpose-built or in ad hoc venues, inevitably involves a further extension of arguments about the viability or otherwise of creating real woodland scenes to match the ways that Shakespeare creates them through his verse. While such productions

---

8 For fairies and magic, see Briggs, *Puck, Fairies, Dictionary*, Latham, *Fairies*, and Thomas, *Religion*.

may have considerable merits, and are referred to occasionally, they remain a minor strand in the developing history of Shakespearean production.[9]

A Midsummer Night's Dream in the Renaissance

The fact that we do not know when, where and for what audience *A Midsummer Night's Dream* was first performed has been no barrier to critical speculation, which has in turn considerably influenced the play's stage history in the twentieth century. The play's 'hymeneal' quality, its action structured around a forthcoming wedding, with contested betrothals, and marital disharmony in the fairy world, all culminating in multiple marriages and celebration, has suggested to a number of influential editors and critics that its first performance was as part of the wedding celebrations of some noble couple, possibly (because of the play's references to the fair Vestal) graced with the presence of Queen Elizabeth herself. Perhaps the most influential of these critical readings was the one promulgated by Arthur Quiller-Couch and John Dover Wilson in their widely circulated and much reprinted 1924 New Cambridge edition of the play, which was taken up most notably at the Old Vic in 1929 and Stratford in 1932, and by Peter Hall in his 1959/1962 Stratford production. The important characteristics of these productions were their use of broadly Elizabethan costuming for the mortals, 'Elizabethan' music and folk tunes, fairy costumes derived from Inigo Jones or Michael Drayton, and the use of a set for the Athenian scenes which resembled an Elizabethan great house. Jan Kott, whose work became widely available in English from 1965, followed a similar line derived from A. L. Rowse's biography of Shakespeare, but invested his putative first performance with a highly charged eroticism which has played some part in subsequent readings and stagings of the *Dream*.[10]

Even if the play was first staged as part of a wedding celebration (and given Elizabeth I's identification with the Fairy Queen, the relationship between Bottom and Titania seems a potentially risky one to present to an audience of

---

9 See Habicht, 'Shakespeare in Germany', for an illuminating discussion of issues of translation. For useful brief summaries of other productions in Britain and North America see the regular surveys in *SS* and *SQ*. Odell ('New York') and Gary J. Williams ('Web' and 'Popular Traditions') discuss aspects of early American productions. Leiter, *Globe*, covers productions between 1945 and 1982, Hamburger, 'New concepts', examines German productions of the 1970s and early 1980s. For a thorough listing of film and television versions of the *Dream* see Rothwell and Melzer, *Screen*.
10 Foakes, *Dream*, gives a useful brief summary of the wedding play argument on pp. 2–3. Kott's theory is promulgated in *Shakespeare Our Contemporary*.

which she was a member), there is no reason to doubt that it was also presented in the Elizabethan period under normal performance conditions. That is, it was presented in daylight in an open-air amphitheatre (presumably The Theatre) in which the atmosphere of a night-time wood was created largely by the play's language rather than by special effects. While Renaissance theatres were technically sophisticated, there would have been no attempt at creating a fully mimetic large-scale representation of a wood and the audience's imagination, responding to Shakespeare's language, would have been a key factor in creating moonlight, wood and diminutive fairies. Although the costumes would have been rich and colourful and the contemporary music would have been performed by more than competent musicians, the play requires nothing very extraordinary in terms of what we know about the technical capabilities of an Elizabethan playhouse.

The meeting between Oberon and Titania in 2.1 clearly exploited the confrontational possibilities of the tiring house doors since the stage direction in the quarto reads 'Enter the king of Fairies, at one doore, with his traine: and the Queene, at another, with hers'. The existence of the permanent set provided by the tiring house façade is also exploited when Quince arrives in 3.1 to declare 'here's a marvellous convenient place for our rehearsal. This green plot shall be our stage, this hawthorn brake our tiring-house' (2–4), presumably pointing to the actual tiring house and stage as he does so. It was possible to winch quite substantial properties in and out, so, although there is no direct evidence that the fairies flew, it is not impossible that Puck might have used the flying apparatus, just as he might have used the trap door to appear in unexpected places.

While there is no direct external evidence about how the *Dream* itself was costumed, we do know that some attempts were made to mimic 'classical' dress in Roman plays, so it is not impossible that Shakespeare's Athenians wore some approximation of current views of period costume. However, the English Renaissance theatre was not archaeologically realistic in its approach to costume and the Athenian nobility may equally well have worn contemporary dress. Certainly, on the internal evidence of Puck's 'hempen home-spuns', we can assume that the Mechanicals were probably dresssed as contemporary tradesmen.[11]

With the presentation of the fairies, however, there is a range of evidence, both theatrical and non-theatrical, that points in several directions. It has been suggested that the play requires a larger number of boys to play fairies than would usually have been available to Shakespeare's company, thus bolstering

---

11 Useful modern accounts of Elizabethan stage conditions are Gurr, *Stage*, Hattaway, *Popular Theatre* and Thomson, *Theatre*.

the argument that it was first performed at some special occasion such as a wedding when augmented resources would have been available. These arguments are often circular and remain inherently speculative. However, the pervasive influence of traditional, basically nineteenth-century, assumptions about the fairies, which crops up in such unexpected places as T. W. Baldwin's presumption that Oberon was a boy's part, is usefully challenged by Ringler's assertion that the fairies in Oberon's and Titania's trains might well have been played by the actors who played Snug, Snout, Starveling and Flute.[12]

Shakespeare's own treatment of the fake fairies in the gulling of Falstaff in *Merry Wives of Windsor* provides some idea of how he may have imagined the fairies in the *Dream*. In *Merry Wives*, the fairies are played by both children and adults, masked, and dressed in costumes of green or white. Ann Page is scheduled to be the Queen of Fairies, dressed in white silk or in green, masked, 'With ribands pendant flaring 'bout her head' (4.6.41), though Mistress Quickly substitutes for her, and Sir Hugh, dressed like a satyr, plays Hobgoblin, another generic name associated with the class of spirits Pucks belong to. Shakespeare could also have drawn on the conventions of fairy costuming used by John Lyly and Robert Greene in their plays. The other sources which have been used most by subsequent theatre directors searching for an authentic Renaissance version of fairydom are the Jacobean masque designs of Inigo Jones, which have been a significant source of ideas for both sets and fairy costumes: his Oberon costume (designed to be worn by Prince Henry in *Oberon*, the 1611 masque written by Jonson) offers us a Renaissance version of a classical hero, with no obvious fairy trappings; other more grotesque fairy designs have been picked up by directors such as Harcourt Williams and John Barton for their rank and file fairies. Although there are descriptions of fairies in literary works such as Edmund Spenser's *Faerie Queene* or William Browne's *Britannia's Pastorals*, their treatment of fairies has not been drawn upon theatrically, but the descriptions of fairies in Michael Drayton's *Nimphidia* (1627) was used, partly, no doubt, on the strength of his Warwickshire background and presumed friendship with Shakespeare, by Patrick Kirwan in 1914.[13]

12 See Foakes, *Dream*, p. 4, for a further consideration of Ringler's arguments. Brook used four fairies in 1970; recent productions to double fairies and Mechanicals include those at Nottingham and Derby in 1987, by the Contact company in Manchester in 1993 and Adrian Noble's for the RSC in 1994. Jan Kott, 'Bottom and the boys', has recently suggested that in the original production boy fairies played the Mechanicals, rather than adult Mechanicals playing fairies.

13 See H. J. Oliver's edition of *Merry Wives*. Lyly's *Endymion* and Greene's *James IV* are particularly relevant. Jones's designs are to be found in Orgel and Strong, *Inigo Jones*; Jonson's *Oberon* is in vol. VII of Herford and Simpson's *Jonson*. Merchant (*Artist* and 'Costume') is also relevant.

The nearest we have to an eye-witness account of an early production of *A Midsummer Night's Dream* appears to be a reference in Edward Sharpham's play *The Fleire* (1607) to a memorable (and long-lived) piece of business: 'Faith like *Thisbe* in the play a has almost killed himself with the scabbard.' With the exception of Dudley Carleton's reference to seeing 'a play of Robin goode-fellow' at court in January 1604, which may refer to *A Midsummer Night's Dream*, the few other pre-Restoration anecdotes that seem to be about the play also concern the Mechanicals: John Gee refers in 1624 to '*Piramus and Thisbe* where one comes in with a Lanthorne and acts *Mooneshine*' and John Taylor quotes from the Prologue to 'Pyramus and Thisbe' in 1630. The play acted at the Bishop of Lincoln's house on a Sunday in 1631 was probably *A Midsummer Night's Dream*, since Mr Wilson who 'did in suche a brutishe manner acte the same with an Asses head' was put in the stocks 'attyred with his asse head, and a bottle of hay sett before him'.[14]

A Midsummer Night's Dream, 1662–1777

The virtual absence of *A Midsummer Night's Dream* from the theatrical repertory in the late seventeenth and eighteenth centuries should occasion no particular surprise. Very few plays have maintained an unbroken or unadapted stage career and the pre-1750 theatre had little need for what the *Dream* had to offer. As A. H. Scouten has shown, the Restoration and eighteenth-century stage used Shakespeare mainly as a provider of tragedies (with the relative popularity of *Twelfth Night* and *As You Like It* resting on their 'breeches' roles), relying for its comic attractions largely on contemporary plays. The lovers' intrigues and the Theseus/Hippolyta frame story had little to offer the eighteenth-century theatre, which had many contemporary comedies with lovers at cross-purposes to draw on and, in a repertory heavily influenced by Sentimentalism, little incentive to address the problems posed by the lovers' language which had the faults of being archaic, indecorous and in verse. So, as the titles of the plays derived from *A Midsummer Night's Dream* in the seventeenth and eighteenth centuries suggest, the play was picked over for elements that might be recycled elsewhere: *The Merry Conceited Humours of Bottom the Weaver*, a droll (a short comic sketch) from the Commonwealth period was published in 1661; Henry Purcell's 1692 operatic adaptation, *The Fairy Queen*, was short lived, partly because its staging was so expensive, partly because its music was lost very early in the eighteenth century; the

---

14 *The Fleire* is quoted from Munro, *The Shakspere Allusion Book*, I, p. 174; Carleton is in Foakes, *Dream*, p. 12n; Gee and Taylor are in Quiller-Couch and Dover Wilson, *Dream*, p. 160; Wilson is in Halliday, *Critics*, p. 169.

metatheatrical farce of 'Pyramus and Thisbe' was twice converted into topical meta-operatic parodies (and shoe-horned into Charles Johnson's adaptation of *As You Like It* in 1723); the fairy elements formed the main attraction of both J. C. Smith's attempt to turn the play into a Handelian English opera and Colman's recycling of his abortive 1763 single performance *Dream* into a musical *Fairy Tale*. Perhaps if the *Fairy Queen* music had not been lost, there might have been more frequent revivals of works adapted from the *Dream*, leading in turn to the same kind of theatrical life enjoyed in the eighteenth century by *The Tempest* in successive broadly operatic adaptations.

THE RESTORATION PERIOD

According to its title page, *The Merry Conceited Humours of Bottom the Weaver*, the earliest known adaptation of the *Dream*, had been 'often publikely Acted by some of His Majesties Comedians, and lately, privately, presented by several APPRENTICES for their harmless recreation with Great Applause'. It was published to match '*the general mirth that is likely, very suddainly to happen about the Kings Coronation*' and '*may be easily acted ... for a private recreation*' (sig. [a2r]). It is basically an abridgment of the Mechanicals scenes, with passages from the original retained or discarded wholesale and few internal cuts in speeches. The fairies lose most of their more obviously lyrical and expansive material and the lovers are discarded altogether, with two lords sharing Lysander's and Demetrius' interventions in 'Pyramus and Thisbe'. The cast list suggests doubling Bottom, Flute and Snout with three fairies, and Oberon, Titania and Pugg (*sic*) with the Duke and Duchess and a lord. It would be interesting to know whether these ideas relate in any way to Elizabethan practice but the droll had no direct influence on the subsequent history of the *Dream*, although the doubling of Oberon and Titania with Theseus and Hippolyta is now a commonplace as a result of the success of Peter Brook's production, and some recent productions, including Adrian Noble's in 1994, have doubled some of the Mechanicals with fairies.

The only direct evidence for a Restoration production of *A Midsummer Night's Dream* is Samuel Pepys's diary entry for 26 September 1662. He was less than impressed by the production he saw at Thomas Killigrew's Vere-Street Theatre: 'we saw "Midsummer Night's Dream", which I had never seen before, nor shall ever again, for it is the most insipid ridiculous play that ever I saw in my life ... some good dancing and some handsome women which was all my pleasure'.[15] Pepys's reaction may be taken as representative of audience reactions, since there is no evidence of any other revival

15 Pepys, *Diary*, III, p. 208.

of *A Midsummer Night's Dream* before the version prepared under the aegis of Garrick and George Colman the Elder which managed a single disastrous performance in 1763. In the intervening period, all the interest in *A Midsummer Night's Dream* as a performance text concentrated on the Mechanicals and the fairies. As well as the positive evidence from what was staged, there is also strong supporting negative evidence from two theatrical preparation copies from the late seventeenth century which appear never to have gone into production.

The first of these preparation texts, possibly associated with the company that performed at the theatre in Hatton Garden, has only been marked up over the first three acts. The editor had little patience with figurative or descriptive passages, emphasising plot framework at the expense of long speeches and amplificatory material, and preferring the Mechanicals to the other mortals. It seems that Titania and her fairies were to be eliminated completely, which meant the omission of the whole theatrically telling incident of Bottom and the ass head. The lovers are cut heavily but, compared to their fate in the nineteenth century, rather haphazardly: the sleeping place dialogue in 2.1 which was always bowdlerised in the nineteenth century is untouched, but the 3.2 quarrel was heavily cut in ways reminiscent of the nineteenth-century approach. The other book, apparently prepared for Smock Alley, Dublin, confirms that the four young lovers were judged the most expendable with the 3.2 quarrels particularly heavily hit, losing about half their lines. Anything not obviously required in immediate plot terms, such as the 'forgeries of jealousy' speech, Puck's retelling of his intervention in the 'Pyramus and Thisbe' rehearsal, Oberon's account of Titania surrendering the Indian Boy or Theseus' lunatic, lover and poet speech, was severely curtailed.[16]

The significance of these early preparation copies is that they show that the down-grading of the lovers and the exaltation of the Mechanicals have been features of theatrical thinking about the play from an early date and that there has been a remarkable continuity in theatrical approaches to the play text: the problematic areas of the seventeenth century remained problematic into the twentieth. Generally the supernatural elements have been better treated than they are in the Hatton Garden book, but the Smock Alley book's tendency to omit the more grotesque and frightening aspects of the fairies has had many subsequent parallels. A growing scepticism in the late seventeenth century about the direct intervention of supernatural beings in everyday life might lie behind some of the Hatton Garden book's changes, but the fact that neither of the books, apparently, led to a production

16 See Evans, *Prompt-Books*, vol. I, pt i, pp. 11–12, 21–3 and vol. III, pt i for discussions of the provenance of these books.

and Pepys's dissatisfaction with the performance he saw indicates that *A Midsummer Night's Dream* was far from obvious theatrical material.

THE FAIRY QUEEN (1692)

The success of the semi-operatic 1674 adaptation of *The Tempest* may have prompted an attempt to achieve something broadly similar with *A Midsummer Night's Dream*. However, unlike the altered *Tempest* which in various forms was a staple of the repertory for well over 150 years, *The Fairy Queen* was to play a very minor part in the *Dream*'s history, mainly because the score was lost in 1701 and was only rediscovered in the twentieth century, but also because its spectacular staging was prohibitively expensive to recreate. As the contemporary prompter John Downes describes it:

> *The Fairy Queen* made into an Opera from a Comedy of Mr *Shakespears*: This in Ornaments was Superior ... especially in Cloaths, for all the Singers and Dancers, Scenes, Machines and Decorations, all most profusely set off; and excellently perform'd chiefly the Instrumental and Vocal part Compos'd by the said Mr *Purcel*, and Dances by Mr *Priest*. The Court and Town were wonderfully satisfy'd with it; but the Expences in setting it out being so great, the Company got very little by it.   (*Roscius Anglicanus*, pp. 42–3)

Although Henry Purcell's music was one of the production's great attractions, he did not set any of the Shakespearean songs. On Roger Savage's estimate some 950 of Shakespeare's line were cut completely and 400 modified in some way (out of a total of just over 2,000) but 200 spoken and 250 sung lines were added, mainly at the end of the acts where there were highly spectacular scenic transformations, dances and musical numbers. Apart from the complete removal of Hippolyta and the initial wedding frame-plot, so that the opera begins with Egeus' arrival, the most important structural change to Shakespeare's play is that a conflated version of the rehearsal and performance of 'Pyramus and Thisbe' is placed in Act Three with Puck given the remaining courtiers' interventions. This leaves a hole in Act Five to be filled with an example of a Chinoiserie, the then fashionable exotic entertainment, although 4.2 also makes a truncated appearance in the final act, so that we last see the Mechanicals heading off to the palace confident that 'Our Play shall be preferr'd' (*Fairy Queen*, p. 46). The adapter, generally taken to be Elkanah Settle, was not always so absent-minded, earlier giving Egeus some lines agreeing to Helena and Demetrius' marriage, and then capping Theseus' abridged lines on fantasy and imagination with 'strange Musick warbling in the Air' and an appearance by Oberon and the fairies 'To cure your Incredulity' (p. 47). Textually the lovers bear the brunt of the cutting and their lines are systematically de-rhymed, but Settle was clearly preoccupied throughout the play with questions of decorum which leads to some limping alterations to Shakespeare: Lysander informs Hermia that 'I have never found / By Observation, nor by History, / That Lovers run a smooth, and even course' (p. 3); Puck's opening lines in 2.1 are 'Tell me *Fairy*, where's our Queen? / And where have you been wandering' (p. 9); and Oberon greets Titania with 'Now proud *Titania* I shall find your Haunts' (p. 10).

Conventionally *The Fairy Queen* has been seen as 'a sort of revue, in which Shakespeare's scenes are merely episodes in a larger and more magnificent whole', in which Purcell's masques 'have so little connection with the play that no one who merely heard the music would have the remotest suspicion that the opera was an adaptation of Shakespeare's *Midsummer Night's Dream*'.[17] More recently, Roger Savage has argued that these masques can be treated not as extraneous non-Shakespearean effects but as serious efforts by the adapters to provide a Restoration equivalent to Shakespeare's thematic interlinkings of effect through patterns of imagery and extended lyrical passages: 'the cuts involving the evocative descriptive poetry make perfect sense in that the role of evocation and description in the semi-operatic proscenium-theatre of the Restoration is taken over by music and decor'. This involves a key assumption, which was, and is, made by many of those who stage Shakespeare that 'there is some kind of parity between spoken drama and dramatic music [or scenery and costuming] which will allow of a balancing of aesthetic books by the paying back into one medium of what one has taken from another'. In the case of *The Fairy Queen*, Savage argues, the adapters were using a doctrine of aesthetic substitution; the idea was that 'whatever Keatsean elements were taken out of the spoken *Dream* by the adaptor would be put back by Purcell ... in a different medium and with a different accent, but without loss' (Savage, '*Fairy Queen*', p. 213).

In the case of *The Fairy Queen* the placing of the performance of 'Pyramus and Thisbe' in Act Three is not compensated for by any of the additions. In 'Pyramus and Thisbe' potentially tragic events are turned to comedy through the performers' incapacity, but *The Fairy Queen* offers no musical equivalent to this parody of the lovers' self-absorption. However, *The Fairy Queen* is by no means a negligible piece of work. It attempted, as Savage has shown, to provide acceptable contemporary equivalents for aspects of Shakespeare's work which were considered to be obsolescent or unsuitable and did so by using the allegorical pageantry associated with opera to cope with the staging problems posed by the play's supernatural characters. In

17 Westrup, *Purcell*, p. 137. See also Zimmerman, *Purcell*, p. 629, White, 'Early performances', and Gary J. Williams, 'Concord'.

assimilating the play into one of the fashionable modes of the time it rather swamped it, yet it did give *A Midsummer Night's Dream* a stage life – a success which the neglect and failures of the eighteenth century were to show was no mean achievement.

THE EARLY EIGHTEENTH CENTURY

A Midsummer Night's Dream owed what little theatrical life it had in the first half of the eighteenth century to Richard Leveridge who spotted the potential of 'Pyramus and Thisbe' as a vehicle for attacking the increasing vogue for Italian opera in his *Comic Masque of Pyramus and Thisbe* (1716) and J. F. Lampe who emulated him in 1745, to Charles Johnson who managed to have 'Pyramus and Thisbe' played to the exiled Duke in *Love in a Forest* (his version of *As You Like It*) in 1723 and, tenuously, to the author of the *Robin Goodfellow* pantomime which achieved many performances in the period 1738 to 1745, although Shakespeare's fairies, including both Puck and Robin Goodfellow, are heavily outnumbered by *Commedia* characters and assorted fruits and vegetables.

Leveridge's idea was to 'Dress out' the piece in 'Recitative, and Airs, after the present *Italian* mode, hoping I have given it the same Comical face, though in a Musical dress'. His Semibreve, Crotchet and Gamut adapt some of the courtiers' interventions in the performance of 'Pyramus and Thisbe' as vehicles for the attack on opera: '*Crot:* I wonder whether the *Lion* be to sing? / *Sem*: Never wonder at that, for we that have Study'd the Italian Opera may do anything in this kind.' The Lion did indeed sing, introducing a musical roar – 'a vocal vibrato' which has amused some later commentators. Leveridge's approach was followed in 1745 by J. F. Lampe, whose *Pyramus and Thisbe: A Mock Opera* used some of Leveridge's songs and his machinery of Semibreve, Crotchet and Gamut commenting on the Mechanicals' performance but discarded the rehearsal and casting scenes.[18]

GARRICK AND *A MIDSUMMER NIGHT'S DREAM*

During David Garrick's long management at Drury Lane he was involved in two *Dream* projects: *The Fairies*, an opera by J. C. Smith (1755), and *A Midsummer Night's Dream* (1763) which rapidly metamorphosed into the rather more successful *A Fairy Tale*.

The Fairies was essentially an attempt by Handel's pupil J. C. Smith to achieve something of Handel's operatic force by using the allegorical mode of opera as an equivalent to Shakespeare's use of fairies. Rejecting the parody

18 The vocal vibrato is from Hoffman, 'Music', p. 97; details of *Robin Goodfellow* are from Avery, *London Stage*, III, pp. 740 ff., 1128 ff. See Odell, *Betterton to Irving*, I, pp. 232, 347, for Leveridge and Lampe.

associated with recent treatments of the Mechanicals, Garrick and Smith concentrated on the fairies and the court. As the Advertisement in the text of *The Fairies* put it, 'Many Passages of the first Merit, and some whole Scenes in the Midsummer Night's Dream, are necessarily omitted in this *Opera* to reduce the Performance to a proper length' (sig. A3v). There were twenty-eight songs, by Milton and Waller among others, together with those taken from other Shakespeare plays, but only 500 lines of the original play make any kind of appearance, sometimes sung or reallocated to another part of the action. Everything to do with the Mechanicals and Titania's love for 'a patch'd fool' was dispatched in six lines (*Fairies*, p. 34). Anything not immediately functional in terms of the barest development of a skeletal plot is omitted to make way for the songs, which are generally not inappropriate. The company was augmented by two Italian singers and by a trained group of children who played all the fairy parts.[19]

Clearly there is a substantial discrepancy betwen the imagined size of the fairies in *A Midsummer Night's Dream* and their actual size in any stage representation. Although this discrepancy is a structural feature of the play which has always been there, it has proved a major problem as successive generations of directors and audiences have convinced themselves that Shakespeare's diminutive fairies capable of crawling into acorns can best be staged by giving some or all of the fairy roles to children. Given the persistence of such beliefs among audiences and managements over some three hundred years, there appears to be some metonymic logic in accepting that, say, a child three foot tall is more credible as a fairy less than an inch high than an adult would be. However, the usual result, as in *The Fairies*, is a reduction of any complexities in the fairy parts, either because the actual dialogue appears unsuitable for children to speak or to reduce demands on the children's memories, or to make space for song and dance.

The Drury Lane management had reason to be very grateful to its child fairies in 1763 when it made a second attempt at *A Midsummer Night's Dream*, since it was only their excellence that allowed it to stagger through its single disastrous performance. William Hopkins, the Drury Lane prompter, had a ringside seat:

> The piece was greatly Cut & Alter'd: the 5th Act Entirely left out & many
> Airs interspers'd all through; got up with a vast deal of trouble to everybody
> concerned in it but particularly to Mr Coleman, who attended every
> Rehearsal & had alterations innumerable to make. Upon the whole never was

19 See Stone, 'Garrick and Colman', for an account of Garrick and Colman's dealings with the play.

anything so murder'd in the Speaking. Mr W. Palmer & Mrs Vincent were beyond Description bad; & had it not been for the Children's excellent performance (& particularly Miss Wright who Sung delightfully), the Audience would not have Suffer'd em to have gone half thro' it. The Sleeping Scene particularly displeas'd. Next day it was reported. The Performers first Sung the Audience to Sleep, & then went to Sleep themselves. Fairies pleas'd – Serious parts displeas'd – Comic between both.[20]

This debacle is of particular interest because for the first time there is some direct evidence how difficult producing a viable version of *A Midsummer Night's Dream* seemed to be to those charged with creating it. Of course we have the eloquent negative testimony of the abandoned Restoration acting version and what we can infer from the textual changes made in *The Fairy Queen*, but the notes George Colman the Elder (Hopkins's Mr Coleman) made when he was entrusted with the project by Garrick reveal his concern with how to create something decorously viable from unpromising material. Colman was much exercised over the lovers who, as Hopkins confirms, were regarded as 'serious'. He objected to the predominance of rhyme in their scenes, since rhyme was 'very uncouth' and the scenes would work better as 'plain blank verse'. Also, de-rhyming all the scenes except the fairies' would 'make the Fairy-scenes appear more characteristically distinguished'. The lovers' quarrel in the wood was particularly problematic, since 'a good deal of the writing in this act is uncouth & wants alteration', but he also had reservations about the last act performance of 'Pyramus and Thisbe': 'The palpable gross play of Pyramus & Thisbe, as well as the interlocutory dialogue of the other characters must be shortened as much as possible – if the Comi-Tragedy c[oul]d be enlivened with 2 or 3 odd songs I think it w[oul]d be safer.' By the time the play was produced, 'Pyramus and Thisbe' had been omitted as had the final fairy scene. Colman had, justifiably, been worried about Garrick's proposal to lose this scene: 'I think it very ill judged to attempt to cut out the concluding Fairy scene', and his concern about the whole project is well conveyed in his less than confident summing up: 'On the whole I think it may with care and attention be made a most *novelle* and elegant entertainment – but may tumble for want of amending a few absurdities, and altering some trifling circumstances w[hi]ch make it uncouth and unsuitable to the taste of the present times.'[21]

Ultimately the play that resulted from Garrrick and Colman's efforts was a heavily truncated version of the first four acts of Shakespeare's original,

---

20 In Avery, *London Stage*, IV, p. 1021.
21 Colman's notes are preserved in a significant collection of material relating to this production in the FSL.

graced with many of the 1755 songs and some new ones, but the net result was lack-lustre in the extreme. The *St James Chronicle* commented, perhaps as much on the play as on the production, that 'the Fairy part is most transcendently beautiful ... but the Love-Story wound up with it, and the celebration of the Marriage of Theseus is very flat and uninteresting' (24 November 1763). Clearly contemporary opinion was less than convinced by the play but Colman's worries about 'Pyramus and Thisbe' seem strange, unless we can extend his concern about the uncouthness of much of the play into a fear that his audience might not have recognised that 'Pyramus and Thisbe' was itself uncouth parody. Nevertheless, given the play's previous history, it seems odd that he should not have recognised the value of these scenes. As Frederic Reynolds remarked, some of the 1763 failure could be put down to the audience's disappointment that the Mechanicals, 'though they decidedly led the Audience to expect the performance of a Play, never performed any Play at all'.[22]

Taking a hint from audience reaction to the fairies, Colman reworked the failed *Dream* production into *A Fairy Tale*, which opened three days after its parent's debacle. According to Hopkins: 'Mr Colman thought it was a pity so much pains and expense as was bestowed on the MND should be thrown away – he luckily thought of turning it into a farce; which alterations he made in one night.' All the court characters were omitted from this piece which was designed to exploit the novelty appeal of the children as fairies and the comedy of the Mechanicals. It became a reasonably successful afterpiece which remained in the Drury Lane repertory until 1767 and was revived at the Haymarket in 1777, when it was set from stock pieces such as a 'Garrett chamber' and a 'Garden'.[23]

'Poetry and the stage do not agree': Frederic Reynolds, 1816 and 1833

The 1763 version of the *Dream* formed the working text on which Frederic Reynolds created one of the last Shakespeare adaptations based explicitly on the supposition that the text required modernisation to make any impact in the theatre. As he put it in his autobiography: 'So many of Shakespeare's fine comedies having been performed no more than once, in two, or three seasons, and others having been altogether withdrawn from the stage, I thought ... that they might be again restored to it (with the assistance of a few alterations and the addition of music) advantageously to the managers, and without

22 Reynolds, *Dream*, pp. iii–iv.
23 In Avery, *London Stage*, IV, p. 1022; the sets are from the *Fairy Tale* promptbook.

injury to the immortal bard.'[24] In practice Reynolds, a competent journeyman at best, laced his adaptations with a cornucopia of crowd-pleasing ploys:
low comedy, disguise, spectacular entrances, musical numbers, pageants and
flying, all topped off with Shakespeare's name to give the show an air of legit-
imacy. His facility in creating opportunities for processions, tableaux and
highly spectacular act endings, was coupled with a tendency to introduce
extra steps into the processes of a scene, thus slowing down its development,
and a tendency to niggle about things Shakespeare left untidy. In Act One,
for instance, he has Egeus properly introduced by an officer rather than
bursting in, and he also makes Theseus instruct an officer to find a forester,
thus accounting for the Act Four hunting scene that Shakespeare introduces
without warning. Reynolds rearranges the play thoroughly with many
wholesale shifts of lines from scene to scene but the general tendency is to
emphasise the low comedy, music and fairy spectacle at the expense of the
lovers, who are given very short shrift indeed.

Reynolds had attributed the failure of the 1763 production partly to the
absence of the performance of 'Pyramus and Thisbe', but he chose to repeat
the *Fairy Queen*'s expedient of placing the performance in the wood in the
middle of the play, rather than restoring Shakespeare's arrangements which
would have given him both the performance of 'Pyramus and Thisbe' and
opportunities for a spectacular dance finale. At one point he wondered 'could
the clouds ascending & the dance of Fairies be brought to conclude the
piece?'[25] in place of the Air and Chorus which made a rather lame ending in
the 1763 text. Instead he contrived a new spectacular '*Grand Pageant, commemorative of the Triumphs of THESEUS*' (Reynolds, *Dream*, p. 57) which combined a
contemporary patriotic tribute to the veterans of the Napoleonic wars
(Hermia welcomed them with a song including the lines 'Warriors! march on!
march on, and hear the praise, / A grateful nation to your valour pays!',
(Reynolds, *Dream*, p. 56)) with such mythological figures as Ariadne (not an
entirely tactful choice for Theseus' wedding), the Centaurs and the Minotaur.

Although there was some unqualified praise for the production and it did run
for a respectable eighteen nights in its first season, it was very heavily criticised,
in ways which laid down battle lines for the whole nineteenth century, mainly on
the grounds that there was a mismatch between the play itself and the methods
which had to to be adopted to stage it. Hazlitt's condemnation is justly famous:

> All that was fine in the play was lost in the representation. The spirit was
> evaporated, the genius was fled; but the spectacle was fine: it was that which

24 Reynolds, *Life*, II, p. 409; the preparation copy is in the FSL.
25 Reynolds, preparation copy of 1763 *Dream*, p. 47.

saved the play ... Poetry and the stage do not agree together. The ideal has
no place upon the stage which is a picture without perspective; everything
there is in the foreground. That which is merely an airy shape, a dream, a
passing thought, immediately becomes an unmanageable reality.

(Examiner, 21 January 1816)

Almost before it had been staged, certainly in its Shakespearean form, *A
Midsummer Night's Dream* was already well on the way to being regarded as
something too fine and precious for the rough trade of the theatre. As *The
Times* argued:

> Story there is none ... it is almost as if the author had grudged labour enough
> on the occasion to construct a consistent plot – but of invention, of imagery,
> and eloquence of the highest order there is enough to beautify the materials
> of an hundred plays ... All this is delicious to a man of poetical feeling in his
> closet. But there is no interest to excite the passions – no event to arouse the
> curiosity – no character to attract the observation of that vulgar and chance
> medley multitude who crowd together within the walls of a theatre. The bad
> judgement of bringing forward such a play at all cannot be cured by any sub-
> sequent or collateral attention to points of secondary importance.

(17 January 1816)

So Romantic anti-theatrical prejudice combined with grudging bardolatry
to dismiss *A Midsummer Night's Dream* from the theatre, though very few
critics explicitly noted, as *The Times* did that 'SHAKESPEAR'S words have
been superseded by more foolish words, and his absurdities have been
disgraced by comparisons more absurd than they are.'

Despite the ferocity of the reactions against his adaptation, Reynolds had
managed to give the play a stage life, something that it had conspicuously
lacked since the Restoration; simply being performed, even in a garbled fashion, brought the play back into theatrical notice and showed that some kind
of production was possible.

Reynolds's version soon disappeared from the repertory but had one further claim to fame when it was revived in the 1833–4 season at Drury Lane. It
was scarcely noticed when it appeared as an afterpiece to George Colman the
Younger's *Poor Gentleman*, 'compressed into Two Acts', mainly by the expedient of removing the whole of Act Two after Bottom's dance with the
fairies.[26] The *Literary Gazette* noted that 'Tawdry as a country barn and
mutilated with the most barbarian recklessness, the spoiling of this beautiful
play would have disgraced the darkest era of the unfortunate drama' (7

---

26 The promptbook is now in the University of Michigan Library.

December). The production did, however, benefit from Mendelssohn's overture, played for the first time in a London production, which was to have such an impact on the future of *A Midsummer Night's Dream* as a performance text.

Reynolds's version of the *Dream* was the last systematically to rework and rewrite lines, plots and characters on a large scale. Thereafter the play would be made theatrically viable by editing the text rather than replacing it. The other elements Reynolds drew on – music, dancing, spectacular scenery and special effects – would continue to be major factors in securing the play's increasing theatrical success in the nineteenth century. Although the *Dream* failed to secure a place in the repertory over such a long period, we ought not to use hindsight to assume that it should have been tackled more often than it was. However, since the theatrical elements that worked in the nineteenth century had been drawn upon in various degrees throughout the *Dream'* ; theatrical history of partial sucesss and absolute failure since 1660, its change of fortune after 1816 must partly rest upon movements in broader intellectual climates which made the Victorian period readier to accept it than earlier ones had been.

Terms such as 'the Age of Enlightenment' and 'Romanticism' must be used with caution since they inevitably simplify many complex cultural issues, yet it is striking that the theatrical eclipse of *A Midsummer Night's Dream* is most marked during the period of the Enlightenment and that it becomes a viable theatrical text after the consolidation of many 'Romantic' values in the 1830s. 'Enlightenment' ideas and practices did not constitute a fertile intellectual matrix for *A Midsummer Night's Dream*, with its emphasis on the supernatural made physically present, its generic mixture of high and low elements within a broadly aristocratic framework, its verse and its treatment of Nature and the country. Shakespeare may have anticipated Locke when Lysander declares himself swayed by Reason four times in six lines, in 2.2, but he is, of course under the influence of magic when he does so! The decline of belief in magic and the direct intervention of supernatural beings in everyday life, the rise of scepticism and empirical science are all factors which contributed to the creation of a hostile intellectual climate in which the *Dream* was unlikely to flourish. Its mixture of elements drawn from different traditions made it peculiarly difficult to assimilate whole into the operatic mode which might have been its logical theatrical home (and no-one in the theatre appears to have seriously considered pantomime), and there were always bits left over once someone had found a theatrical use for parts of it. Such attempts to create a viable stage play out of the *Dream* by resolving it into its constituent parts can also be read as implicit responses to neoclassical objections against Shakespeare's fundamental lack of attention to the Unities. Both structurally and linguistically, the *Dream* posed similar problems to those that Thomas Warton raised in his 1785 discussion of the reasons for the neglect of Milton's early poems during the Augustan period: 'wit and rhyme, sentiment and satire, polished numbers, sparkling couplets and polished periods, having so long kept undisturbed possession in our poetry, would not easily give way to fiction and fancy, to picturesque description, and romantic imagery'.[27] Similarly, the lovers' scenes, subject from the earliest known post-Restoration records to cutting, shaping and reordering, clearly posed considerable problems of decorum throughout the eighteenth century. Comedy in the Restoration and eighteenth century was predominantly contemporary in subject matter and literary style, and increasingly concerned with the urban bourgeoisie, and no-one seems to have seen a potential in the lovers for the kind of lovers' intrigue that graced the altered *Tempest* or many post-Restoration comedies.

The gradual flowering of 'Romanticism', for all its cross-currents and contradictions, began to create intellectual and theatrical climates which were more favourable to the play. Although Dryden, Addison and Rowe had all made favourable comments about Shakespeare's delineation of supernatural characters, the growth of an interest in the gothic and the fantastic, exemplified in Hurd's *Letters on Chivalry and Romance* (1762) and Mrs Montagu's defence of the 'Praeternatural beings' (1769), laid the ground for a reconsideration of the viability of the *Dream*. By the time Reynolds adapted the play in 1816, there had been a major shift in the intellectual climate as a result of 'Romanticism' which meant that the play could be valued for the author's originality and for those lyrical qualities that Roger Savage has revealingly labelled as Keatsean. The negative side of this change was that the theatre was to be castigated for its temerity in attempting to stage the unstageable, but the Victorian theatre would find methods to keep many critics at bay by creating a more coherent kind of synaesthesia than any previous versions of the *Dream* had managed by drawing on the intellectual and technical vocabularies of Romantic ballet, music and scenography.

Restoring Shakespeare: Madame Vestris, 1840

Whereas in the eighteenth century various factors that might have given *A Midsummer Night's Dream* a theatrical life failed to coalesce, so, conversely, the nineteenth century brought together a number of elements at Covent Garden in 1840 which would not only combine into a successful production, but also establish a template for the rest of the century. When she went into management

27 Quoted in Amarsinghe, *Dryden and Pope*, p. 33.

at Covent Garden Madame Vestris was uniquely well placed to bring together a whole range of factors which would enable her to reverse the theatrical fortunes of *A Midsummer Night's Dream*. She could apply the lessons learned with the fairy extravaganzas she had staged in her management of the Olympic with the polymathic dramatist and antiquary J. R. Planché, who had not only written the libretto for Weber's *Oberon* (1826) in which she had appeared, but was also to advise on the *Dream* production. She also took with her from the Olympic her machinist E. M. Bradwell who had first hand experience of flying fairies from his work there (he had also worked on the Reynolds staging). Her first marriage, into the French Vestris family of ballet dancers, had given her direct first hand insights into significant developments in dance in Europe. She could draw on devices developed to express the supernatural in Romantic ballet, such as dancing on points (which gave an impression of weightlessness appropriate to nineteenth-century ideas about fairies) and the early long-skirted version of the tutu, apparently introduced by Marie Taglioni in *La Sylphide* (1832). The Romantic stress on dreams and the supernatural, of which *La Sylphide* is but one example, coupled with a delight in wild landscapes expressed in poetry and painting, were significant factors in creating an intellectual climate which helped to make a successful production of *A Midsummer Night's Dream* more likely. With her own skills as a singer (which probably explains why she herself played Oberon), with her scenery in the hands of the Grieve family, one of the great theatrical dynasties (John Grieve had already worked on the 1816 production, Thomas would work on Kean's 1856 staging as well), and with the Mendelssohn overture to set the scene, the technical and intellectual ingredients were in place to establish a tradition which would dominate the nineteenth-century approach to staging *A Midsummer Night's Dream*.

Unlike Reynolds and the rest of her predecessors, Vestris did not add textual material, although she did set precedents for the rest of the century with her editing practices. Bottom became the character with the most lines and Helena was relegated from second place to fifth, while the Mechanicals' proportion of the lines spoken rose to 24 per cent (they lost only about 10 per cent of their lines) and the lovers fell to 30 per cent (they lost about one-third of their total). Although there were some cuts and transpositions elsewhere, Madame Vestris was mainly concerned with questions of propriety and focussed on the lovers' scenes, particularly 3.2. She cut some 400 lines from Shakespeare's text overall, but nearly half of these came from this scene which only constitutes a fifth of Shakespeare's play. Like Colman and Francis Gentleman in the eighteenth century, Vestris's concern was with decorum and the avoidance of what Gentleman, commenting in Bell's edition of the play, had called 'warm ideas' (Bell, *Dream*, p. 159). Inevitably the cuts to these scenes reduce the vitality, energy and earnest sincerity of the lovers' language, thus making them even more suitable targets for cutting. The lovers' contribution to the play now seems to lie precisely in the comic seriousness with which they regard themselves and with which they conduct their affairs, but at this point, and into the twentieth century, they were more often thought of as serious rather than comic characters.

Scenically Vestris used three main locations: the Athenian court, Quince's cottage and the woods, using a diorama to change the scene from one part of the wood to another. After Bottom's wakening which, as always in nineteenth-century productions, takes place before Theseus' discovery of the sleeping lovers, there was a slow sunrise effect over the lake which became an inevitable concomitant of Victorian *Dream* production, presumably because of the visual opportunities for moonlight reflecting off the watery surface which developing lighting technology made increasingly attractive. However, the sunrise effect also ties in very well with the return to daylight normality after the night-time misrule and is one instance of a highly appropriate spectacular effect. The staging of the final scene, in which the fairies were to be seen 'darting from side to side, flying round and round, now here, now there, on the ground, in the air, waving their tiny lamps till the entire palace seems sparkling with the countless hues of light' (*Theatrical Journal*, 1 May 1841) was much praised. Planché's account of its genesis reveals that the economic and the aesthetic were closely linked: 'When this revival was first suggested, Bartley said: "If Planché can devise a striking effect for the last scene, the play will run for sixty nights." I pointed out that Shakespeare had suggested it himself, in the words of Oberon to his attendant fairies' and so they devised a staging for the last act with fairies dancing and singing 'as indicated in the text, carrying out implicitly the directions of the author, and not sacrilegiously attempting to gild his refined gold'.[28] Although this account appeared many years after the event, it is an important testimony to how far attitudes had changed between what Reynolds was trying to do in 1816 and the Vestris management's approach.

Planché may also have played an important part in Vestris's costuming decisions since he had been involved with earlier experiments in historical costuming, such as Charles Kemble's 1823 *King John*. Reynolds, working under the management of John Philip Kemble who was interested in questions of historical costume, had made some attempt at Athenian costuming and setting with his 'Grand Doric Colonnade appertaining to Duke Theseus' Palace' and Madame Vestris followed this with a set of a room in Theseus' palace with a distant view of Athens and conventional classical Athenian dress for the Athenian court (with Amazon tunic and pantaloons for

28 Planché, *Recollections*, p. 274.

Hippolyta). She dressed the fairies in variations on Greek themes but, given the need for them to be able to dance, these came out very close to the standard fairy dress of the Romantic ballet. In subsequent stagings the Athenian setting was to become both a reflex and a major part of the play's attractions, as the surviving accounts and illustrations of both Charles Kean's and Beerbohm Tree's productions demonstrate.

Vestris's production was very well received critically: 'complete justice was done to the text of the great bard in all the appliances of scenery, costume, and music' (TM cutting). Even those with reservations about the *Dream* as a stage play were prepared to concede that 'in the conception of the whole, a fine poetical feeling was apparent, a consciousness of the difficulties with which the struggle was to be made, and a resolution to conquer them if possible' and that 'as far as theatrical representation of this ethereal drama is possible, it was achieved last night' (*Times*, 17 November 1840). However, despite making a strong impact in its own day and establishing the framework which was to dominate stagings of the play for more than half a century, this production has only recently begun to receive the recognition it deserves. Partly this is because Vestris's two successors as *Dream* producers, Samuel Phelps and Charles Kean, had longer managerial careers and more effective partisans and publicists, partly it is because Vestris herself, the object of erotic speculation as 'a woman with a past', was a dubious figure for a theatre that was bent on establishing its own respectability in order to attract a more respectable audience.[29]

MENDELSSOHN

Vestris used Mendelssohn's overture (1826) to *A Midsummer Night's Dream* as an important part of her staging in which music played a significant part in the overall effect. The key difference from previous productions was that she used only settings of lines and songs from the *Dream* itself, although some came to her via the Reynolds adaptation. Mendelssohn's overture and incidental music (1843) became a virtually indispensable part of productions of the play for more than a hundred years and substantially influenced production traditions, becoming a major cause of contention when directors tried to remove it in the twentieth century. The music itself is of high quality, drawing on the Shakespearean play with great sensitivity, but it is very much of its period and a decision to use it almost presupposes other kinds of decisions about the nature

29 Jorgens 'Criticism and stage history'(PhD), Griffiths ('Pioneer production'), and Gary J. Williams ('Web') all discuss Vestris's production and each independently identify Vestris's text as that published by J. Pattie, rather than Lacy's, as Odell thought (*Betterton to Irving*, II, p. 204). See Davis, *Actresses*, for illuminating comments on costuming and on Vestris's image.

of the production, the treatment of the fairies and the amount of time available to the production. The musical treatment of the fairies allied them with the supernatural characters of Romantic ballet, the musical evocation of woodlands encouraged ever more romantically realistic woodland scenery and the need to accommodate nearly an hour of Mendelssohn's music (including the overture) inevitably led to textual cuts to make room for it, a situation exacerbated in the many productions which also used other music.

Mendelssohn and spectacular scenery were, in the first place, both an attempt to honour Shakespeare by lavishing on his play the best and most up-to-date aesthetic tributes and, in some senses, a defence against the perceived likelihood of theatrical failure with a difficult text. Their continued presence is a powerful testimony to the influence of the pictorial in Victorian culture and to their efficacy as an insurance policy. When directors like Granville Barker or Harcourt Williams dispensed with Mendelssohn they took on a powerful tradition, as Williams reveals in his paraphrase of a letter from one of the Old Vic gallery regulars protesting at his innovations: 'I have always told my friends that if they came to see *A Midsummer Night's Dream* at the Old Vic, they would see a play and an opera at the same time. I can't say that now.'[30] This battle over Mendelssohn came to incorporate and symbolise all the other battles between traditionalists and innovators in the first half of the twentieth century. Although Mendelssohn's music is now more likely to be quoted ironically in professional productions (as with Brook using the Wedding March to celebrate Bottom's coupling with Titania or Caird's 1989 punk pastiche), or to be played as the main attraction, accompanied by a truncated version of the *Dream*, it still casts a long shadow.[31]

Phelps and Kean, 1853–1875

Samuel Phelps and Charles Kean were dominant but contrasting figures in Shakespearean production in the 1850s. When Kean retired from management in 1859 he stated that his theory in staging Shakespeare was that 'historical accuracy might be so blended with pictorial effect that instruction and amusement would go hand in hand', thus making the theatre 'a school as well as a recreation'. Phelps was never so theoretical on his own behalf but critics consistently praised his productions for their intelligence which 'pervades the entire scenes of the play, and adjusts all the relations of the characters, and the saliences ... of the

---

30 Harcourt Williams, *Saga*, p. 84. See also Gary J. Williams ('Concord').
31 The City of Birmingham Symphony Orchestra staged such a version in 1973 (with Sara Kestelman fresh from Brook's production reprising Titania in rather different circumstances) and in 1989; the Finchley Children's Music Group and the London Mozart Players did a semi-staged version based on Kean's edition at the Barbican in 1988.

various situations. Hence the completeness of all and each and the harmonious working together of the company.'[32] Kean worked inwards from the circumference, from historical accuracy and pictorial effect to Shakespeare, whereas Phelps worked outwards, his effects radiating from a Shakespearean core. Each, however, developed his ideas for the *Dream* within the Athenian model established by Vestris, bolstered by the availability of the Mendelssohn incidental music which offered an important linking element in their productions.

Both, of course, approached Shakespeare with due regard for the dictates of Victorian propriety, finding potentially blasphemous material more troublesome than had their predecessors who tended to concentrate on questions of sexual decorum. One can almost gauge the spread of Victorian morality arithmetically, as both Phelps and Kean remove even more lines in sensitive passages than Vestris had. More individual words also come under suspicion, so that Phelps removes Titania's 'To have my love to bed, and to arise' (3.1.149) and Theseus' 'To wear away this long age of three hours / Between our aftersupper and bedtime' (5.1.33–4) and his 'Sweet friends, to bed' (5.1.346), all kept by Vestris, presumably on the strength of the arousing potential of 'bed'. Similarly Kean had a 'Minstrel' rather than a 'eunuch' offer the 'Battle of the Centaurs', Pyramus had a 'heart' rather than 'paps', and Theseus' sweet friends go 'away' rather than 'to bed'.[33]

PHELPS AND *A MIDSUMMER NIGHT'S DREAM*, 1853–1875

Phelps's *Dream* achieved an immediate success on its first production in 1853 and remained in his repertory throughout his Sadler's Wells management. His production was broadly similar to Vestris's with realistic woodland scenes, fairy dances, music and dioramas, and like Vestris he removed passages which expanded points already made, either verbally or visually, or recounted events the audience had already seen (thus reducing the number of occasions when a verbal and visual version of the same moment are offered for contrast). He cut many of the less appealing aspects of the fairies' lines so that they become simply mischievous sprites who make life difficult for the mortals. Like Vestris, Phelps reserved his heaviest cuts for the lovers, reducing the amount of confused quarrelling, and making them both less changeable and less interesting than in the original text, but he did better than Vestris in allowing them to discuss the nature of what they have experienced when they wake up in 4.1.

Critics were near unanimous in discovering a unity of approach in

---

32 Kean's speech is in Farquharson Sharp, *History*, p. 152; the comment on Phelps is part of a review of his *Dream* in the *ILN*, 26 August 1854.

33 In the commentary I have indicated where Bowdler's *Family Shakspeare* suggested cuts should be made for reasons of propriety.

Phelps's production which ensured its success in the face of post-Hazlitt critical orthodoxy. Henry Morley was prominent in his praise for Phelps who 'never lost sight of the main idea which governs the whole play' which was 'to present merely shadows'. Douglas Jerrold made a similar point with reference to the 'beautiful dreaminess' of the production with its woodland scenes characterised by 'a misty transparency about the figures that gives them the appearance of flitting shadows more than of human beings'. In fact the misty transparency was literal as well as metaphysical, since Phelps treated the whole of the wood scenes as a dream played behind a huge gauze that filled the proscenium opening. It was decorated with giant flowers that made the characters appear smaller, and it clearly played a significant part in emphasising the different nature of events in the wood and in Athens.[34]

Phelps's approach to the fairies was unconventional for his period: 'the fairies, as they glide in and out of the trees and foliage, give you a notion that they have actually stepped out of them, as though the trunks and flowers were their natural abiding-places, and by long residence, they had become imbued with the colour of them. There were none of your winged, white muslin fairies with spangles and butterfly wands.' While this unconventional element seems to have worked well, Phelps was less successful with his lovers, since Morley took them to task for being too funny and unable to adapt to the dream elements in the play. Although the surviving promptbook for Phelps's 1861 revival shows that Phelps's editing had toned down the quarrel, Morley thought that 'the arguing and quarrelling and blundering that should have been playful, dreamlike, and poetical, was much too loud and real' and it was 'a very great mistake' when 'the dream so worked out into hard literalness as to create constant laughter' during the scenes when Helena is wooed by both Lysander and Demetrius. Apparently 'the merriment which Shakespeare connected with those scenes was but a little of the poet's sunlight meant to glitter among tears'.[35] The lovers' self-absorbed seriousness in scenes framed by the fairies' intervention is now usually treated as comic, but Morley's was a representative nineteenth-century view.

Phelps's own playing of Bottom was the focus of his unified approach. Although, as we have seen, Bottom is only one of a number of roughly equal parts in the play, Phelps's success with the part over a period of more than

34 Morley is in Rowell, *Dramatic Criticism*, p. 102; Jerrold is in May Phelps, *Life*, pp. 131–2; for the gauze see comments by Frederick Fenton (Phelps's designer) in Moyr Smith, *Dream* , p. xiii. Lloyds, *Scene Painting*, explains how many nineteenth-century effects were achieved.

35 The fairies are from May Phelps, *Life*, p. 133; Morley is in Rowell, *Dramatic Criticism*, p. 104.

twenty years fuelled the conventional view throughout the nineteenth century that 'with the exception of Bottom, the cast of *A Midsummer Night's Dream* contains no parts with great opportunities' (*Era*, 13 January 1900) and made the role the choice of most male actor–managers (except Benson whose classical profile made him stick to Lysander and latterly Theseus). However, Phelps's approach was unusual in its refusal to play for easy laughs, as Westland Marston's representative praise demonstrates:

> The calm self-conceit of his Bottom, who finds so many things within
> his range, because his ignorance conceals their difficulties, was far more
> humourous than if his vanity had been made broader and more boisterous.
> His absolute insensibility to the ridiculous was more mirth-moving than the
> most grotesque means by which inferior actors would have italicized the
> absurd conceit of the character. His quiet, matter-of-course belief that the
> parts of Thisbe and the Lion are equally within his grasp, and that, as to the
> latter, he could roar, with equal sucess, either 'terribly' or 'as gently as any
> sucking dove,' was more telling than would have been a violent and highly-
> coloured expression of his self-complacency. The same may be said of his air
> of contented superiority in contriving means to protect the ladies from fears
> of the drawn sword and of the lion in the play, of his ready assumption of the
> ass's head, of his light fingering of it, as if it had been the most natural of
> head-gears, and his satisfaction with his own wit in fathoming and baffling
> the designs of Puck, who had imposed it. In all this, the sense of acquiescence
> in the absurd was far more ludicrous than extreme wonder or excitement
> would have been. As a picture of intense self-conceit, expressed generally
> rather by signs of inward relish of his acuteness than by more open display
> – of ridiculous fastidiousness and equally ridiculous devices to satisfy it –
> as a parody of sense and ingenuity by a shallow brain, – Bottom must be
> ranked as one of this actor's most original conceptions.[36]

Phelps's decision to play Bottom was both risky, since Bottom's failings are those traditionally ascribed to the actor–manager (particularly self-satisfaction, arrogance and building up his part at the expense of others), and an interesting indication of one of the difficulties actor–managers had in finding suitable parts for themselves in *A Midsummer Night's Dream* because of its unusual construction. Phelps's influence in this respect was double edged: by making Bottom an actor–manager's part and by playing it in his own and others' productions between 1853 and 1875 he established his interpretation as normative. However, at the same time he paved the way for an increasing elaboration of business in the Mechanicals scenes which in some versions seems to have swamped everything else in the production. Certainly the 1861

36 In Rowell, *Dramatic Criticism*, p. 108.

promptbook has very elaborate stage directions for the company falling out with one another during the performance of 'Pyramus and Thisbe'.

Phelps played a major role in the acceptance of Shakespeare's *Dream* as a performance text. Although his success with Bottom led to a concentration on the Mechanicals which would distort some future productions, his emphasis on subsuming all the elements in his productions to a common end built on Vestris's foundation, combining as much of the original text as propriety allowed with an expression of the text's implied musical and spectacular possibilities, in marked contrast to Charles Kean's pedantically pictorial production.

CHARLES KEAN AND *A MIDSUMMER NIGHT'S DREAM*, 1856

Kean was, as the German novelist Theodor Fontane described him, very much 'a cross between a professor and theatre director',[37] whose archaeological interests led to his election as a Fellow of the Society of Antiquaries and towards informatively tortuous overjustifications of his archaeologically spectacular production decisions. Michael Booth has shown the centrality of the educationally pictorial and of the archaeological in Victorian culture, but in Kean's case the spectacular imagination itself had serious implications for *A Midsummer Night's Dream* since it led to a concentration on the visual at the expense of the aural, and to the play becoming a site for even more elaborate decorative effects, to the exclusion of nearly half of the Shakespearean text.

As well as removing potentially offensive material Kean also pruned lines which amplified points already made in action or by the scenery, but the scale of his changes was much greater than either Phelps's or Vestris's. Like other managers he cut very little from the Mechanicals, but he was ruthless with the lovers: Helena's 225 Shakespearean lines dwindled to under a hundred, the lovers' total from nearly 700 to under 350, and Lysander narrowly overtook Helena as the lover with the most lines, whereas Shakespeare had him third, a long way behind Helena and just behind Hermia. Moreover Kean's archaeological exactitude necessitated other changes: Periclean Athens was not a duchy, so Theseus (who was not its ruler anyway) is referred to as 'Prince' throughout Kean's version. In general, Kean reduced the number of short speeches, thereby creating a static mood which rendered the play more suitable for the various set pieces as a kind of series of Shakespearean *tableaux vivants*, and like his predecessors he consistently reduced the elements of dislocation and transmutation throughout the play. Although some of Kean's changes may have produced a neater and smoother narrative, others, such as only referring to the Indian Boy in Oberon and Titania's first quarrel, obscure the narrative development of the play.

37 Fontane, *Aus England*, p. 48n.

1 Oberon and Titania's 2.1 confrontation in Charles Kean's production at the Princess's, 1856. Note the flying fairies, the influence of ballet on the women's costumes, the picturesque woodland scene, Ellen Terry as Puck (seated at Oberon's feet), and the presence of the Indian Boy. Oberon and her/his fairies wear 'classical' costume.

One of the problems Kean faced was that his concern with archaeological accuracy could not readily be reconciled with *A Midsummer Night's Dream*, since Theseus' court belongs to a mythological rather than a historical past and there is no obvious historical costume for Athenian fairies. Thus any attempt to be 'historically accurate' in *A Midsummer Night's Dream* must always involve some complicated decisions about period authenticity. Kean was silent about the inspiration for his fairies, who were securely within the balletic tradition, with white-winged female *corps de ballet* sylphides and crimson-winged male Athenian warriors, benefiting from five pairs of clock-work wings to enhance the illusion of flight (promptbook). However, despite the fact that from the time of Reynolds managers had staged the *Dream* in settings that reminded their audiences of classical Athens, Kean worried away at the issue in revealing ways. His playbill for *A Midsummer Night's Dream* gives a full account of his reasoning:

the general character of the play is so far from historical, that while I have made Athens and its neighbourhood the subjects of illustration, I have held myself unfettered with regard to chronology. Indeed, sufficient is not known of the details of Greek life and architecture to render complete (or proximate) accuracy possible, even if a theatrical representation of the period were attempted. Influenced by these considerations, I have selected a later period, in the hope of conveying an idea of Athens as it would have appeared to one of its own inhabitants, at a time when it had attained its greatest splendour in literature and art.

Kean's audience were, therefore, educated with pictorial recreations of the Acropolis, the Theatre of Dionysus and 'that memorable hill from whence the words of sacred truth were first promulgated to the Athenian citizens by apostolic inspiration'. Although the Mechanicals' furniture and tools were supposedly 'Copied from Discoveries at Herculaneum' (playbill), his stage manager's workbook reveals that many of the props had already been used in *Winter's Tale* (interestingly, Tree cannibalised his *Dream* mise-en-scène for a production of *Winter's Tale*, a clear indication of the intellectual space the two plays shared in the theatre).

In return for the more than 40 per cent of Shakespeare's text that Kean omitted, he provided a wealth of dances and tableaux conceived on a monumental scale, with sixty fairies involved in the first confrontation between Oberon and Titania, a shadow dance of fairies dancing in the moonlight to lull Titania to sleep, and a maypole dance after Puck's 'naught shall go ill' speech to provide a spectacular act ending. Although Kean's biographer rightly ascribed the production's success to 'an endless succession of skilfully-blended, pictorial, mechanical, and musical effects, [which] overpowered the faculties of the spectators with the influences of an enchanting vision',[38] critical opinion was far more divided about this than about Phelps's approach. The *Illustrated London News* believed that Kean did not 'indulge in scenic and decorative magnificence for the mere sake of dazzling by show to baffle competition. His purposes are more lofty and intellectual: they aim at truth, propriety and instruction' (18 October 1856). On the other hand, the *Illustrated Times* believed that Kean did not approach Shakespeare 'with the zeal of an enthusiastic admirer' but used the plays as 'vehicles for the display of much good taste and many beautiful effects' (25 October 1856). The problem that this led to the displacement of part of the play is not simply a modern perception. Henry Morley was infuriated by the maypole dance because of the textual sacrifices that had to be made to accommodate it: 'From the third act we miss a portion of the poem most essen-

38 Cole, *Kean*, II, p. 199.

2 The final scene of Charles Kean's production at the Princess's, 1856, with Ellen Terry
as Puck. The architecture gives a strong visual impression of classical Athens. Some of
the fairies were painted figures on the back-cloth. The fairies give 'glimmering' light
with flower-shaped lanterns, but all appear to be female, in contrast with 2.1.

tial to its right effect – the quarrel between Hermia and Helena; but we get, at
the end, a ballet of fairies round a maypole that shoots up out of an aloe, after the
way of a transformation in a pantomime, and rains down garlands.'[39] Extending
critical generosity to Kean, one might argue that the dance in which the fairies
unwound streamers and 'threaded the needle' in a complex dance pattern might
offer a visual compensation for the removal of much of the lovers' complexities
(and of all textual references to the rite of May), but it would surely be an over-
extension of Savage's doctrine of aesthetic substitution to see the dance as an
adequate balancing of the aesthetic books.

Doubts and cross-currents, 1875–1895

From Hazlitt's impassioned response to Reynolds's adaptation onwards,
there had been considerable critical doubt as to whether *A Midsummer*

39 In Rowell, *Dramatic Criticism*, p. 101.

Night's Dream was a viable stage play but the argument was complex and multi-faceted. Some argued that the play was simply unsuited to the stage, others suggested that an approach like Phelps's was better than Kean's, others believed that Shakespeare would have approved of Kean's approach because 'had the wonderful appliances now within the reach of the theatres been known in Shakespeare's day, it is thus that he would have had it played' (*Era*, 9 October 1856), and yet others took the view that the play was seldom performed, 'not because, as it is vulgarly supposed, of it being too poetical, but on account of it requiring too extensive an interpretation. It demands a large company, and a variety of talent to give it with grace and effect' (*Illustrated London News*, 15 October 1853).

By the time of Phelps's last London performance as Bottom in 1875, Dutton Cook was extending that argument to suggest that contemporary theatrical conditions were 'fatal to the grace and delicacy of such a poem as "A Midsummer Night's Dream"'. The play was written 'at a time when scenic illusion and stage artifice depended almost entirely upon the imagination of the spectators' but 'the scenic embellishments ... and the musical accompaniments, without which the work could hardly be presented to the playgoers of today' reduced the play 'to the level of a fairy spectacle of commonplace quality' in which 'the poetry of the subject lies hidden under stage carpentry'. He could see no alternative to such staging methods and so the *Dream* 'might fairly be dismissed from the catalogue of acting plays'.[40] Indeed this was virtually the case in London between 1875 and 1900 since only Edward Saker's 1880 production (which originated in Liverpool), F. R. Benson's touring version (first seen in London in 1889), and Augustin Daly's staging (which had had a distinguished New York history before its 1895 London engagement) appeared in London during that period.

Saker's 1880 production was characterised not only by heavy textual, spectacular and musical debts to Kean but also by the rediscovery of the 1763 ploy of having all the fairy parts played by children. Saker's intention was to find a viable method of creating a contrast between the mortals and the fairies: 'In the substitution of CHILDREN for adults who have hitherto filled the parts in the fairy Scenes, I have hit upon an idea that I think and hope will convey that necessary contrast between the Mortals and Immortals, so desirable: and more thoroughly embody the effect intended by Shakespeare in this exquisite conception' (programme). While Saker's conception of the fairies follows the traditional nineteenth-century reading in which their sensual and sexual aspects are played down, he carried it to a Garrick-like extreme by using children to play all the

40 Dutton Cook, *Nights*, pp. 273–6.

fairy parts: their language was pruned, their behaviour was childlike and their function in the play trivialised. However, Saker's arrangement toured successfully to Dublin, Brighton and London, largely on the strength of the novelty value of the children and its very full list of scenic, balletic and musical attractions, including the whole of Mendelssohn's score as well as 'compositions of Sir H. Bishop, C. Horn, Cooke, Stevens, Werner and John Ross' (programme).

While Augustin Daly occupies an important position in the history of American theatre, his production of *A Midsummer Night's Dream* was already something of an anachronism when it appeared in London in 1895. Its basic conception was some twenty years old, it was subject to some chauvinistic carping, and it also suffered the misfortune of being in a head-on collision with George Bernard Shaw in full polemical flight. However, although Daly was condemned as a 'hacker and slasher' of Shakespeare, there was nothing innovatory about his editorial practices: he removed offensive matter, descriptive passages that could be visualised and, as William Winter, who edited his texts, put it, literary passages that 'neither facilitate exposition of character nor expedite movement, and by which sometimes the action is impeded'.[41] Since Ada Rehan, Daly's star, played Helena, her part was given greater prominence than usual by ending Act One with her declaration that she would follow Demetrius into the wood and by allowing her to be the last lover to enter in Act Three, but basically it was the spectacular and musical mixture as before.

Unlike some traditionalists, who believed that the play was inherently undramatic and would always have to presented as a spectacular pageant, Shaw, as one might expect, was in the vanguard of those who attacked the older methods of staging Shakespeare. He argued that Daly had 'a systematic policy of sacrificing the credibility of the play to the chance of exhibiting an effective living picture', that he was 'unable to conceive that there could have been any illusion at all about the play before scenery was introduced' and that 'every accessory he employs is brought in at the deadliest risk of destroying the magic spell woven by the poet'.[42] This was a minority view in the nineties and had little immediate effect.

F. R. Benson and Beerbohm Tree

Frank Robert Benson had *A Midsummer Night's Dream* in his repertory throughout his long managerial career, and although the appearance of his touring production changed over the years with new scenery (particularly after

41 'Hacker and slasher' is from the *Sketch*, 10 January 1900: Winter's criteria are quoted in Felheim's excellent *Daly*, p. 221.
42 Shaw, *Nineties*, I, p. 179.

3 Hippolyta and Hermia share a moment of sympathy in the opening scene of Beerbohm Tree's 1900 staging at Her Majesty's. Hippolyta's costume combines an Amazon breast-plate with a skirt. Tree's staging offered classical dress and a massively 'authentic' Athenian set in the fashion of Alma Tadema.

a fire destroyed much of the company's equipment) and music and cast changes, its overall conception remained broadly the same from the 1880s into the 1920s.[43] Essentially Benson's was a modestly spectacular traditional Mendelssohnian–Athenian *Dream* in the Victorian manner, using the Vestris–Phelps approach to the text, rather than the more radical one favoured by Kean and Saker. There were some thoughtful detailed innovations which enhanced audience comprehension such as Oberon using his powers 'to summon such as the lovers whose presence is desired' (HTC cutting, 1900) as well as other features which were less welcome. Chief among these was a deaf Starveling, an initially amusing innovation which rapidly became both a tradition and an irritation in the context of the tendency for Benson's Mechanicals

43 Benson's staging is discussed in Moyr Smith, *Dream*, pp. xiv–xvi. Trewin's *Benson* is the standard survey of his career.

to indulge in gags and over-elaborate business. Benson was enormously influential because of his role as a mainstay of the early days of the Stratford Festival, which led eventually to the formation of the Royal Shakespeare Company,[44] and because of the number of those who, having passed through his company, staged their own productions under his influence, either positive as in the case of Oscar Asche (1905), or negative as in the case of Harcourt Williams (1929). He was also influential by virtue of his very long touring career which meant that his production was staged over many years throughout the British Isles. Indeed, traditional conceptions of *A Midsummer Night's Dream* today, as represented in a parody like the 1991 *Pocket Dream*, are a fair indication of the longevity of a sub-Bensonian approach.

Herbert Beerbohm Tree's 1900 production of *A Midsummer Night's Dream*, whose rabbits remain a byword for the excesses of the Victorian tradition, was very firmly located within that tradition with its Athenian views, woodland glades, Mendelssohn music and dancing. As Gordon Crosse, who kept a diary recording his responses to fifty years of Shakespearean productions, put it, 'unlike Daly, Tree had a real devotion to Shakespeare ... and really thought that he was honouring the poet by embellishing his works with all the magnificence the theatre could supply'.[45] Tree was an articulate and thoughtful self-publicist who produced trenchant defences of his general approach to Shakespeare, which was largely traditional although he was to invite the radical William Poel to direct for him. According to Tree, the actor–manager's enemies believed that he was capable of 'every shameless infraction of every rule of dramatic art, provided only that he stands out from his fellows and obtains the giant share of notice and applause'. To this end they thought that the text was 'ruthlessly cut in order to give an unwarranted predominance to certain parts'. Tree answers this criticism by pointing out that, given the need for scenery, which he justifies by reference to the prologue to *Henry V*, it would be impossible to present the plays within Shakespeare's 'self-imposed' three-hour time limit without cutting. Of course, 'the scenic embellishments should not overwhelm the dramatic interest', but they 'should be as beautiful and costly as the subject of the drama being performed seems to demand; ... not subordinate to, but rather harmonious with, the dramatic interest, just as every other element of art introduced into the representation should be'.[46]

Tree develops his arguments cogently and at length, and the majority of

44 Beauman, *Royal Shakespeare Company*, is the standard history of the RSC.
45 Crosse, *Fifty Years of Shakespearean Playgoing*, p. 43. Crosse also published *Shakespearean Playgoing 1890–1952*. Both books are based on his manuscript diary which is now in the BSL.
46 Tree, *Thoughts and After-Thoughts*, pp. 51, 52, 57–8, 56.

critical responses to his production of the *Dream* are testimony to the effectiveness with which he pursued his goals. Richard Dickins, who was to be appalled
at the excesses of Tree's *Tempest* only four years later, thought it was a 'triumph
of stage art' which 'never became operatic'.[47] Similarly, another critic commented that 'this scholarly manager has been led into no excess... There is no
mere weight of spectacle... Mr Tree gives us a full stage "with a difference".
The difference lies in the poetic spirit, the fine interpretive capacity, to which
we owe these lovely realisations of some of Shakespeare's more rare and elusive
conceptions' (HTC cutting, 18 January 1900). Many of the critics are aware of
the dangers of the spectacular approach but, with the exception of a very few
dissenters like Percy Fitzgerald, who argued that Tree's performance as
Bottom was 'distended till it spread over the whole play' with a resulting 'lack
of proportion',[48] they assert that Tree overcame them on this occasion.

A good example of Tree's method is his treatment of the final scene, which
sounds reminiscent of Phelps's approach:

> Instead of the epilogue, Mr Tree employs an effect, which he, no doubt,
> regards as symbolical of the dream of which Puck speaks... At the first when
> the curtain rises, the woodland scene grows out of gloom. So, at the end,
> the pomps and splendours of Theseus' Court fade from sight and complete
> darkness steals over the stage. Not suddenly, however. The mortals leave,
> Oberon and Titania and their train come on, and then the palace yields a
> magical change. Pillars and columns keep their shape, yet lose their solidity.
> They stand out translucent, aglow, and the whole space is mysteriously
> suffused with light... Then the soft song dies down and light and fairies
> seem to fade away together, and there is darkness impenetrable.
>
> (HTC cutting, 18 January 1900)

The presence of Benson's company at the Lyceum with their *Dream* for a
week during the run of Tree's 1900 production only pointed the moral that,
as Richard Dickins put it:

> Whatever views may be held regarding the vexed question of scenic display,
> there can be no doubt that when the eye has become accustomed to artistic
> stage surroundings, anything approaching ugliness is instinctively resented,
> and my personal experience is that while a lovely background assists the
> imagination, such eye-sores as an obviously cardboard rock or badly painted
> statue irritate the nerves and distract the attention from the acting.[49]

47 Dickins, *Forty Years*, pp. 93–4.
48 Fitzgerald, *Representation*, p. 74.
49 Dickins, *Forty Years*, p. 95.

By 1911, when Tree staged what was to be the last pictorial *Dream* before the outbreak of the First World War, he had learned from Oscar Asche (whose 1905 production was operatically Bensonian) that traditional Shakespearean productions could benefit from quicker scene changes if only one designer was employed,[50] but otherwise the mixture was broadly as before. The managerial consensus about staging *A Midsummer Night's Dream* had changed little from the pioneering days of Madame Vestris, seventy years before. The ingredients for a successful production were Mendelssohn's music, a forest as beautiful and realistic as possible, some child fairies, heavily cut texts which gave prominence to the Mechanicals and the fairies at the expense of the lovers, and a large amount of gagging and business for the Mechanicals. There was no discernible disagreement about characterisation or about the play's meanings from production to production. A manager staging the play strove to surpass his contemporaries with the sumptuousness of his production within the traditional guidelines, not to challenge them.

The nineteenth century strove for 'authenticity' in staging *A Midsummer Night's Dream*. One aim was to reproduce an Athens which would fit in with Victorian notions of Athenian culture, identifying Britain with a composite Graeco-Roman civilisation, and thereby offering an educationally satisfactory mixture of cultural tourism and cultural imperialism. At the same time, while the search for fairy authenticity involved assimilation of ballet and Mendelssohn's music to create a Keatsean synaesthesia, the ever more realistic but essentially English woodland glades satisfied an urban fantasy of lost preindustrial innocence. This innocence, which was associated both with the origins of empire and with childhood, may partly lie behind the stress on child fairies.[51] Marrying these elements was always difficult and Shakespeare was sometimes at best a secondary element in the resulting show, the aesthetic figleaf for an extravaganza of dancing, music, massed numbers and scenery.

Challenging the consensus: William Poel and Granville Barker

The ossifying Victorian consensus was broken by a combination of factors, as scholarship revealed more about the nature of the Elizabethan stage (particularly after the discovery of the de Witt drawing of the Swan theatre), as William Poel's often eccentric attempts to recreate Elizabethan stagings opened up the possibility of other approaches, and as new technological and

50 Asche, *Oscar Asche*, p. 122.
51 See Beatrice Phillpotts's excellent introduction to *Fairy Paintings*, and Jeremy Maas, *Victorian Painters*, p. 148 for incisive and highly relevant accounts of the role of fairies in nineteenth-century art and Victorian culture.

economic factors combined with new approaches to theatre in general to exert an influence on Shakespearean staging.[52]

Poel's experiments with allegedly Elizabethan staging from the later years of the nineteenth century complicated the historical fidelity argument by suggesting that productions could be faithful to Shakespeare's period rather than that of the supposed period of the play's action. This laid down a framework which is still very influential today: the 1970s BBC/Time–Life television Shakespeare, attempting to be non-controversial with an eye to American video sales, was still committed to setting plays either 'in Shakespeare's time or in the little period that tradition has assigned to the play'.[53]

Poel was the doyen of the Shakespearean radicals, who generally explored his sometimes eccentric vision of a more authentically Elizabethan method of staging with predominantly amateur casts in non-theatrical venues. Although he did not stage the *Dream*, his influence percolated into the mainstream through those who had worked with him. Harley Granville Barker acted for Poel, acknowledged his influence, and in turn influenced others both through his Shakespeare productions in 1912–14 and through his *Prefaces*; Ben Greet was associated with Poel in reviving *Everyman* and passed many of his ideas on to such directors as Robert Atkins, Andrew Leigh and Russell Thorndike. The ever increasing network of those indebted, at whatever remove, to Poel, began to dominate productions of *A Midsummer Night's Dream* in the 1920s and 1930s to the discomfort of those who preferred real woods, Mendelssohn and balletic fairies, although the tendency would be to substitute a new fantasy of Elizabethan authenticity for an old Athenian one.

GRANVILLE BARKER, 1914

The greatest impetus for this movement away from the traditional consensus came from Granville Barker's productions of *Winter's Tale*, *Twelfth Night*, and *A Midsummer Night's Dream* at the Savoy Theatre in 1912–14. His major innovations for all three plays were similar: he used a full text and non-realistic scenery, and he reinstated the forestage. Although Barker's methods were innovatory in Britain, they may have owed something to developments in Germany and an apron built out into the auditorium had already been seen when Poel staged *Two Gentlemen of Verona* for Tree in 1911.[54] Nevertheless,

---

52 See Styan for an excellent account of *The Shakespeare Revolution*. Speaight's *Poel* and *Shakespeare on the Stage* are also useful.

53 A comment by Elijah Moshinsky, who directed an 'Elizabethan' version for the BBC/*Time–Life* series (in Elsom, *Contemporary*, p. 116).

54 Byrne, 'Fifty years', p. 8. Dymkowski (*Granville Barker*) and Kennedy (*Dream of Theatre*) offer overviews of Barker's achievement.

Barker's attempt to stage a full text of the *Dream* meant that he had to dis-
mantle the vast accretion of musical and scenic conventions that were
swamping the play, using new approaches to scenery, costuming and music.
An attempt to present a full text inevitably involved an innovatory mise-en-
scène which cut out the complicated scenery and long waits for scene
changes characteristic of the traditional approach, in which text had to be
removed wholesale to accommodate the scenery which supposedly illustrated that text. Similarly, Mendelssohn's music had become associated with
the spectacular production style, so it too had to be rejected, in Barker's case
in favour of Cecil Sharp's compilation of English folk tunes.

Productions between Vestris's and Barker's offered anything from around
60 per cent to around 80 per cent of the text of *A Midsummer Night's Dream*;
Barker made two brief omissions, a few slight verbal adjustments, and added
a song after Titania's 'Will we sing and bless this place' (5.1.378) taken from
The Two Noble Kinsmen because he believed that 'there is a lyric missing at the
end of the play, and to set a tune to the rhythms of Oberon's spoken words
seems absurd'.[55] Opinions differ about whether a song is actually missing
and whether Barker adopted the best approach to deal with the problem, but
finding a method of staging the play with a virtually unaltered text represents a major breakthrough that allowed the play to emerge as a dramatic
rather than a lyrical entity.

Barker's stage business was inevitably a mixture of old and new – in many
places he followed the general approach of his predecessors, in others he
offered something new.[56] In the case of the Mechanicals, Desmond
MacCarthy had no difficulties in assigning traditional attributes to 'the fussy,
nervous accommodating Quince' and 'poor timid old Starveling' amongst
others. Indeed Barker's Starveling was H. O. Nicholson, who played the role
in major productions over more than twenty years for Benson, Granville
Barker, Benson again, J. B. Fagan and Basil Dean, and always played a deaf
old Starveling, whatever the style of the production. On the other hand,
Gordon Crosse observed that 'in the play scene they rather underacted – I
suppose for fear of exaggerating', not a common critical stricture on interpretations of this scene, and the *Pall Mall Gazette* hoped that they would 'set
up a new standard for the English stage, and that the old depressing imbecili-
ties sacred to "acting versions" have at last and forever been swept away'.[57]

Certainly Barker's use of a full text would have led to an increase in the

55 Granville-Barker, *Prefaces*, p. 39.
56 See Griffiths, 'Tradition and innovation', for a more extended analysis.
57 In Rowell, *Dramatic Criticism*, p. 160; Crosse, *Diary*, V, p. 167; quoted by Byrne,
    'Fifty Years', p. 8.

lovers' prominence, at the expense of the traditional tendency for Bottom and the Mechanicals to dominate the whole play. The lovers, generally played as 'straight romantics' into the twentieth century, were also generally regarded as tedious. Although they pose nothing like the perceived threat to established order associated with the 'New Woman', and their language is not nearly as sexually explicit as that of Restoration comedy, it is probably no coincidence that the theatre began to find ways of dealing with fuller versions of the lovers as contemporary plays began to present versions of the 'New Woman' at the end of the nineteenth century and as Restoration comedy returned to the stage after the First World War. Benson actually pioneered the robust comic approach successfully, building on Phelps's unappreciated innovations: at Stratford in 1892 his 'ladies' were castigated for being 'a little too demonstrative in the third act, where bitter words pass between them' (*Stage*, 21 April) and Dickins saw Benson's lovers 'playing with spirit and a fine sense of comedy' in 1900. Asche, a former member of Benson's company, continued in his vein with 'the dramatic scenes of criss-cross comedy ... played with uncommon energy' (*Sketch*, 6 December 1905). With Granville Barker's return to the full text, the lovers' position was further strengthened, though even Desmond MacCarthy's praise suggests a suspicion that he was being conned somehow: Barker's female lovers 'revealed more dramatic comedy in the situation than any reader, however imaginative, is likely to feel in it'.[58]

If the restoration of the lovers to their Shakespearean proportions was, in itself, a significant innovation, the treatment of the fairies was revolutionary, although Barker did still use children in some of the fairy parts. Barker believed that the fairies were the director's main test and that Shakespeare's 'chief delight' in *A Midsummer Night's Dream* lay in the 'screeds of word music to be spoken by Oberon, Titania, and Puck'. Barker himself realised that concentrating on the fairies had its dangers: 'they must not be too startling. But one wishes people were not so easily startled. I won't have them dowdy. They mustn't warp your imagination - stepping too boldly between Shakespeare's spirit and yours. It is a difficult problem.'[59] While Puck was comparatively easy (even if a male Puck was highly unusual), since Barker stressed his Englishness and clothed him in red, the other fairies offered the most radical of challenges to the balletic tradition. They seemed to MacCarthy to be 'ormolu' fairies, 'detached from some fantastic bristling old clock' and to the *Era* (February 11) they were

---

58 'Straight romantics' is from Sprague and Trewin, *Shakespeare's Plays*, p. 97; they suggest that the major change in approaches to the lovers came with Dean in 1924 but this is not borne out by the evidence. Dickins, *Forty Years*, p. 94; MacCarthy in Rowell, *Dramatic Criticism*, p. 160.

59 Granville-Barker, *Prefaces*, pp. 37, 38.

4 Granville Barker's production (Savoy, 1914). Oberon and the 'ormolu' fairies watch Helena and Demetrius. The curtains make no attempt to recreate a real wood, and Oberon and the fairies make no attempt to hide, creating a convention of invisibility, rather than attempting to be invisible. Design by Norman Wilkinson.

'heavy little idols of gold with shiny yellow faces'. After the initial shock had worn off, however, MacCarthy concluded that:

> the very characteristics which made them at first so outlandishly arresting now contribute to make them inconspicuous. They group themselves motionless about the stage, and the lovers move past and between them as casually as though they were stocks or stones. It is without effort we believe these quaintly gorgeous metallic creatures are invisible to the human eyes. They, therefore, possess the most important quality of all from the point of view of the story and the action of the play. Dramatically, they are the most convincing fairies yet seen upon the stage.[60]

To make the extra room for Shakespeare's text, Norman Wilkinson, Barker's designer, used curtains for all the scenes except Theseus' palace in Act Five which was fully built-up. The play opened in white silk curtains with a conventional gold design for the early scenes with Theseus and Hippolyta, in place of the traditional Athenian palace or Periclean panoramic view of Athens, moved to salmon-pink curtains with steel-blue masses supposed to represent the roofs of the city for the Mechanicals scene and thence to the

60 In Rowell, *Dramatic Criticism*, p. 159.

wood which had nothing resembling a realistic tree: 'none of those tiresome, flat, gauze-tethered bough-and-blossom cut-outs'.[61] From the wood the scene reverted to the Mechanicals curtain set and then to the palace where the performance of 'Pyramus and Thisbe' took place against solid columns and the fairies reappeared to blend mortal and immortal worlds against a star-spangled backdrop. The purpose of Barker's approach quite escaped G. C. Odell, the great historian of Shakespearean production, who saw the 1915 New York revival:

> This was all supposed to be very much more artistic than the kind of thing
> Augustin Daly aimed at, and far more suggestive. It was thought to be full
> of illusion. Of course it was not. Anyone who has imagination can get the
> poetic illusion by seeing these things acted on a bare stage or on a stage hung
> with curtains or with just a conventional unchanged setting... No human
> being, however, can be expected to be anything but worried and annoyed by
> pink silk curtains that are supposed to be the roofs of houses, or green silk
> curtains that are supposed to be forest trees; especially when they blow and
> stream out in the gales of the stage.   (*Betterton to Irving*, II, p. 468)

If Barker intended the change from curtains to architectural set to act as some kind of visual parallel to the stability which had descended on the characters after the turmoil in the woods, then Odell certainly failed to grasp all the nuances of the mise-en-scène. Moreoever, he was not the only critic to express reservations about Barker's scenery in terms which point up one of the inherent paradoxes of Barker's new approach to the text. Perhaps it was inevitable that a radical textual approach should be judged on what might be regarded as its unfamiliar accidentals, rather than its fundamentals, but in the auditorium the impact of a full text might well be smaller than the impact of the other aspects of the production. Certainly Desmond MacCarthy believed that 'the majority of the audience thought as much about scenery at the Savoy Theatre as ever did an audience at His Majesty's. It was a different kind of scenery, but just as distracting to most people.'[62]

An even more serious criticism was voiced by John Palmer, in the *Saturday Review*:

> Even those who do not resent Shakespeare being slaughtered to make an
> intellectual and post-impressionist holiday will find it rather difficult to
> endure the dissonance of the inharmonic intervals between Mr Norman
> Wilkinson's unfamiliar vision in purple and green; Mr Barker's entirely

---

61 Quoted in Trewin, *Shakespeare*, p. 57.
62 In Rowell, *Dramatic Criticism*, p. 159.

Gallic vision of Shakespeare's comic people; and Mr Cecil Sharp's old
English music. The production as a whole is more like a battle field than a
collaboration.   (14 February)

It might, of course, be equally difficult to defend organising theatrical interpretations of a sixteenth-century English writer's play around a nineteenth-
century German composer's music, if that had been tried for the first time in
1914. However, if Barker was aiming to achieve that 'unity of emotion and
atmosphere throughout' which was an 'explicit aim of the newer aesthetic
theory of the time' it seems that he failed.[63] So great and so varied was the
critical response to the fairies that it tended to obscure other elements of the
production: the Shakespeare text had been completely restored, the music
and the scenery were reasonably well accepted, but one element of the costuming seized the audience's attention. If Barker saw the fairies as his test, he
may be open to criticism for substituting the dictatorship of one element of
mise-en-scène for another. However, the true measure of his achievement
lies in the way that through finding a means of presenting the whole text
within acceptable time limits, he was able to demonstrate, as MacCarthy
stated, something which the play's stage history had left in real doubt: 'how
dramatic also passages and scenes are which seem to the reader to be entirely
lyrical'.[64] The closet play had given way to the spectacle play and now the
spectacle play gave ground to the whole text production. Other battles
remained to be fought, often over old ground, but a decisive claim for
Shakespeare's text had been made.

New methods of staging Shakespeare also made themselves felt at
Stratford, previously a Benson preserve, in 1914 with the unfortunately little
documented Patrick Kirwan offering a season which tried, in his own words,
to 'get the flavour of Elizabethan and Jacobean England into the air' by cutting
intervals and act waits to what he regarded as a minimum, using period costumes and music and announcing the performances by trumpet in the High
Street. On the basis of Kirwan's account, his production of the *Dream* seems
to have been distinctive and innovative: for the mortals he used Greek costumes which bore 'the impress of Elizabethan influence' and the fairy costumes were based on descriptions in Michael Drayton's *Nimphidia*. While all
this is innovatory, it should be noted that Kirwan's Elizabethanism did not
extend to casting: both Puck and Oberon were female parts in his production.

In performance the innovations were generally tolerated rather than
admired: the *Morning Post* missed Mendelssohn but found 'every

63 Byrne, 'Fifty years', p. 9.
64 In Rowell, *Dramatic Criticism*, p. 159.

justification for substituting the native music of the Sixteenth Century when the general aim is to be as primitive as is reasonably possible', but also objected to the 'many liberties [that] were taken with the text', including, amazingly enough in view of its past history, objections to the removal of parts of the 2.1 sleeping-place dialogue (23 April). The Stratford *Herald* (21 and 24 April) took a conservative line, arguing that 'the comedy was scarcely presented with the adjuncts a Stratford audience is accustomed to', even if, and presumably glancing at Barker's production, it welcomed the lack of surprises and 'indigestible morsels of brain disturbing artistry – such as eccentric costuming and far-fetched devices in scenery and lights'. Kirwan clearly inclined towards some of the newer developments in Shakespearean staging, particularly in his attempts to create quasi-Elizabethan theatrical conditions, but his influence was limited;[65] Barker and the Old Vic, combined with changing economic conditions, played a larger part in developing the ways in which *A Midsummer Night's Dream* was staged.

Tradition and innovation, 1914–1945

J. C. Trewin has characterised the period 1919–24 as one of confusion in Shakespearean staging,[66] a judgment which is amply confirmed in relation to *A Midsummer Night's Dream* productions over a much longer period. Well into the twenties many productions remained strongly influenced by a selective reapplication of the older methods in the light of changing economic conditions. Alongside the traditional strand there were some post-Barker Modernist stagings but Barker's production, like Brook's in 1970, offered principles for approaching Shakespeare, rather than a model to be directly emulated. Productions with Elizabethan sets and costumes also emerged as a significant factor from 1929. The general conditions under which Shakespeare was produced also changed significantly, with the gradual decline of the actor–manager system and the rise of the Old Vic, and with economic developments which made the old spectacular approach increasingly expensive.

Perhaps the most striking feature of the decade after the First World War is the sheer number of productions of *A Midsummer Night's Dream*, compared to any period before or since: it was staged seven times at the Old Vic between 1918 and 1929, there were three other major London productions and Bridges Adams directed it at Stratford on six occasions between 1919 and 1928. In the thirties, as the immediate need for fantasy as an antidote

---

65 Mazer takes a much less sanguine view of Kirwan's Elizabethanism (*Shakespeare Refashioned*, pp. 75–6).
66 Trewin, *Shakespeare*, p. 92.

to the horrors of war receded, the number of productions dropped and became exclusively the preserve of the Old Vic and Stratford.

THE OLD VIC, 1914–1926

Although Benson continued to tour his increasingly anachronistic production of the *Dream* throughout the First World War and into the twenties, there was little incentive for a manager to produce a new traditionally spectacular production during the war, so *A Midsummer Night's Dream* was left to the emerging Old Vic under Ben Greet. Greet produced the *Dream* many times over the years in many venues, often in the open air and, although there are few details of his Old Vic staging available, it seems on the evidence of other accounts that it fell well within the established tradition with Mendelssohn and fairy dances, gagging Mechanicals, a senile Starveling and heavily cut lovers, all presided over by Greet as Bottom. However, there was little in the way of spectacular scenery. Peter Roberts sums up Greet well: 'If the productions seemed reformist compared to the splendours of Irving or of Tree's Shakespeare, it was due to a combination of the pastoral staging tradition and sheer lack of money with which to embark on anything fussier' (Roberts, *Old Vic*, p. 120).

Greet's successor at the Old Vic for 1918–19 was George Foss whose production of *A Midsummer Night's Dream* was so disastrously hit by the great influenza epidemic that 'the performance could only hope to be a creditable get-through' and much of the 'rehearsed business had to be abandoned'. This is particularly unfortunate since his 1932 book *What the Author Meant* reveals him as a thoughtful and conscientious director who attempted to grapple with the various challenges of the play without resorting to easy, conventional or traditional solutions. Perhaps the most striking aspect of Foss's account of the *Dream* is his stress on Shakespeare's informing central theme, which is 'the Emancipation of Women'. Foss clearly saw Shakespeare as his contemporary, developing an interesting and plausible reading that opens up significant ways of approaching the relationships between Theseus and Hippolyta, Oberon and Titania and the four young lovers, both in general terms and in detail. On the evidence of his book, Foss had much to offer as a director.[67] His successors Russell Thorndike and Charles Warburton appear to have staged a straightforward but reduced traditional *Dream*.

Although Robert Atkins was reponsible for removing the footlights and adding a movable platform over the Old Vic's orchestra pit to serve as a kind of apron, [68] his three Old Vic productions of *A Midsummer Night's Dream* seem to have been in the reduced traditional mode with Mendelssohn, gag-

67 Foss, *Author*, pp. 130, 123.
68 Roberts, *Old Vic*, p. 160. see also Atkins, *Autobiography*.

ging Mechanicals, dances and sunrise effects. Although Bottom was to become one of his best parts, Atkins did not play the character in these productions which were inherently pragmatic in their approach: Oberon, for example, was a female part in 1923, but male in 1921 and 1924, although the female understudy in 1924 likened the role to 'a sort of principal boy's part of the classics' (VW cutting). Atkins's 1924 staging was also notable for developing the idea of the lovers as comic figures: the *Era* noted 'how often the four lovers seem out of key with the rest of the play, for they are so often presented as semi-tragic figures. The quarrel scene is always taken much too seriously. Mr Atkins has realised that the *Dream* is a comedy even in the lovers' parts' (19 November).

In 1926 Andrew Leigh, Atkins's successor at the Old Vic, was generally agreed to have 'sacrificed the fairies to the comics' (St John Ervine, VW cutting), despite fairy dances choreographed by Ninette de Valois. General reaction to the production was confused and uncertain about the right way to deal with the play post-Granville Barker and there was quite widespread nostalgia for the less intellectually complicated days of Tree, well exemplified in the *Star*'s reactions:

> these fairies are always rather difficult to manage. You may make them bizarre creatures with gilded faces, as did Granville Barker, memorably, or you may be content to present them as little elves straight from an obvious dancing academy, and still not satisfy the imagination. It is perhaps best to stick to the conventional kind, as is here done. But what a pity it was that these fairies were not allowed a little more of that perfectly matching Mendelssohn music to which to trip.   (VW cutting)

STRATFORD-UPON-AVON, 1919-1931

Stratford, despite brief flirtations with Patrick Kirwan and Ben Greet, had remained largely Benson's territory for nearly thirty years. When W. Bridges Adams succeeded him in 1919 he began a tenure that was to last another fifteen years, pursuing a cautiously radical path, pragmatically tempered by financial stringency and the demands of the repertory system. He directed *A Midsummer Night's Dream* ten times, trying permutations of most approaches to the play, from a pictorial Athenian–Mendelssohnian version in 1919 to an Elizabethan country house wedding staging in 1932. In these productions he gradually took Stratford away from the nineteenth-century norm towards the mainstream of contemporary practice, but generally at a respectful distance.[69] Moreover, if an innovation was successful, it tended to become a

69 See Speaight, *Shakespeare*, pp. 158–9.

tradition, so that the successful Elizabethan costumes and set of 1932, for example, were bequeathed to subsequent directors who were forced to use them as late as 1944, with or without Mendelssohn according to taste.

Bridges Adams remained broadly true to the principles he outlined in an early interview with the Stratford *Herald:* his plan was to aim for '*real* adequacy without stylistic eccentricity or shabbiness' and to 'do whatever will most quickly and unobtrusively make the majority of your audience feel at home in the play' (25 July 1919). He also stated that there would be a few cuts but no transpositions or mutilations, and a reduction in traditional business to get in more text, although that proviso hardly applied to his *Dream* productions, in which the Mechanicals' traditional overplaying was a dominant feature.

After a 1919 production with Greek costuming, realistic scenery, Mendels-sohn music and a female Puck, Bridges Adams replaced Mendelssohn with selections from *The Fairy Queen* in 1921, eliciting a response from the Stratford *Herald* that indicates the production's main attraction was the Mechanicals: 'this broad dramatic comedy is always appreciated, in as much as it is replete with humours and incident, and has so little to do with fancy and romance' (29 July). Mendelssohn was back in 1923 and the Mechanicals were in the ascendant, but in 1924 they were criticised for being less funny than previously. In 1924 Stratford's first male Puck caused the *Herald* to wonder 'why the part is so generally given to an actress' (2 May) but in 1926, in the cinema used after the Victorian theatre had burned down, it reverted to being a female part. A further gender realignment in 1928 established it as male until wartime exigencies once more led to a sex change. Bridges Adams's continuing emphasis on the Mechanicals is substantiated by the promptbook first used in the Mendelssohnian 1928 revival, in which the curtain call is so arranged that Bottom appears last for a solo call.

OTHER STAGINGS, 1920–1924

When J. B. Fagan offered a modestly reformist staging of the play in a relatively full text, without Mendelssohn but still with gagging Mechanicals (and still with H. O. Nicholson as Starveling), at the Court in 1920, he arranged his production in three parts, with all the wood scenes as Act Two. He thereby not only minimised scene changes but stressed a symmetry which Gordon Crosse, for one, had not been aware of previously.[70] While some critics were impressed by the stylised wood set, described by the *Athenaeum* as 'just tree trunks and a wide star-studded sky of infinite sugges-

70 Crosse, *Diary* , VII, p. 84.

tiveness' (17 December), the *Daily Telegraph* objected to its permanence since it confined 'to one part of the wood, action which in the original supposes three different settings'. In full-blown realistic settings the action had, of course, moved to 'Another Part of the Forest' in consonance with eighteenth-century editorial stage directions. On the small stage at the Court, according to the *Telegraph*, 'We get the feeling that at any given moment the scene is bestrewn with sleepers, all blissfully and incredibly unconscious of one another; and when towards daybreak, Hermia and Lysander lie down in the same spot where they have already had their earlier sleep, the effect is that our imagined vast forest dwindles to the size of a spinney' (6 December). What irritates the *Telegraph* seems both fitting, since the lovers return to the spot where their troubles began, and probably closer to what would have happened on Shakespeare's stage, but it is indicative of the persistence of erroneous ingrained assumptions about what 'the original supposes', based on anachronistic understandings of Shakespeare's stagecraft.

Donald Calthrop had played Puck for Barker, so it is not surprising that Crosse saw his 1923 Kingsway production as 'another experiment in the modern style', with Cecil Sharp's music and Norman Wilkinson as designer, even if there was still a deaf Starveling. The *Birmingham Post* commented that the production was based on 'the entire text played through quickly with the simplest scenery, speedily changed' (15 November) and Crosse was pleased that there was 'very little processioning, singing or dancing in the fairy scenes'.[71] Others, however, were less impressed. The *Illustrated London News* wondered if 'perhaps there are just a few plays of Shakespeare, this pre-eminent among them, which really gain in effectiveness from the help of spectacle' (21 November), while the conservative critic James Agate missed 'the leafy sense and the tinkle of the fairies' and found it difficult 'to dispense with the least of the sumptuosities which it has been customary to lavish upon this play, or to forgive Mr Calthrop one single note of the Mendelssohn which he withheld' (Agate, *Chronicles*, p. 39).

Basil Dean's production gave Agate everything he thought he wanted, and more. Opening at Drury Lane on Boxing Day 1924 as a substitute for the usual pantomime, it used, according to Dean, a full text and Mendelssohn's music as well as 'more colour and movement than usual: two ballets by Fokine and a wood scene which would change in full view of the audience to one of enchantment, after the manner of the transformation scenes of long ago' (Dean, *Seven Ages*, p. 237). Dean had once been Tree's stage manager and the production owed something to his methods, although even Tree at

---

71 Ibid., VIII, pp. 97, 99.

his most expansive had never included Mendelssohn's *Italian Symphony*, two string quartets and seven other items amongst his incidental music. Herbert Farjeon, who was on the side of the radicals, objected along pre-dictable, but highly appropriate, lines which sum up the anti-Mendelssohn, anti-pictorial case effectively: 'because it would take up too much time to give *all* Mendelssohn and *all* Shakespeare, and because it is Mendelssohn's *Dream* that he is bent on producing rather than Shakespeare's, Mr Dean con-demns us to sit through the Wedding March while his prize blue pencil gets to work on "irrelevant" – because so purely musical! – passages in the text'. Not only did Mendelssohn involve cutting Shakespeare, it also meant that the whole production was arranged in 'a setting favourable to the intention of the nineteenth-century composer rather than to that of the sixteenth century poet' with a 'classical wedding-marchy, Alma-Tadema palace', 'ballets undreamed of in Shakespeare's stage philosophy', and a large-scale forest 'designed for the accommodation of masses of fairies, because masses of fairies are clearly demanded by Mendelssohn's *chichey-chichey* fairy motive'. Ultimately Farjeon's argument was that Dean overlooked the fact that Shakespeare created 'the illusion of a forest full of fairies in words', that his 'loveliest lines were written through sheer necessity' in order to create that illusion, so that 'to give them a production by which the necessity is removed, turns the play into a succession of disregarded superfluities and redundan-cies' (Farjeon, *Scene*, pp. 39, 42–3).

Dean's staging of the wood scenes in a single set was as problematic on the broad acres of Drury Lane as Fagan's had been on the small stage at the Court. Farjeon again usefully summarised a whole history of staging problems in his response:

> In *A Midsummer Night's Dream* ... we are continually being transported to what editors describe as 'Another Part of the Forest'. Victorian producers tried up to a point to follow these instructions, which were true to Shakespeare's imagina-tion, but since they employed pictorial scenery, the result was a desolating suc-cession of waits, while the scene-shifters made the journey. Then came the out-cry against waits. We have now reduced the waits by employing a single picture forest scene, and so conveying the impression – and this is in no way true to Shakespeare's imagination – that the action all takes place on one and the same spot ... The lovers stumble mazily through the tangle of the wood, now here, now there. Yet always – at Drury Lane – they are in the same place, cribbed, cabined, and confined by the same trees. (Farjeon, *Scene*, p. 43)

Despite his emphasis on the spectacular, Dean, like Atkins in the same year, 'intended to have the lovers' parts played in a lighter comedy vein than was usual' (Dean, *Seven Ages*, p. 239), and achieved comic results by playing their scenes quickly and with a kind of exaggerated seriousness, which allowed the audience to see the humour in the lovers' self-obsession. This rapidly became theatrical orthodoxy, presumably helped by changes in the status of women after the First World War which allowed fuller texts to be played with less concern about the 'unwomanliness' which might be revealed by those texts and by partial analogies with Restoration comedy (Edith Evans was Dean's Helena) and contemporary society comedy (in Dean's production: 'once launched upon their quarrel, they are independent of the forest, they make of it a sort of mock drawing-room', *Times* cutting).

Agate, as one might expect, found much to admire in Dean's staging, although even his enthusiasm for Mendelssohn paled in the face of a three-and-three-quarter-hour running time, which he thought could be reduced by cutting the ballets ('We began to think that M. Fokine's perfect ballets were perhaps not designed in the same age as Mendelssohn's perfect music') and the 'penitential entr'actes'. He sees Dean's great achievement as creating a unified narrative: 'Theseus, Oberon, and Quince's Amateur Dramatic Society all meet in the same wood and in the same century – impossible if you like, but always the same kind of impossibility' (Agate, *Chronicles*, pp. 41, 40). Dean's methods may not match modern ideas, but Agate is a powerful witness to their effectiveness, even if we might cavil that the century the actors met in was not Shakespeare's but Mendelssohn's.

Heavily cut texts liberally decorated with music and scenery may have given way to fuller texts and more modest production values but with Mendelssohn under siege the fairy scenes appear to have become a lesser element as the Mechanicals came to predominate in twenties productions of *A Midsummer Night's Dream*. No consensus had emerged to replace the pre-war innocence shattered by Barker, and the critics had no firm ground on which to base their responses to the productions of the twenties, just as even the most traditional stagings could not escape awareness of Barker's innovations.

Few directors or critics were, as yet, raising serious questions about the play's meanings or themes; it was valued for its beautiful verse by neo-Elizabethan bare-stagers and Mendelssohnian pictorialists alike, and their disputes were about methods of staging, not about the meaning of the play itself. The important Cambridge edition of the play, itself published in 1924, reveals the same untroubled assumption that everyone knew what it was about, although the editors, Arthur Quiller-Couch and John Dover Wilson, had a significant impact on the stage history of the *Dream*, not only through their discussion of an ideal set for the play, based on an Elizabethan great hall, but also through their editorial stage directions which insisted on such a presentation. Although Peter Hall's 1959 Stratford production is perhaps the most famous of all those that utilised this approach, the enormous world-wide success of the Cambridge edition ensured its widespread currency, particularly among those who assumed that the editors' stage directions had some kind of Shakespearean authority.

ELIZABETHAN STAGINGS: HARCOURT
WILLIAMS AND BRIDGES ADAMS

Mendelssohn was anathema to Harcourt Williams, a former member of Benson's company who had had his fill of 'muslin-clad fairies from the bottom of the garden and the suburban dancing school', who directed the *Dream* at the Old Vic, in 1929. Williams, inspired by his reading of Masefield's *Shakespeare*, opted to make his production English and Jacobean in reaction against 'washy Athenian-cum-classic mortals and muslin fairies'. This was a major break with Old Vic traditions – Lilian Baylis liked her fa ries 'gauzy'.[72] Williams, however, used the Cecil Sharp folk tune compilation originally used by Barker, to the dismay of the *Daily Mail*, which compared the *Dream* without Mendelssohn to 'lamb without mint sauce' (10 December). Ivor Brown, however, approved wholeheartedly and revealingly:

> Mr Harcourt Williams has taken 'A Midsummer Night's Dream', and
> scoured it clean of the greasy Mendelssohnian atmosphere with which the
> familiar score and modern sentiment have so long invested it. He has taken
> this sorely used thing of loveliness and laughter, and put it straight where it
> belongs – into the very heart of a moonstruck Warwickshire, where ruffed
> nobles go a-marrying, bumpkins go a-playing, and Puck, who is an English
> Robin, hops from twig to twig of mischief. An air or two from the Cecil
> Sharp collection of folk-tunes sets the note, as it did in the Granville Barker
> production, but there are no 'fantastications' of decoration. Mr Owen
> Smyth has worked for the fairyland dresses on designs of Inigo Jones, and
> Titania and Oberon are Elizabethans who have wandered from some gay
> masque of make-believe. Shake the play thus free of pseudo-classic trap-
> pings and later sentimental whims, and nothing can go wrong. Even the
> quartette of jarring lovers, who can be so tedious, become natural wanderers
> in a world of pastoral magic and madrigal.   (*Guardian*, 10 December)

Although the Mechanicals continued to overplay, Williams's approach meant that even Egeus and Philostrate made more of their parts than Gordon Crosse had ever seen before and 'the result was not to interfere with the rest but to improve the general effect'.[73] The general verdict on Williams's staging

---

72 Harcourt Williams, *Saga*, p. 157, and *Four Years*, p. 52; Trewin, *Shakespeare*, p. 117.
73 Crosse, *Diary*, XII, p. 53.

was that it was 'a triumph of courageous and imaginative production' (*Morning Post*, 10 December). With the weight of the Cambridge edition's authority also behind a Renaissance setting, a major strand in twentieth-century interpretations of the *Dream* had been established.

Financial problems meant that Williams used his old promptbook for his 1931 revival, concentrating on the Mechanicals scenes in order to give scope to his new Bottom, Ralph Richardson, who duly gained the lion's share of critical attention. Agate, as one might expect, continued to lament the loss of his beloved Mendelssohn, but praised Richardson's 'very fine' performance:

> In the fairy scenes he abandoned clowning in favour of a dim consciousness of a rarer world and of being at court there. This was new to me, and if Mr Richardson had not the ripeness of some of the old actors, his acting here was an agreeable change from the familiar refusal to alternate fruitiness with anything else. Most of the old players seem to have thought that Bottom, with the ass's head on, was the same Bottom only funnier. Shakespeare says he was 'translated', and Mr Richardson translated him.
>
> (*Sunday Times*, 8 November)

One of Richardson's advantages over previous Bottoms was the nature of his ass head. The traditional large fully built-up head, even if it had moving ears and jaws, tended to muffle the actor's voice, and encourage broad playing in the translation scenes. Williams 'substituted a light mask of my own devising' which left Richardson's eyes visible and 'added greatly to his powers of expression as the donkey'.[74] Critics who do not actually mention the technical innovation often, like Agate, praise Richardson's subtle and original playing. Gordon Crosse pinpointed the difference between old and new approaches exactly when he compared Richardson's waking speech with that of George Weir, Benson's longtime Bottom: Richardson 'showed that he was still half in a maze, thinking of Titania and the wondrous fairyland he had been in, not of his tail and ears as Weir did'.[75]

The other aspect of Williams's 1931 revival that attracted comment was his treatment of the fairies. Although Gordon Crosse remarked that they were 'the same as when I last saw the play here',[76] when Williams had based his approach on Inigo Jones designs, the *Morning Post* took exception to 'a heavily-skirted and panniered brigade of dames in an elderly make-up with wigs of long rough grey hair and smudged and gilded faces' who were 'just ugly and

---

74 Harcourt Williams, *Four Years*, p. 128.
75 Crosse, *Diary*, XIII, p. 31.
76 Ibid., p. 27.

pretentious'. The newspaper believed that 'nothing is more obvious than that Shakespeare imagined his fairies light and little' (3 November). Once again the old problems resurface as some of the more startling innovations in productions of the *Dream* begin to be tolerated, if not wholly accepted: how does a director cope with characters whose dialogue insists on a diminutive stature which no human form, be it child or adult, can accurately represent? Once again we find that the *Dream* is 'a poem rather than a play; it is magnificent but it is not drama' (*Saturday Review*, 14 November) and that 'this masque is of too wafer-like and remote a texture (except for the comics) and too dependent on rich but undramatic poetic utterance, for satisfactory staging' (*Era*, 4 November). Despite these strictures, Harcourt Williams's productions do represent a breakthrough for the new approaches to staging the play. The 1929 production compelled respect for the quality of its acting throughout the cast and general approval, even from those who mourned Mendelssohn's music, and the 1931 revival consolidated that success.

Under Bridges Adams, Stratford had moved rather slowly away from the old methods of presenting *A Midsummer Night's Dream*, with only minor excursions like the Purcell music of 1921 disturbing a basically Bensonian pattern. In 1932, however, with the opening of the new theatre, Bridges Adams threw out the traditional Athenian–Mendelssohnian setting and, like Harcourt Williams, opted for a lightly cut text staged in an Elizabethan–Jacobean mise-en-scène designed by Norman Wilkinson (who had designed Barker's and Calthrop's productions), parts of which were to remain a feature of Stratford productions for over a decade. The scenes in Theseus' court were played in an Elizabethan great house, Quince's shop was set in front for its scenes, and the wood featured a Duke's Oak which could be moved on the new theatre's rolling stage so that the scene changed without lengthy waits and spectators were offered some visual variety in the wood scenes. The *Birmingham Mail* welcomed the new approach:

> No longer were we afflicted with the picture-book fairies of flowing draperies, bare legs and recognisable kinship to someone's clever little Joyce or Rosemary. They were replaced by a silver-and-blue troupe of mannikins whose keynote was unearthliness – quaint little people with grey faces, witches' hats, spangled garments, chattering tongues, who served a dusky red-lipped queen beneath a magic oak accommodatingly moving from side to side of the stage as the scene demanded. (28 April)

There seems to be something of both Kirwan's and Williams's Renaissance conception of the fairies here, but there was surprisingly little agonising about either this change or the loss of Mendelssohn. As in Williams's production the lovers also benefited from the Elizabethan staging with

Crompton Rhodes finding them really credible for the first time (*Birmingham Post*, 29 April).

In many ways this production did, as the *Birmingham Mail* put it, bring 'real distinction to the Festival for the first time', certainly as far as productions of *A Midsummer Night's Dream* are concerned. It fared less well in 1934 when the *Evening Despatch* declared that the costumes, 'formal almost to monotony, add their quota to Mr W. Bridges Adams's success in changing this comedy of mortals, immortals, and rude mechanics into a poetic and polite conversation piece of rare beauty' (6 June). In Stratford as in London, increased familiarity with new methods of presentation simply allowed old doubts to re-emerge: 'the mortals seemed ... the least convincing' (*Evening Despatch*); 'the comedy side ... has but little connection with the romantic element' (*Yorkshire Post*, 6 June); 'The quarrels of the lovers ... become somewhat tedious. It is in the comical portion of the play that Shakespeare reveals his dramatic genius' (Coventry *Herald*, 8 June). Whatever production methods were adopted – pictorial, Athenian, Elizabethan, or stylised – the perennial problem of producing *A Midsummer Night's Dream* remained one of balancing the elements of the plot against one another and whatever degree of scenic, balletic or musical accompaniment was considered appropriate. While Bridges Adams may have inclined towards the newer styles of Shakespearean production, circumstances at Stratford did not favour radical innovation and thus his stagings of the *Dream* tended towards a compromise middle ground with the generally unrestrained treatment of the Mechanicals tipping the balance in favour of the old.

When E. Martin Browne staged *A Midsummer Night's Dream* at Stratford in 1937 he inherited Bridges Adams's scenery and costumes, explaining to the *Observer* why he was not using Mendelssohn:

> I should like nothing better than to produce the play with it. But in considering this year's production I had to take into account Norman Wilkinson's lovely decor and costumes, which are bequeathed to me for use this year. And it seems clear that, with a setting which places the play in an Elizabethan country house, one cannot use Mendelssohn, but must have music based on the Elizabethan style.   (28 March)

Perhaps unsurprisingly, neither Browne's production, nor Andrew Leigh's in the following year using the same mise-en-scène, made a significant impact, but when Ben Iden Payne, who is usually regarded as a rather academic follower of Poel, staged the play in 1942 it was Athenian and Mendelssohnian. The return to Mendelssohn probably owed something to political pressure, since the *Evesham Journal* records that Mrs L. T. Evans,

5 E. Martin Browne's 1937 Stratford production, using Norman Wilkinson's
Elizabethan costumes and set, originally designed for Bridges Adams's 1932 staging.
The aim of the design was to recreate an impression of an Elizabethan country
house wedding.

one of the theatre governors, claimed to have 'forcibly spoken her mind on
many occasions and by pushing hard had done much to bring about the
return of the Mendelssohn' (25 April). However, the most interesting aspect
of the production was Jay Laurier's approach to Bottom. Although this
Bottom still dominated the production, Laurier, a music-hall artist who had
played the part in the 1938 production, not only played his awakening with a
Richardson-like sensitivity but also, somewhat controversially, broke the tradition that Bottom remained confident in the performance of 'Pyramus and
Thisbe'.

A further production by the very experienced Baliol Holloway 'in the
moonlight and Mendelssohn manner' (J. C. Trewin, *Observer*, 25 April
1943) preceded the final appearance of Norman Wilkinson's Elizabethan
costumes in Robert Atkins's 1944 revival, which still owed something to
Bridges Adams's conception (the *Stage* referred to 'the celebration of a
nobleman's wedding', 11 May) but also included the Mendelssohn music.
The most interesting aspect of this staging was that Atkins stressed the interpenetration of the worlds of Athens and the wood: even in the opening scene,

6 Norman Wilkinson's Elizabethan fairies and wood set, Stratford, 1937. These were Wilkinson's third *Dream* designs and they were originally used in Bridges Adams's 1932 staging

'the magic moonlit wood showed in shadowy silhouette' behind classic pillars (*Theatre World*, June) and at the end, 'the fairy-haunted palace melts into the starlit woods' (Ruth Ellis, Stratford *Herald*, 12 May). As with Leigh and Holloway, it is virtually impossible to say at what point Atkins might have introduced an individual piece of business or approach to a specific aspect of the play and it may well be that Stratford in the forties was only seeing what the Old Vic had already seen in the twenties.

In general, change at Stratford between the wars was evolutionary rather than radical and the Festival tradition probably meant, for good and ill, that there was greater continuity between old and new than was the case in London, exemplified perhaps by the fact that while there were fifteen productions of *A Midsummer Night's Dream* between 1919 and 1945, only five actors played the part of Bottom.

Harcourt Williams's departure from the Old Vic in 1933 and Bridges Adams's from Stratford in 1934 in many ways marked the end of the first period of reaction to the Victorian Shakespearean tradition. Beerbohm Tree had written in 1913 of 'the slow process of elimination of unessentials' in staging and of 'the maze of complexity' which obscured the goal of simplicity. The elimination of unessentials which characterised much of Poel's and Granville Barker's work once more tended to be lost in a maze of complexity as their successors grappled again with problems that had apparently been eliminated by the newer methods, only to resurface as these methods themselves became more familiar.

The search for viable conventions within which to stage *A Midsummer Night's Dream* had led away from the pictorial tableaux of the nineteenth century to less elaborate productions in which more emphasis could be given to individual characterisations and interpretations. Old conventions were often shed reluctantly long after their useful life was over, with many false starts, blind alleys, and guerilla warfare from the Mendelssohn partisans. Nevertheless, by the time Williams left the Old Vic, it was reasonable to expect a production of *A Midsummer Night's Dream* to offer a fairly full text in which machinery, music, spectacle, lighting and dancing were at the service of, rather than displacing, the text, and where choices between different approaches to specific aspects of the staging would have to be made and even defended in terms of choices between, for example, Mendelssohn or Cecil Sharp and Elizabethan or Athenian sets.

BACK TO THE FUTURE? MAX REINHARDT AND TYRONE GUTHRIE

Max Reinhardt had been staging *A Midsummer Night's Dream* for some thirty years when he co-directed the 1935 Warner Brothers film with William Dieterle. Reinhardt's treatment, mixing Expressionist and realistic elements with considerable panache, preserves many features of the nineteenth-century tradition, with spectacular effects, gagging for the Mechanicals, many extras to play crowds and fairies, lengthy ballets to Mendelssohn music, live animals and very realistic wood sets. In many ways, then, it is the nearest thing we have to a film of the old spectacular tradition of staging the play, although Shakespeare's text is very heavily simplified, rewritten and redistributed throughout the film to accommodate the perceived needs of the new medium.

The film was not a hit, and tends to be referred to dismissively, because of its reliance on star names (James Cagney as Bottom, Joe E. Brown as Flute, the young Mickey Rooney as Puck, Dick Powell as Lysander, Olivia de Havilland as Hermia), Mendelssohn, lengthy ballets staged by Bronislawa Nijinska and Hal Haskin's special effects. However, it is noteworthy for the fairy scenes in which Reinhardt sometimes, as John Russell Taylor points out, managed to 'distil precisely the slightly cruel, slightly sinister poetry that Shakespeare achieved in words, often by cutting the words and replacing them with visual equivalents of startling beauty'.[77] In this way, then, the film raised once more the abiding issue of how best to present Shakespeare's plays in media that offer significantly different technical possibilities from those of the Renaissance theatre.

While film as a medium offered a whole range of radical technical differences from theatre, the film of *A Midsummer Night's Dream* drew heavily on Victorian theatrical values associated with Mendelssohn and 'gauzy' fairies. Similarly, one of the more radical of the new theatre directors, Tyrone Guthrie, reverted to a Victorian approach in his 1937 production of *A Midsummer Night's Dream* at the Old Vic. Guthrie himself was well aware of the dangers of a Mendelssohnian staging. In a 1954 edition of *A Midsummer Night's Dream* he would argue that 'we have a tendency these days to senti-mentalize all our ideas of fairies and personifications of Nature' which 'found a powerful ally in Mendelssohn', whose music 'has proved good enough to impose a particular conception of the play upon at least three generations'. That conception meant that the fairies 'cease to contrast with the other two groups of characters' and the play loses 'a great deal of its meaning if it is robbed of a magic which springs, not from the glittering tip of a department-store wand, but from the earth, the trees, the stones, the very air of the wood; and a magic which is not merely pretty but dark and dangerous'.[78]

In 1937, however, since the Old Vic was still a proscenium arch theatre, it was 'illogical and annoying if a stage which has been designed as a peep show, which has all the mechanism ... for creating visual interest, is then denied its whole function'.[79] So, as a programme note declared, the production's 'early Victorian' style was not merely an attempt to be amusing, but 'one more attempt to make an union between the words of Shakespeare, the music of Mendelssohn and the architecture of the Old Vic'. To contemporary critics the union of Mendelssohn music, *corps de ballet* and flying fairies seemed blessed, but in many ways the production was a restatement of the values that Guthrie was to reject in his subsequent career.

Although this was a 'Victorian' production, Guthrie played a full text, and consequently there were some significant differences within the overall Victorian impression. Gordon Crosse noted that the lovers, 'followed the

---

77 Quoted in Manvell, *Film*, p. 27. For Reinhardt's *Dream*, see also: Leonhard M. Fiedler's 'Reinhardt, Shakespeare, and the "Dreams"', in Jacobs and Warren, *Reinhardt*, pp. 79–95; Manvell, *Film*, pp. 24–7; Jorgens, *Film*, pp. 36–50; Simon Williams, *German Stage*, pp. 203–11.

78 Guthrie, *Dream*, pp. 16, 15, 17, 18.

79 Guthrie, *Life*, p. 185.

good new custom of taking their scenes in the wood rapidly & in an almost far-cical style'.[80] Even the very traditional fairies, who included flying fairies with lighted tapers in the finale, had some of the sinister elements that Guthrie was to refer to in 1954: W. A. Darlington saw Robert Helpmann's Oberon as 'sat-urnine in a sort of stag-beetle dress', and he was 'a majestic, ominous and most romantic figure' according to Farjeon (Farjeon, *Scene*, p. 47). Darlington expressed the majority viewpoint in praising Ralph Richardson for discarding Bottom's traditional business and making his points for himself (*Daily Telegraph*, 28 December). Richardson, who played Bottom for Williams and Guthrie, was noteworthy for playing the part with a degree of restraint, along somewhat Phelpsean lines that gave due credit to Bottom being the only mor-tal who actually sees the fairies. As with Phelps, critical comments drew atten-tion to his freshness of approach: 'Bottom can either be a music-hall clown or a pathetic figure. Mr Richardson makes him neither. This Bottom is a know-ing rustic, a shade out of his depth' (*Yorkshire Observer*, 28 December); he played 'with an elemental wonderment that sets him in the front rank of Shakespearean clowns. It is a sweet bully, a tender lout, and the ass he becomes is almost radiant with its own gentleness' (*Glasgow Herald*, 28 December). Twenty years later, his performance was still being invoked as a benchmark: 'no one before Richardson, and no one after him either, guessed that there was in this weaver so deep a well of abused poetry, such an ineradicable vision of uncomprehended wonder' (*Sunday Times*, 29 December 1957).

James Agate, inevitably, took Guthrie to task for his defensiveness in a gloriously conservative review:

> Mr Guthrie has protested too much, particularly in view of the fact that it is all so very easy. First you dress your Athenians like Athenians, your workmen like workmen, and your fairies like fairies. Second you hire Mendelssohn's band-parts. Third, you send for the most old-fashioned scene-painter you can think of, and then tell him to imitate Conrad

---

80 Crosse, *Diary*, XVI, pp. 137, 139. In 1951 Guthrie tried the *Dream* again, this time without Mendelssohn and with only one female fairy, Titania, with less happy results. The *Guardian* thought that Guthrie was 'so anxious that we should not think of Mendelssohn or Taglioni fairies that he eclipses the magic with the sentiment' (28 December), and the critical consensus was that the Mechanicals overdid their scenes with irrelevant and elaborate clowning. For T. C Worsley, the result was to make 'the least interesting part – the mortal lovers – stand right out' as a result of 'an imaginative reading of the lines, and out of the situation itself developed to its height' (*New Statesman*, 5 January 1952). Much of the critical dissatisfaction stemmed from Guthrie's failure to repeat his previous spectacular strategy at a time when theatre was being looked to for a colour and excitement that was not available in daily life.

Tritschler's setting for this play in Mr Robert Courtnedge's Manchester production some thirty years ago, which means plenty of imitation grass and fairy lamps à la Southend. At least that is what I should have done without a second thought. (*Sunday Times*, 2 January 1938)

Although Farjeon cavilled that it remained to be seen 'how they did *A Midsummer Night's Dream* in periwigs, or how (if it had been written then) they would have done it in the Stone Age' (Farjeon, *Scene*, p. 47), nevertheless, both in the traditional *Dream* role as a Shakespearean Christmas pantomime and as a witty statement of the problems facing a director of the play, Guthrie's production was a huge success. It was well summed up by the *Sketch*:

A delicate balance must be held 'twixt text and scene, if the poetry of language and of motion is to harmonise. Mr Guthrie has brought to his problem an original and individual mind, and in his explanatory note sets forth his argument... The play takes on a new dress, and it fits the frame and gives us an enchanting picture. The style has been intelligently determined by the conditions and therefore does not offend as a freakish and arbitrary imposition, but delights because it establishes a unity. (19 January 1938)

Stagings 1945–1959

Unsurprisingly, for most of the Second World War, the fate of *A Midsummer Night's Dream* was left in the hands of old stagers like Robert Atkins, Baliol Holloway, Ben Iden Payne and Donald Wolfit who offered productions within established patterns. Although contemporary critics would detect significant differences between individual post-war productions, in retrospect it is clear that the majority of those before 1967 were offering limited variations on Mendelssohnian Athens or settings, costumes and music in the Renaissance idiom. Even Peter Hall's 1959 Elizabethan country house staging was largely recapping on ideas developed in the thirties and it was left to Peter Brook to provide a paradigm shift in 1970.[81]

In January 1945, the Oxford don Nevill Coghill staged *A Midsummer Night's Dream* as part of John Gielgud's Haymarket season. The production played the traditional *Dream* function of a Shakespearean pantomime, but Coghill used a Granville Barker style arangement of the full text, adapted Inigo Jones designs for the lovers' costumes, developed the scenery from two of Jones's designs for fairy palaces, and used music in Elizabethan style by

81 Hugh Grady's *The Modernist Shakespeare*, an account of developments in Shakespearean literary criticism, offers some relevant parallels to these processes. See particularly pp. 193–4.

Leslie Bridgewater. Moreover, Coghill also had ideas about the play's meaning. His aim was to present 'a sort of dramatic paean in praise of young and mature (Theseus) love', in which 'the flight of the young lovers into the forest was intended to symbolise the idea that marriage meant being dipped in pure Nature and returning under the blessing of nature ... full of nuptial love'. Oberon represented 'all things green and growing', Titania 'all things blue and blowing' and the production was intended to 'express the great Wordsworthian truth "Let Nature be your Teacher"'.[82] Although critics found much to praise in the production, there was a certain suspicion of Coghill's theatrical credentials, a general view that the parts were greater than the whole, and a suspicion of director's theatre: 'the fact that it has been directed is so apparent and so insistent that it keeps the spell of the piece from falling upon us' (*Evening Standard*, 27 January 1945).

Perhaps inevitably in a period of austerity, Michael Benthall's 1949 Stratford production of the *Dream* appealed 'to the eye rather than to the ear' (*Guardian*, 25 April) with something of a mixture of visual styles including a Veronese palace and Renaissance Greek costumes on one hand, and Mendelssohn, 'spangled starlight' and 'tulle-draped ballerinas' on the other, all mixed with 'a black garbed cohort that waited on Oberon ... from a Fokine production' (*Birmingham Post*, 25 April). Benthall's productions often straddled the narrow line that divides cluttering and over-embellishment from imaginative use of theatrical resources, splitting the critics between those who applauded his pictorialism for being at the service of Shakespeare and those who felt it drowned the play. Although the 1949 production seems on the evidence of the reviews and the promptbook to have been fussy, over-elaborate and ponderous, yet there was considerable praise for the lovers and for Theseus which indicates that Benthall was no thoughtless Shakespearean upholsterer.

His second version of *A Midsummer Night's Dream*, produced for the Edinburgh Festival and an Old Vic tour to the USA in 1954, appears to have been something of a marketing exercise: J. C. Trewin declared that the play had not been produced 'more elaborately in our time' and that New York was 'likely to be impressed by Michael Benthall's stage pictures and by the romantic profusion of the whole affair, complete as it is with the full Mendelssohn score, but it seems to me in some ways to have taken English production back to the Edwardians' (*Birmingham Post*, 1 September 1954). In 1954 Benthall used Stanley Holloway as Bottom with considerable success, in 1957 he tried Frankie Howerd with equally good results in a production which seems to have been 'much less massive, more selective' (*Birmingham Post*, 27 December) than his

---

82 All quotations are from a letter to the author from Nevill Coghill, dated
9 September 1977.

earlier ones and in which 'not only are all three parties "Athenian", but Athens would not be its proper self if one of them were missing' (*The Times*, 27 December).

Where Benthall tended towards fussiness and pictorial display, George Devine's 1954 Stratford staging infuriated many critics with its sinister treatment of the fairies. Curiously little attention was paid to what appears at this distance to have been an innovative approach to the play which emphasised its own commentary on the nature of theatricality by such devices as having Quince set up his own interior set for Act 1, Scene 2 and using a permanent symbolic wood set for the rest of the play. While some critics were prepared to concede that 'hoards of the Mabel Lucy Atwell species, cherubs with tiny wings, Falstaffian stomachs and hearts of gold' were not the best way to to deal with the folklore elements in the fairies' make-up, the general view was that Devine had gone too far the other way. Critics vied with one another to describe the 'Mephistophelean atmosphere' in which 'the hobgoblins of a midsummer nightmare' indulged in 'waspish incantations' with 'barely concealed malevolences'. Oberon seemed to be an 'Aztec bird of illish omen' or a pantomime 'Demon Rat' and Puck, 'dressed like a bird and equipped with claws', resembled 'Caliban's cousin', 'Pan in a toad's skin', or 'a rough-spoken bandy-legged creature of the woods, half-Panda, half-chameleon'.[83] Although the fairies attracted much attention, it was generally agreed that, of the three strands in the play, Devine had emphasised the Mechanicals without allowing them too much licence.

Peter Hall's production of *A Midsummer Night's Dream*, which opened at Stratford in 1959, and was revived there in 1962 and at the Aldwych in 1963, was conceived along Quiller-Couchean Elizabethan great hall wedding celebration lines. Hall enhanced this atmosphere by not curtaining the proscenium arch, so that the audience entered a theatre transformed into the hall of an Elizabethan manor house with a permanent set graced with a double staircase. The transformation to the wood was mainly accomplished by the use of gauzes and back lighting, with Titania's bower and Quince's shop set in an inner stage under the landing formed by the junction of the staircases, which remained in the wood as a rustic bridge. The finale very closely matched Q's prescriptions: 'The homely and the supernatural are cunningly combined when the fairies invade the great hall after the wedding festivities to give their blessing. Tapers are lit from the last flickers of a log fire as they flit up and down the stairs and along the galleries chanting their moving verses, the play's enduring magnetism is again fully captured' (*Morning Advertiser*, 6 June 1959).

83 *Leamington Courier* (26 March), *Daily Mail* (26 March), *Gloucester Echo* (24 March), *Leamington Courier* ('incantations' and 'malevolences'), *Punch* (31 March), *Observer* (28 March), *Birmingham Mail* (24 March), *Observer*, *Gloucester Echo*, *Guardian* (25 March).

Although either the production or the critics' attitudes to it mellowed over the years, initial reactions were that Hall's self-declared attempt to break away from 'balletic fairies, high-powered scenic effects and the Mendelssohn music' resulted in a loss of 'the magic and sense of wonder evoked by some of the loveliest lines that Shakespeare wrote' and the replacement of 'the author's poetic conception' with 'robust, mocking exploitation of comedy, played at a fast pace',[84] so that the fairies became more impish than usual and the lovers less sentimental. In fact, the change to the lovers was more apparent than real, since it had been pursued by many directors since F. R. Benson, but critical horizons of expectation seem to change with glacial speed.

Dreams and the unconscious, 1960–1994

It is a peculiarity of the stage history of *A Midsummer Night's Dream* that few directors have explicitly related their own theatrical practices to the element of 'dream' in the play's title and that the rise of modern psychological thought has had such limited overt effect on productions of the play. However, the relationship between the conscious and the unconscious was to become the key factor in interpretations of the play in the last decades of the twentieth century, particularly after the idea of doubling Theseus and Hippolyta with Oberon and Titania took off with Dunlop's and, more importantly, Brook's adoption of the device.[85] Obviously neither the idea of doubling, which goes back at least to the *Merry Conceited Humours of Bottom the Weaver*, or the idea of exploring the 'dream' elements in the play, was completely new. What was new was the application of ideas about the therapeutic nature of the experience in the wood to the framing relationship between Theseus and Hippolyta as well as to the four lovers, so that the play's psychological journey begins to be seen as involving all the mortals.

This process began tentatively with Michael Langham's 1960 Old Vic production, which was dominated by lovers who were even more athletic than Hall's and eschewed Mendelssohn in favour of 'an impression of Athens

---

84 Hall is quoted from the *Daily Worker* (4 June), the other quotations are from the *Warwick Advertiser* (5 June). Hall's production was revived at Stratford in 1962 and in London in 1963. Jorgens, *Film*, pp. 51–65, and Manvell, *Film*, pp. 119–27, discuss the rather different film version which Hall eventually made in 1969. Hall also directed Britten's *Dream* at Glyndebourne in 1981. For an illuminating discussion of the opera in the context of Hall's developing approach to the *Dream*, see Warren, 'Interpretations', pp. 144–6.

85 Leopold Lindtberg had used the device in a German language production at Salzburg in 1966 (See Habicht, 'Shakespeare in Germany', p. 161n). Whether for aesthetic or economic reasons, it is now virtually universal in British productions.

seen through late Renaissance eyes'.[86] Where Hall's Elizabethan wedding celebration staging appears to have been based on formal and stylistic considerations, Langham was following similar lines to Coghill in seeing the therapeutic value of the trip to the wood:

> In *A Midsummer Night's Dream* the war amongst the fairies has resulted not only in a loss of control of elements and seasons: human beings also have become at odds with each other. It is a kind of cold war and all life as well as all nature has been set a-jangling. It seems that the mortals can find peace only when Oberon and Titania have found it. And more than this – they can find it only after being drawn into the world of Dreams back to the roots of mythology and folklore and into Oberon's domain of half-light – more revealing by far in its fantasies than the world of Reality. After the dreamers have reawakened, their dreams, like most dreams, prove elusive. But the magic has been worked. The mortals have been touched by it, and Jack has found Jill, and wedding rite and consummation must follow.
>
> (programme note)

Little of this made much of an impact on the critics who sniped at the standard of verse speaking (a common complaint of this period) and the almost farcical vigour of the lovers. However, Langham had begun to raise issues which would become the key to *A Midsummer Night's Dream* production for the rest of the century, finally beginning to explore the relationship between the mortals and the fairies in terms of the relationship between the conscious and the unconscious. While Langham's programme note seems to be mainly concerned with the four lovers' immersion in the world of dreams, he also recognised that Hippolyta 'is by no means reconciled to the idea' of marrying Theseus although 'she gradually softens' (J. C. Trewin, *Birmingham Post*, 21 December). Although other critics were not as perspicacious as Trewin, with *The Times* complaining about gimmicks such as 'a manacled Hippolyta' (21 December), Langham had made a significant breakthrough.[87]

Frank Dunlop took a further step forward along these lines by doubling the mortal and fairy rulers in a 1967 modern dress production for his Pop

---

86 Speaight, *Shakespeare*, p. 273.

87 Langham's production may also have influenced critical responses to the 1962 revival of Hall's staging, when the fairies were linked to another dream play, *Peter Pan*: 'the sprites are Barrie's Lost Boys (augmented by a Lost Girl or two); and Oberon and Titania are unmistakably Peter and Wendy. Their row is a nursery tiff, conducted with all the determined vindictiveness that that implies: Oberon deprived of his changeling behaves with the icy petulance of Pan deprived of his shadow' (*Observer*, 22 April 1962).

Theatre Company at the Saville.[88] The programme carried a discussion of the play which shows the rationale for Dunlop's treatment of it: pointing out that *A Midsummer Night's Dream* had 'only recently ... become a seriously considered play', the programme mentions Jan Kott's references to 'its extremely sensual and violent nature' and quoted David Young's 1966 discussion of the thematic and plot parallels between Oberon and Titania and Theseus and Hippolyta, Philostrate and Puck, suggesting that 'what is emerging from new work on *The Dream* is a play with sharper more jaggged edges, in which extremes mirror each other and then converge'. The legacy of Victorian sentimentality meant that the fairy world 'which commands a half of the play' was still allowed 'to elbow out the mirror-image symmetry of the court of Theseus – great hero to the Elizabethans – a court which has already achieved balance and reason before the play commences'.

While the supposed stability of the Athenian court at the beginning of the play rather undercuts the value of doubling Oberon and Titania with Theseus and Hippolyta, it is noteworthy that Dunlop's innovation attracted very little more comment from most critics than a bare acknowledgment of its existence, apart from an incidental sideswipe that 'the fairies don't really fit into a contemporary version, even though Theseus and his queen double as Oberon and Titania in a desperate attempt to add point to their presence' (*Daily Mail*, 27 September). Peter Ansorge thought it was a neat idea to introduce 'an element of Kott's midsummer madness' by doubling Oberon and Titania, 'green-skinned monsters who cackle over their voyeuristic activities in the dark', with 'the authoritarian and fox-hunting rulers of Athens', but complained that Dunlop failed to develop the idea and looked elsewhere for comic effects (*Plays and Players*, December).

PETER BROOK, 1970–1973

It was left to Peter Brook's production of *A Midsummer Night's Dream*, which opened at Stratford on 27 August 1970, to bring together many of these new insights and some of his own in a revival which was immediately, and properly, recognised as an achievement to stand beside Granville Barker's *Dream* as one of the great Shakespearean revivals of the century and 'a historic landmark in the interpretation of Shakespeare's plays' (Robert Speaight, *Tablet*, 12 September). Brook's staging was neither Elizabethan nor Athenian, nor did he have any truck with mimetic woods: the permanent set was a white box which reminded critics of a circus ring, a gymnasium and

88 Modern dress Shakespeare, like psychological Shakespeare, was a child of the inter-war years, but no-one thought to apply it to *A Midsummer Night's Dream*. See Styan, *The Shakespeare Revolution*, passim.

7 Titania is impressed by the translated Bottom, who is being chaired by the fairies in Brook's Stratford production (1970). The translation includes a cap with ears, a false nose and boots, as well as the phallic arm.

an operating theatre, to quote the most common analogies. Two doors at the back offered entrances in basically Elizabethan positions, two ladders at the front edges of the side walls gave access to a catwalk around the top of the set from which musicians and fairies looked down on the action below. The

8 4.1 in Brook's Stratford production (1970). The sleeping lovers are on the trapezes, Bottom is at the foot of Titania's flying bower, which has turned from horizontal to vertical, depositing him on the floor. The absence of furniture and properties is noteworthy. The doors in the back wall are clearly visible and the space above the walls occupied by musicians and offstage characters runs across the top of the picture.

fairies flew on trapezes, Titania's bower was a flying concoction of scarlet feathers and the trees which snagged the lovers in the wood were coils of wire flown in on fishing rods by fairies on the catwalk.

Although a tiny but vociferous minority of critics condemned Brook's production as no more than a bag of tricks,[89] to the vast majority of critics and audiences, the physical ingenuity and invention were functions of an overall conception of the play which was entirely Shakespearian. Brook stated that:

> today we have no symbols that can conjure up fairyland and magic for a modern audience. On the other hand there are a number of actions that a performer can execute that are quite breathtaking. So we went to the art of the circus and the acrobat because they both made purely theatrical statements. We've worked through a language of acrobatics to find a new approach to magic that we know cannot be reached by 19th century conventions.

> (*Daily Telegraph*, 14 September 1970)

89 John Russell Brown expressed his opposition in *Free Shakespeare*. David Selbourne's account of the rehearsal process in *The Making of A Midsummer Night's Dream* is, at best, agnostic.

The performers' physical dexterity thus became the magic, the spinning plate dropped from Puck's magic wand to Oberon's did not represent the flower 'love-in-idleness', but the act of passing it, in itself, became the magic of the flower. Crucially, Brook and his designer Sally Jacobs had created 'an environment for the *Dream* which removes the sense of being earthbound: it is natural here for characters to fly' (*Times*, 28 August). Here there was no attempt to hide the mechanism and this removed the traditional difficulties of theatrical flying in which, as the *Observer* had unpityingly remarked about Tony Richardson's disastrous 1962 Royal Court production, 'beams of light unfailingly pick out the wires from which the elfin fliers dangle' (28 January 1962).

Instead of the traditional apparatus, Brook had provided what Robert Speaight described as 'the blank page upon which imagination can play its tricks' (*Tablet*) and many critics picked up on the way in which the set had liberated the imagination and allowed a concentration on the possibilities of the text where other more traditional stagings had been more limiting. Gavin Millar spoke for many:

> When we smile at the patient Quince discussing with Bottom the problems
> of representation – how a lion can be Snug the joiner, how Snout can be a
> Wall – we smile at ourselves, for they echo humbly the act of imagination
> that makes the play work at all. And something beyond that. The play itself
> mimics the act of imagination which enables mortals to dream, to purge
> their dross, to hold at bay the fearsome goblins and sprites of 'black-browed
> night', the 'blots of Nature's hand'. For the *Dream* is a fearful play. Brook
> has doubled Theseus/Oberon and Hippolyta/Titania in order to underline
> the salutary function of imagination. When day returns Oberon must slip
> back into that mortal coil, and it's at this point that he asks for the house to
> be blessed and protected against the malign hand of Nature. Mortals are
> made of gross stuff. They are born deformed, a prey to disease; at the mercy
> of blind passion, they fall in love with the wrong people, their foolish
> excessses are exposed by the absurd tragi-comedy of Pyramus and Thisbe,
> not so far removed as you might suppose, Hermia and Lysander, Helena and
> Demetrius, from your own grotesque carryings-on ...
>   It wants only the act of imagination to see not just 'what fools these
> mortals be' but what depths of feeling and beauty their foolishness conceals.
>
> (*Listener*, 3 September 1970)

The sheer length of this discussion of what the play might actually be about is one indication of the magnitude of Brook's achievements: no previous production of the play, even Granville Barker's, had focussed critical attention so forcibly on its significance rather than on individual facets of the production.

The doubling of Oberon and Titania with Theseus and Hippolyta, and of Puck with Philostrate, was applauded as part of a process in which social cohesion was expressed 'by means of emphasizing the parallels betwen the three groups of characters' so that Titania's line 'This same progeny of evils comes from our debate' came to embrace the whole action (*Times*). However, since 'Titania and Oberon are the night-thoughts of Hippolyta and Theseus' (J. C. Trewin, *The Lady*, 17 September 1970), it also allowed Brook to explore the idea that the homeopathically therapeutic happenings in the wood changed not only the young lovers but also Theseus' ability to temper the excesses of patriarchal law.

Brook's *Dream* has been described as completely different from any earlier production of the play, but this is to do both it and its predecessors a disservice. Other directors of *A Midsummer Night's Dream* had already seen the need to remove various sentimental accretions, others had made the fairies a strong physical presence in the lovers' quarrels, others had seen possibilities in doubling the mortal and fairy rulers or stressing the therapeutic value of the events in the wood. Similarly, some aspects of the work of Meyerhold, Piscator and Brecht provide other, non-Shakespearean, antecedents for Brook's achievements, but his triumph lay in creating a powerful crystallisation of these various elements into a unified and cohesive whole which impressed not only young radicals but also more traditionally minded figures such as Robert Speaight:

> For all its breath-taking virtuosity, this left the impression not of a man asking himself what he could do with a play grown too familiar, but what the play could do with him – stranded as he was without magical beliefs in the middle of the twentieth century. And the magic had been found, far beyond the spinning saucers and Titania's bright-red feather bed, where Shakespeare had put it and where it must always be rediscovered – in the alchemy of the spoken word. (*Shakespeare*, p. 294)

Brook's triumph was not an easy act to follow, and the Royal Shakespeare Company did not stage the play again until 1977 when John Barton offered a fairly conventional staging with no doubling and no attempt to emulate Brook. Barton used Renaissance costumes for the mortals and had rank and file fairies in the Inigo Jones mode, which, as always, caused critical unhappiness since few critics appeared to recognise their provenance.

When the RSC tried again in 1981, Ron Daniels sought inspiration for his version of theatrical magic in a homage to Victorian toy theatre which doubled the mortal and fairy rulers but also used puppets manipulated by onstage handlers for all the other fairies except Puck. Although Nicholas Shrimpton thought that Daniels was doing no more than hide 'a conventionally rumbustious mid-twentieth-century production behind a thin Victorian

9 The Mechanicals in John Barton's Elizabethan production (Stratford, 1977) with the traditional figures of an elderly Quince (with script), a substantial Bottom (next to Quince in hat) and a tall, thin Starveling.

veneer' (*TLS*, 31 July), the Victorian setting worked well in bringing out the patriarchal attitudes of Athens, and setting up a situation in which 'aristo-cratic pretensions are shed as all four lovers progressively lose their outer clothes in the snags and snares of the forest' (*Sunday Times*, 19 July).

The designer Maria Bjornson had created this forest out of cloud and tree flats but also left chairs, ladders and a property basket gracing the set. According to *The Times*, 'the effect is extremely sophisticated thanks to Mr Daniels's additional trick of evoking the Victorian stage and then denying any pretensions to illusion ... The trick is to let out all the secrets and still weave a spell' (16 July). Although some critics were less convinced that Daniels had actually achieved such an effect ('There seemed no reason why lovers fleeing from even a straitlaced society should wander on to the stage of a deserted theatre', Warren, 'Interpretations', p. 146), the sharpest divi-sion of opinions was about the fairies. Sheridan Morley thought they were 'magically and wonderfully performed by stick puppets operated in almost Kabuki fashion by black-garbed attendants' (*International Herald Tribune*, 30 July), whereas others wondered if the Victorian conceit should be extended to 'a distracting fourth social class in the play, the puppeteers, whose black working clothes and dirty faces suggest an industrial proletariat of mill-hands and matchgirls' (*Sunday Times*, 19 July). As Shrimpton remarked, 'if a point is being made about the class structure, however, it remains obscure' (*TLS*, 31 July).

Daniels similarly divided critics with his doubling of the mortal and fairy rulers, albeit with an unusual extra-theatrical edge encapsulated by Benedict Nightingale: 'the new *Dream* has been described as the RSC's salute to the Royal Wedding [of Prince Charles and Lady Diana Spencer]; but, if so, it's an ambiguous one [because of the doubling]. In other words, Chuck might feel better about Di if he imagined her having sex with a prole with a donkey's head' (*New Statesman*, 24 July). Daniels's programme stated that the marriage between Theseus and Hippolyta was 'at first, a marriage of convenience between two strangers', but in the course of the staging, according to Nightingale,

> out come the unspoken fears and resentments of Theseus and Hippolyta, out in the form of the quarrel between Oberon and Titania; and having thus constructively freaked out, the two of them can marry with serenity. Such at any rate, is the inference I take from the transformation of the faces Mike Gwilym and Juliet Stevenson present each other: cold, wan, almost funereal at first, and then, after they've swapped their courtly blacks for leprechaun shimmer and flitted through the glades, surprisingly warm and friendly.
>
> (*New Statesman*, 24 July)

His view is diametrically opposed to Shrimpton's: 'the account of the imagination, the sense of disrupted natural harmony, the comments on love, the exploration of theatrical illusion, even the psychological points made (following standard modern practice) by the doubling of Theseus and Hippolyta with Oberon and Titania – all these things are scrambled and diminished' (*TLS*, 31 July). On balance, the critical consensus was closer to Shrimpton's reading of the production, probably because for most critics the various innovations did not add up to a coherent approach to the play.

HIPPOLYTA S DREAM: BILL ALEXANDER, 1986

In 1986 Bill Alexander tried for a spectacular variation on the idea that the action in the woods is in some way the working out of the Athenian unconscious, by doubling only Hippolyta and Titania. The key to Alexander's Stratford staging lay in an unscripted encounter between Hippolyta, who was discovered sitting in the half-light in the room where the Mechanicals were to rehearse: Bottom entered and they 'exchange a long, appraising look across a social chasm. What follows is, in effect, Hippolyta's Dream' (*Daily Telegraph*, 9 July). In that dream, according to Shrimpton, a woman who was being 'forced into respectable marriage with a dull bureaucrat... fantasized about alternative relationships – first with a glamorous cad and then with a rough plebeian' (Shrimpton, 'Shakespeare', *SS* 40, p. 173). When Hippolyta appeared in the wood, fairies removed her gown to mark her entry into the dream world and transformation into Titania. The wood that Hippolyta arrived in included 'a gigantic cobweb stretching above the kind of flowers and foliage evoked in the verse' (*Daily Telegraph*, 9 July), suggesting Spielberg in collision with Rackham and Greenaway (*City Limits*, 17 July) or 'Tenniel's "Alice" and the disorienting botanical dream-world of Richard Dadd' (*Observer*, 13 July). Both the 1920s period setting of the Athenian scenes and the nursery connotations of the forest appear to have been aimed at creating a sense of 'nostalgia and loss through a glimpse of what might have been' (*Financial Times*, 9 July).

The doubling of Hippolyta and Titania allowed Janet McTeer alone 'to express an inner life – a slinkily clad ice-maiden whose hidden fantasies are realized by transformation into a fairy queen of bewitchingly tender sexual desire' (*City Limits*, 17 July), and Shrimpton thought that Alexander had dealt with 'the problem of the play's benign ending by implying that once Hippolyta has had her satisfying piece of rough trade (albeit in a dream) she is reconciled to the thought of marriage' (Shrimpton, 'Shakespeare', *SS* 40, p. 173). However, the general verdict was, rather unfairly, that 'exotic design has become a substitute for a directorial concept' (*Guardian*, 10 July). Whereas the Brook doubling can be accommodated without any changes to the existing text, and without any additional entrances, Alexander's relied not only on Hippolyta's appearance in 1.2 but also on 'a daring but odd manoeuvre in the last scene when sleek society-girl Hippolyta steps incongruously into the fairy ring' (*Jewish Chronicle*, 25 July). Clearly the concept was not a success, since neither the sets nor the doubling survived the production's transfer to London.

Although John Caird reverted to the more usual double doubling in 1989, his production will probably be best remembered for its post-punk irreverence, with St Trinian's fairies, Ilona Sekacz's reworking of Mendelssohn and a forest set that looked like a junkyard of the imagination. Perhaps taking his cue from Titania's 'we are their parents', and from the gap between the mortal generations, Caird treated Oberon and Titania as a harassed pair trying to keep their unruly charges in some kind of order, but their doubling made little impact in the face of the production's other more carnivalesque attractions. A similar fate befell Simon Roberts and Siobhan Redmond in Kenneth Branagh's 1990 production: 'there is no mysterious carry over from one world to another. You get no sense here that the human couple have been through the dream experience by proxy, or learned anything by it' (*Independent*, 15 August 1990).

10 Titania caresses the translated Bottom in Caird's 1989 Stratford production. Oberon
looks on from a spiral staircase and one of Titania's fairies, dressed in parodic tribute to
the balletic tradition, wears an ass head in solidarity with Bottom.

THE NATIONAL THEATRE, 1982 AND 1992

The National Theatre has made few attempts at staging *A Midsummer Night's
Dream* and has eschewed the doubling of Oberon and Titania and Theseus

11 The translated Bottom confronts his colleagues in the Renaissance touring production (1990). The class differentiation of individual characters is noticeable, with Kenneth Branagh's notably young Quince dressed as a parody of a Hollywood director.

and Hippolyta. In 1982 Bill Bryden staged a quasi-promenade version in his post-*Mysteries* Cottesloe style with John Tams and the Albion Band offering an Edwardian music-hall version of the Mechanicals alongside some Elizabethan-clothed fairies, which never quite seemed to know what it was trying to do.

However, the 1992 staging by the Canadian director Robert Lepage was the most important since Brook's in terms of applying an overall concept to the production. In many ways Lepage adopted similar approaches to Brook in terms of using the extraordinary physical skills of his Puck, the circus performer Angela Laurier, to create the atmosphere of magic. Where Brook had created a clinical white box, Lepage took his hint from Lysander's reference to the night 'when Phoebe doth behold / Her silver visage in the watery glass' (1.1.209–10) and Titania's reference to the Nine Men's Morris being filled with mud to create a set which consisted of a wide but shallow pool of water filling the greater part of the Olivier stage, surrounded by wet mud flats in and on which the lovers' quarrels were conducted. The first scene took place on a

12 The lovers in Lepage's National Theatre production (1992), watched by Puck and Oberon (stage left). The central pool surrounded by mud banks recalled the seasonal distortions referred to by Titania and allowed striking opportunities for the thematic exploitation of moonlight reflecting from water, as well as operating as a visual representation of the treacherous territory of the unconscious.

bed poled like a punt on the Indus, stressing the importance of the dream elements from the beginning since Theseus presided over the mortals' uncoiling from a scrum of bedclothes. At the end of the wood scenes the lovers took a very necessary shower, Lepage's equivalent to the traditional sunrise effect, but the sense of a movement away from the swamps of the unconscious was somewhat undercut by the impossibility of changing the set, so that the performance of Pyramus and Thisbe perforce took place on the mud flats. Although the actors' sheer physical difficulties in coping with the mud certainly predominated in some audience responses to the production, the great virtue of the set was that it placed moonlight and reflection at the centre of the staging, and provided an extraordinary physical image of the quagmire of unconscious and repressed desires that lurked in its glutinous shallows.

ADRIAN NOBLE, 1994

When Adrian Noble staged his *Dream* at Stratford in 1994 he appeared to be drawing on many of the developments of the preceding twenty-four years,

13 Puck meets the First Fairy in Noble's 1994 Stratford staging. The forest was created by pendant light bulbs and the flying umbrellas, perhaps echoing Magritte, not only allowed the fairies to fly, but reinforced the sense of a dream world.

both in the way that he and his designer Antony Ward approached the details of his mise-en-scène and, more crucially, in the ways that his production expressed a grasp of 'the central metaphor of the play, which is that the forest is a place of transformation where, as in troubled dreams, you come to value things through deception, degradation, and a sense of loss' (John Peter, *Sunday Times*, 7 August). The play was particularly well spoken, with a strong verbal stress on words associated with moon and dream, and the re-appearance of the Mechanicals as fairies helped to underpin the sense of the interpenetration of conscious and subconscious worlds which the doubling of Theseus/Oberon, Hippolyta/Titania and Philostrate/Puck created.

Noble established the rift between Theseus and Hippolyta in her reaction to his treatment of Hermia and this was picked up in the characterisation of Oberon and Titania: 'that night in the forest becomes the couple's pre-marriage dream of anxiety: they must experience their warning vision of love's torments and follies, its illusions and fine madnesses before their own nuptials' (Nicholas de Jongh, *Evening Standard*, 4 August).

The play opened in a red box set with a central rear door and a stage right swing for Hippolyta which recalled Brook's white box and trapezes, while the lovers wore costumes that were both vaguely oriental and resembled fashionable sleepwear, bringing together elements that had been used by Brook and Lepage on the one hand, and Alexander and Caird on the other. The staging of the first Mechanicals scene with driving rain outside reinforced Titania's claim that the seasons had altered. This theme was carried through into the wood scenes where the forest was created by softly glowing, gently pulsing, hanging yellow lightbulbs, presumably inspired by the play's reference to dewdrops, and Puck and the First Fairy entered on inverted umbrella trapezes. As Irving Wardle saw it, the four upstage doors in the forest 'convert neutral space into an area of enchantment and surprise. For the lovers' quarrel, they operate farcically. Locked against the fleeing mechanicals they become a source of terror. Arising from floor level, they become surrealistic pedestals for the immortals. But above all they concentrate the action in one space to secure an interpenetration of re-ality and dream' (*Independent on Sunday*, 7 August). Titania's bower was also a giant inverted flying umbrella, and the four sleeping lovers were ultimately wrapped in canvas slings and dismissed to suspension high above the stage.

Although some critics felt that the 'design sometimes seems to do the actors' work for them: the transfiguration the lovers should experience in the forest is achieved by their aerial suspension rather than felt in human terms' (Michael Billington, *Guardian*, 5 August), the production generally worked well in conveying what Carole Woddis described as 'a haunting sense of wonder and a properly modern senses of disjunction' (*What's On*, 10 August 1994). Ultimately the interpretation may have lacked the consistency of imaginative vision that characterised Brook's production, but it was a powerful testimony to the continued potency of the interpretative seam that he had begun to mine.

'No epilogue, I pray you'

Plays achieve their fullest existences on stages, yet any interpretation of a play, be it a staging or a reading, is necessarily partial and selective. Each production inevitably responds to Shakespeare's challenge in ways that are determined by the assumptions, sensibilities, and working practices of its times – whether it accepts them or reacts against them. Although many of the strategies adopted for presenting *A Midsummer Night's Dream* by previous generations may now appear curious or mistaken to late twentieth-century eyes, our understanding of the play's potential will be enriched by an informed awareness of the wide variety of interpretations it has sustained. With very few exceptions, the diverse stagings represent thoughtful and considered responses to the play itself, aimed at creating an effective theatrical event in a specific theatrical milieu. Whenever an adapter alters a line or a director changes an established approach to an aspect of the play, they call into question settled assumptions about the meanings of the whole play and force us to re-examine our responses to it. As we examine successive productions in our attempt to see what was gained or lost by different tactics, we glean not only incidental insights into a particular individual's attitudes towards the minutiae of a text, but also fuller understandings of the whole complex of meanings available in the printed text of *A Midsummer Night's Dream*, of a society's understanding of itself, and of the role of Shakespeare in creating, underpinning and challenging that understanding.[90]

The search for authenticity has bedevilled the stage history of the *Dream* because it has tended to find that authenticity in the external trappings of recreating the impossible and the unrecoverable, whether it be a long-vanished Athens and a real wood, a putative first performance, or a Renaissance interpretation, rather than in the live transaction between a contemporary audience and a performance text. One of the reasons why Granville Barker's and Peter Brook's productions of *A Midsummer Night's Dream* were so important is that they decisively rejected modes of interpretation which located meaning in the authority of tradition, in superannuated conventions,

90 Some recent examples include Lindsay Kemp's dance version, a film by Woody
   Allen and Peter Whelan's reframing of the play. Originally staged in Rome in 1979
   and filmed by Celestino Coronado in 1984, Kemp's work is a 'Jacobean gallimaufry, a
   gay fairy tale where time, order and reason have gone awry and sexual desire changes
   its object in a flash', presided over by Kemp as Puck and The Incredible Orlando
   doubling Hippolyta and Titania. The lovers paired off homosexually ('Demetrius
   rises naked from sleep to advance upon an appalled Lysander who lets his sword
   meekly fall and Helen and Hermia become similarly entwined') and 'the changeling
   becomes a focal figure, an engigmatic almost hermaphroditic item of universal
   desire' (*Guardian*, 27 April 1985). Woody Allen's 1982 *A Midsummer Night's Sex
   Comedy* has three major connections to the *Dream* : 'the exchange of partners
   during a single hectic period, the spirits and fairies, and Mendelssohn's famous score'
   (Rothwell and Melzer, *Screen*, p. 199). Peter Whelan's *Shakespeare Country* (1993) is
   'very broadly based on William Shakespeare's "A Midsummer Night's Dream" with
   the two actors playing Oberon and Titania for the RSC who are about to be married
   on Midsummer's Day disagreeing about whether to have a big wedding or not'
   (Questors Theatre publicity handout).

in what the author had originally meant or in what an original audience might have understood him to mean, rather than in the renewed and renegotiated transactions between performers and audience in a theatre on a specific occasion when:

> The actors are at hand; and by their show
> You shall know all that you are like to know.

LIST OF CHARACTERS

THESUES, *Duke of Athens*
HIPPOLYTA, *Queen of the Amazons, betrothed to Theseus*
EGEUS, *father of Hermia*
LYSANDER, *in love with Hermia*
DEMETRIUS, *preferred by Egeus as a match for Hermia*
HERMIA, *in love with Lysander*
HELENA, *in love with Demetrius*
PHILOSTRATE, *Master of the Revels at the court of Theseus*

OBERON, *King of the Fairies*
TITANIA, *Queen of the Fairies*
PUCK *or* ROBIN GOODFELLOW, *Oberon's jester and attendant*
PEASEBLOSSOM
COBWEB
MOTH ⎱ *Fairies attending on Titania*
MUSTARDSEED
A FAIRY, *in the service of Titania*

PETER QUINCE, *carpenter (Prologue in the play of 'Pyramus and Thisbe')*
NICK BOTTOM, *weaver (Pyramus)*
FRANCIS FLUTE, *bellows-mender (Thisbe)*
TOM SNOUT, *tinker (Wall)*
ROBIN STARVELING, *tailor (Moonshine)*
SNUG, *joiner (Lion)*

'*Lords and Attendants*' *on Theseus and Hippolyta*

A MIDSUMMER NIGHT'S DREAM

ACT I, SCENE I

The tiring house façade in an Elizabethan public playhouse would have provided a background ornate, formal and symmetrical enough to suggest a ducal palace to any contemporary spectator concerned about location, as would the hall screen in one of the great houses postulated as the play's original venue by supporters of the theory that it was first staged as part of a private marriage ceremony. The Hatton Garden preparation copy, like George Colman in the eighteenth century, assumed the use of a stock palace set here. Throughout the nineteenth century, from the 1816 'Grand Doric Colonnade appertaining to Duke Theseus' Palace' (Reynolds, *Dream*, p. [5]) an exterior Athenian setting was *de rigueur* in order to allow the scene designers and painters to display their knowledge of Greek architecture. In 1840 Vestris started with Theseus' palace with a distant view of Athens; Charles Kean, 'unfettered with regard to chronology' since 'the general character of the play is so far from historical', chose to present his audience with 'The Acropolis on its rocky eminence, surrounded by marble Temples, ... together with the Theatre of Bacchus' (1856 playbill); Benson opened in front of the Ionic portico of Theseus' palace, painted in an 'archaic style of colouring' with 'deep Egyptian coving which crowns the entablature' (Moyr Smith, *Dream*, p. xv); for Tree, 'Temple towers above temple in grand proportions, the entire composition rich in colour and grandly kept together with a row of cypress trees' (HTC cutting).

In 1914 Granville Barker, reacting against this tradition, dispensed completely with built-up sets here, using white silk curtains with a conventional design to represent Athens. In 1920 Fagan adopted a simplified version of the Athenian staging with 'a loggia with two great fluted pillars' (*Birmingham Post*, 6 December) 'against a sky of blues, purples, and reds; low broad steps leading into a foreground that convey an excellent effect of space' (*Era*, 8 December) but Basil Dean, who had to fill the vast Drury Lane stage as opposed to Fagan's intimate Royal Court, adopted the traditional approach with his 'classical, wedding-marchy, Alma-Tadema palace' (Farjeon, *Scene*, p. 42).

The Old Vic and Stratford, where (despite Patrick Kirwan's brief Elizabethan incursion in 1914) Benson's influence lingered for many years, remained essentially Athenian until Harcourt Williams pioneered an Elizabethan country house approach at the Old Vic in 1929 and Bridges Adams similarly threw out his classical Athenian setting in 1932. Thereafter, with the exception of Tyrone Guthrie's deliberate pastiche Victorian production in 1937, broadly Elizabethan stagings predominated until Brook's white box revival in 1970, sometimes combining the Athenian and Renaissance strands, as in Benthall's 1949 Veronese palace with Greek costumes drawn from Renaissance painting or Langham's costumes and sets which gave 'an impression of Athens seen through late Renaissance eyes' (Speaight, *Shakespeare*, p. 273). Hall's powerful 1959 Quiller-Couchean Elizabethan manor house treatment, with a double staircase joining to form a balcony, also, unusually for the period, did not use the house curtains so that the audience had a sense of entering a theatre transformed into the hall of an Elizabethan manor house. Tony Richardson set the play 'very definitely in Greece' but had very little scenery, with 'a few columns for the Palace' (*Plays and Players*, February 1962).

Generally both Athenian and Renaissance stagings contrast the world of the opening and closing scenes with the world of the wood. However, attempts to suggest the interpenetration of the worlds of the play include Robert Atkins's 1944 Stratford production where, in the opening scene, 'the magic moonlit wood showed in shadowy silhouette' behind classic pillars (*Theatre World*, June), with a similar effect at the end (see 5.1.400); Barton's Renaissance-costumed 1977 staging with 'mottled shadows, leaf-patterned' which faded 'to invisibility during the opening scene' and then reappeared for the rest of the play (*Observer*, 15 May) and Bryden's 'sleek gauze façade of trees and moonlight wih one solid doorway' (*Financial Times*, in *LTR*, 1982), as well as Brook's and Lepage's.

Nevill Coghill developed his 1945 scenery from two Inigo Jones designs for fairy palaces and Devine had a permanent set of 'a few symbolic trees and a moonblanched forest painted on a gauze screen' (*Times*, 24 March 1954) so that scenes traditionally played as interiors, except 1.2 (see below), were taken as exteriors. This apparently radical innovation elicited little critical discussion, although the *Nottingham Guardian–Journal* did find it hard to accept 'an earthy slope decorated with unearthly trees and a glimpse of unglazed green-houses through the distant gauze' as the ducal palace (25 March).

Brook's permanent white box set dispensed completely with Athenian trappings, though it quoted the Elizabethan stage with its two doors in the back wall, and there were also ladders in the walls leading to a catwalk on the top of the set which housed the musicians and offstage members of the cast who could watch the action below. Brook added flown-in wire trees for the wood scenes, trapezes and a flying bower for Titania, but otherwise the set remained unchanged, with the interpenetration of worlds further underpinned through doubling.

Although Brook's production freed the play from either Elizabethan or Athenian histori-cism, there have been few achronological productions and other historical periods have been in vogue latterly for the court scenes, with Ron Daniels trying to create his sense of magic by drawing on the Victorian toy theatre tradition for the RSC in 1981–2 ('Swags of canvas cloud hang stiffly in the heavens. Flats and cut-out wings present a palace of Theseus in the highest Victorian taste' (*TLS*, 31 July 1981)) and Bill Bryden at the National in 1982 going for roughly the same period. Bill Alexander (cocktail-bar white sofa and Art Deco lamps in the style of Lonsdale in 1986), and John Caird (Greek-poled white wedding marquee in 1989), both used inter-war settings, although Caird was deliberately anachronistic with a spatted Egeus matched with a Doc Martened Helena, and an interrogative reworking of the Mendelssohn overture.

While there may have been a conceptual or thematic intent behind Kenneth Branagh's touring 'tilted saucer encircled by a lower rim – faintly resembling a shallow-brimmed boater' with its 'Olympic flame' burning centre stage to differentiate it from the same set when it was used for *King Lear* (*Financial Times*, 11 August 1990), with 'a high wall of curved metal into which star-shaped holes have been punched' (*Independent*, 15 August 1990), the stars and moon connotations of the saucer appear to have escaped most critics, unlike the central use of a circular pool of water in Lepage's 1992 production, which placed moonlight and reflection at the centre of the staging. Adrian Noble in 1994 paid homage to Brook's design with a red box and a swing for Hippolyta.

Costumes have usually reflected sets, with variations on the current version of classical or Renaissance or Victorian/Edwardian or twenties/thirties according to the period of the set. Bridges Adams's Elizabethan costumes, designed by Norman Wilkinson for the 1932 production, were used as late as 1944 with different sets. Coghill dressed his lovers in authentic Inigo Jones designs in silks and satins. Archaeological approaches long survived Kean's: 'For the mortals' costumes, Motley has sought inspiration in antique jars, so that Theseus and his bride really do look like vigorous warriors from the ancient world and not at all like a middle-aged English headmaster and lady dealing with the parents on speech day' (*Stratford Herald*, 26 March 1954). Brook, Lepage and Noble used generic Orientally inspired elements in their court characters' costumes.

Reinhardt's 1935 film begins with a written proclamation which explains the situation, with specific mention of the pension for those whose play is performed at Theseus' wedding celebration. The whole of Athens is gathered to celebrate Theseus' return in song, thus providing the camera with an opportunity to pick out the main mortal characters: Egeus intervenes as the four lovers indulge in waving and counter-waving, singing and counter-singing, smiling and pouting, to establish their relationships, while the Mechanicals prove as incompetent a glee club as they will be a dramatic society. Theseus and his returning army (which includes Lysander and Demetrius) are initially dressed in a Renaissance interpretation of classical military dress, with the Athenian sets maintaining this dual focus, although the dress code is basically Hollywood Renaissance.

ACT I, SCENE 1

Enter THESEUS, HIPPOLYTA, PHILOSTRATE, with others

0 SD   In the Renaissance theatre Theseus and Hippolyta could have entered together through one
        door or, like Oberon and Titania in 2.1, at different doors. Benson's opening is typical of the
        processional beginnings that predominate in later productions: the set showed the Ionic
        portico of Theseus' palace with two marble lions guarding the steps, with 'foliage of various
        kinds spread over the sides and top of the scene'. There were men with dogs, women at a
        water fountain, a man sleeping, children playing and then a flourish of trumpets as Theseus
        and his retinue appeared from behind the colonnade at the central door at the top of the
        steps. A crowd of about twenty entered and shouted 'Hail Theseus' as the ducal procession
        arrived, so that the first scene was played in public in front of a large crowd (Moyr Smith,
        Dream, p. xv and promptbook). Barker, too, had a processional opening with stewards, and
        courtiers and Amazons who ranged themselves to either side of a central throne, Amazons
        on Theseus' left, Hippolyta to Theseus' right and courtiers to Hippolyta's right (prompt-
        book). Shaw, objecting to Daly's similar staging, believed that the dispute should take place
        in private. Although the public inevitably dwindled in more financially straitened times,
        Shaw's view came to the fore again in the 1980s: Alexander staged the first exchanges as a
        private scene with Philostrate the only person in attendance on Theseus and Hippolyta;
        Caird opened with Hippolyta alone and pensive, so that Theseus' speech was an attempt to
        cheer her up but she remained angry, with a mocking curtsey at 'revelling'; Noble began
        with Hippolyta on a swing alone, with Philostrate on briefly only to leave again immediately.
        Lepage's 1992 staging offered a radical reading, with the night/dream element stressed from
        the beginning as 'a tiny figure in red hops and slithers towards a central pool of water, while
        gamelans and strings begin to play. It is Angela Laurier as Puck, walking on her hands, her
        legs hung over her shoulders. She reaches up to grasp a single light bulb hanging from the
        flies – and turns it *out*' (*Sunday Times*, 12 July). After that, 'Theseus and Hippolyta, about as
        lively as statues, are seen perched on the end of an iron single bed, which is being punted in
        circles by a turbaned servant. Asleep on it, top-to-toe, are the four young lovers who stir
        back to consciousness bemusedly as each is required for the scene with the irate Egeus. All
        of them are dressed for bed' (*Independent*, 11 July).

Theseus has generally been regarded as having 'little to do but look the hero' (TM cutting, 1816), dress well, and speak sonorously. *The Times*, objecting to the role being played as 'a solemn buffoon' at the Old Vic in 1926, saw it as 'a delightful decoration of a formal kind' (28 September) and the *New Statesman* simply declared 'the character is empty' (10 February 1945). Since 1945 there have been some attempts to follow up the (Shavian?) 'almost raisonneur' at the Old Vic in 1931 (*Stage*, 5 November): Keith Michell had 'a pleasantly sardonic air' for Devine (*Daily Telegraph*, 24 March 1954); Jack Gwillim, for Benthall in 1957, was 'somewhat pompous' (*Stage*, 27 December); Robert Lang was 'more an ascetic philosopher than a passionate warrior–duke' for Tony Richardson (*Independent*, 28 January 1962); Robin Bailey's colonial governor gave 'Theseus a Shaftesbury Avenue suavity which quickly becomes a succulent parody of the style' in Dunlop's 1967 modern dress production (*Daily Mail*, 27 September), Edward De Souza was 'a first-rate, upper class snob' for Bryden (*Guardian*, in *LTR* 1983) and Robin Easton was embarrassed and vacillating in Alexander's Barbican staging (*Daily Telegraph*, 20 August 1987).

Hippolyta, like Theseus, has traditionally been expected to be more decorative than active, often dressed to suggest her exotic otherness and eastern origin, as for Vestris, when she wore an Amazon tunic and pantaloons. From Kean's Miss Murray, who 'looked the part to perfection, and that is about all that the Queen of the Amazons is called upon to do' (*Era*, 19 October 1856) to Hall's allegedly untraditional, because Elizabethan, Stephanie Bidmead, 'chosen for her looks and high dignity' (Stratford *Herald*, 5 June 1959), the keynotes remained remarkably similar, with the emphasis on diction and deportment. Even minor variants such as Helen Cherry's 'testy lady of the manor' (Stratford *Herald*, 12 May 1944), Yvonne Bonnamy looking like 'Queen Victoria eyeing a departing minister' (*Guardian*, 18 April 1962), or Cleo Laine as 'a hard-riding country lady' for Dunlop (*Daily Mail*, 27 September 1967) were unusual until Langham began to develop the sympathy often shown by Hippolytas to Hermias into a more extended reading in 1960.

Theseus and Hippolyta had traditionally been presented as reconciled at the opening of the play – Tree rebuked his Thesus in rehearsal for waking the languorously dozing Hippolyta with too chaste a kiss (HTC cutting) – but by 1981 Daniels's programme stated that the marriage betwen Theseus and Hippolyta was 'at first, a marriage of convenience between two strangers'. Although the 1935 film Hippolyta, wearing a snake-decorated dress, initially looks frosty and unreconciled to her fate, the substantive process of change seems to have begun with Langham's 'hymeneal chant and pseudodervish dance' (*Times*, 21 December 1960) preceding Hippolyta's entrance as a captive. J. C. Trewin saw this as reclaiming some long-buried implications of the text which allowed Jennie Goossens to develop a Hippolyta who softens gradually over the course of the play (*Birmingham Post*, 21 December). Brook's extensive exploration of possible discords in the relationship between Theseus and Hippolyta, through the doubling of the roles with Oberon and Titania, helped to popularise the idea of an initial disharmony between Theseus and Hippolyta – a harmony which is rectified by the processes of the wood. However, the doubling has not

THESEUS Now, fair Hippolyta, our nuptial hour
              Draws on apace; four happy days bring in
              Another moon – but O, methinks, how slow
              This old moon wanes! She lingers my desires,
              Like to a step-dame or a dowager   5
              Long withering out a young man's revenue.
HIPPOLYTA Four days will quickly steep themselves in night;
              Four nights will quickly dream away the time;
              And then the moon, like to a silver bow
              New bent in heaven, shall behold the night   10
              Of our solemnities.
THESEUS   Go, Philostrate,
              Stir up the Athenian youth to merriments,
              Awake the pert and nimble spirit of mirth;
              Turn melancholy forth to funerals;
              The pale companion is not for our pomp.   15
                                                              [*Exit Philostrate*]
              Hippolyta, I wooed thee with my sword,
              And won thy love doing thee injuries;
              But I will wed thee in another key,
              With pomp, with triumph, and with revelling.

          Enter EGEUS *and his daughter* HERMIA, LYSANDER *and* DEMETRIUS

EGEUS Happy be Theseus, our renownèd Duke!   20
THESEUS Thanks, good Egeus. What's the news with thee?

found favour with all directors and critics: 'To try to make the degree of discord between the
human pair match that between the fairy couple, Ms Higgins has to flounce around the wedding tent, snorting contemptuously at her husband like some discontented proto-feminist
from Ibsen' (*Independent*, 13 April 1989, on Caird's production). In 1986 Alexander
attempted a new variation on this gambit when he doubled only Titania and a black-clad
Hippolyta 'in search of a neo-classical tragedy by T. S. Eliot' (*Sunday Telegraph*, 13 July).

4–6   Kean cut from 'She', as did Saker (whose version is heavily dependent on Kean's) and Tree.

7ff.   Langham 'piles on the discord by having Hippolyta play the opening scene in a tremendous
       pet, as if sickened by the prospect of marrying Theseus' (*Observer*, 12 December 1960).

11   Coghill 'ordained that Philostrate should rhyme with "illustrate"' (*Daily Mail*, 26 January
       1945). This appears to have been one of his donnish crimes, although it is a more metrically
       apposite pronunciation than what was clearly the accepted form with a long final 'e'. Since
       Philostrate has no lines here, he is discussed at 5.1.38.

20   Egeus has generally been treated as venerable, unsympathetic and testy, sometimes as in
       Asche's production with a 'touch of senile fussiness' (*Era*, 2 December 1905). Greet saw him

EGEUS Full of vexation come I, with complaint
        Against my child, my daughter Hermia.
        Stand forth, Demetrius! – My noble lord,
        This man hath my consent to marry her.   25
        Stand forth, Lysander! – And, my gracious Duke,
        This man hath bewitched the bosom of my child.
        Thou, thou, Lysander, thou hast given her rhymes,

as 'the stupid parent who has his eyes on the money bags only' (1915 programme note, Old Vic), he was 'Pantaloonish' at the Old Vic in 1931 (*Stage*, 5 November) and a 'well-outraged and aged rheumatic' for Hall in 1959 (Stratford *Herald*, 5 June). Occasional voices have queried the tradition: in 1943 the Stratford *Herald* asked 'Why must Egeus (Aubrey Danvers) be such a silly old man?' (30 April), and Robert Speaight noted that the Egeus in Langham's 1960 staging resisted 'the heresy that no Shakespearian father can be under seventy' (*Tablet*, 31 December). In Dunlop's modern dress version, he was 'an indignant senior Civil Servant, whose anger with his daughter Hermia obviously springs from her flouting of convention rather than concern for her wellbeing' (*Financial Times*, 27 September 1967). Brook's doubling of Quince and Egeus attracted relatively little attention: Clive Barnes saw it as an attempt to 'bring the play within the play more closely into the main structure, for just as Egeus initiates the real action, so Quince initiates the inner play', although it worked less satisfactorily than the other doublings (*New York Herald Tribune*, 30 August 1970). Howard Goorney, in the Lyttelton transfer of Bryden's production, was 'the usual irksome fusspot' (*Guardian*, in *LTR* 1983).

As Athens only became a duchy in the middle ages, the classical Theseus could not have been a duke and he was thus addressed throughout Kean's archaeologically pedantic production as 'Prince'. Benthall's 1949 Egeus intervened from a balcony and his speech was punctuated by crowd reactions, a stir of conversation, gasps and a big stir at line 44 (promptbook). Daniels had all his male characters bow to Theseus here (promptbook): 'all is decorum and drawing room manners. The Duke reclines on a chaise-longue to receive his troublesome deputation, and admonishes Hermia in the clipped tones of a premature Noel Coward' (*TLS*, 31 July 1981). Alexander's Egeus dragged Hermia on and threw her down on the floor in front of Theseus. Caird's Theseus was preoccupied and dismissive in his attitude to Egeus.

24, 26 On Egeus' commands, Lysander and Demetrius advanced left and left centre in Kean's production (promptbook); most directors use some form of contrapuntal kneeling and/or advancing and retiring by the three lovers during the scene. In Alexander's staging, Hermia, still prostrate, banged the floor when Demetrius was mentioned. Caird's Lysander, who was languid and scruffy (Demetrius was priggish), had been whispering to Hermia, but took his hands out of his pockets as he stood forth.

28–40 Egeus' expansion on Lysander's tactics and tokens was severely truncated by nineteenth-century directors and by some, including Atkins and Hall, in the twentieth, although it can be

And interchanged love-tokens with my child.
Thou hast by moonlight at her window sung 30
With feigning voice verses of feigning love,
And stolen the impression of her fantasy,
With bracelets of thy hair, rings, gauds, conceits,
Knacks, trifles, nosegays, sweetmeats – messengers
Of strong prevailment in unhardened youth; 35
With cunning hast thou filched my daughter's heart,
Turned her obedience, which is due to me,
To stubborn harshness. And, my gracious Duke,
Be it so she will not here, before your grace,
Consent to marry with Demetrius, 40
I beg the ancient privilege of Athens;
As she is mine, I may dispose of her;
Which shall be either to this gentleman
Or to her death, according to our law
Immediately provided in that case. 45
THESEUS What say you, Hermia? Be advised, fair maid.
To you your father should be as a god,
One that composed your beauties; yea, and one
To whom you are but as a form in wax
By him imprinted, and within his power 50
To leave the figure, or disfigure it.
Demetrius is a worthy gentleman.

used as an occasion for comedy at the expense of his pedantry: Brember Wills did 'the splut-
tering rage' of Egeus very well for Dean in 1924 and Adeney, in Harcourt Williams's staging,
was 'fussy & choleric' (Crosse, *Diary* IX, p. 44 and XII, p. 51). Devine's Egeus produced the
jewellery with which Lysander wooed Hermia from his waist satchel. Langham's Lysander
interrupted in the middle of 38 (promptbook). At 'bracelets' Caird's Egeus took a laundry
bag from Hermia; at 'knacks' he emptied it on the floor.

41   Bryden's production raised some problems of period: 'one can't help wondering why a chap
     in hacking-jacket and gaiters is begging the "ancient privilege of Athens"' (*Guardian*, in *LTR*
     1982).

42–3 Kean's Egeus went up to Demetrius and took his hand (promptbook); Caird's joined
     Demetrius' and Hermia's hands.

44   Benson had a 'sigh' at 'death'; Daly's crowd expressed terror; Barker's and Benthall's crowds
     also reacted (promptbooks). Caird's Hippolyta broke to the side unhappy.

45–57 Cut by Kean; Saker cut from 'Be advised' to 51, Phelps and Tree from 47 to 51; Atkins from 46
     to 57. The cuts preserve the narrative outline of the predicament while limiting its expansion.
     Daniels's 'courteous, considerate Theseus seated Hermia beside him to try to persuade
     rather than bully her out of opposition to her father' (Warren, 'Interpretations', p. 147).

HERMIA So is Lysander.
THESEUS   In himself he is;
    But in this kind, wanting your father's voice,
    The other must be held the worthier.   55
HERMIA I would my father looked but with my eyes.
THESEUS Rather your eyes must with his judgement look.
HERMIA I do entreat your grace to pardon me.

53   The little nineteenth-century comment on Hermia shows that she was no exception to
the general treatment of the lovers as serious but not particularly interesting: for Vestris,
Mrs Nisbett 'delivered the exquisite poetry appertaining to the part with a listlessness of
manner' (*Era*, 22 November 1840), while Helen Douglas at the Gaiety in 1875 was 'nowhere
wanting in intelligence or pathos' (*Era*, 21 February). Shaw's comment that Benson's 1889
Hermia was melodramatic and lacked 'the indispensable classic grace' (*Shaw on
Shakespeare*, p. 133) might be a misreading of an early attempt to play the part as comic,
since by Tree's 1900 production the *Era* was talking of both 'the combative characteristics'
and 'the sentimental side of the rôle' (13 January). Thereafter critics draw on the discourse of
vixens, tartars, shrews and viragos, fieriness and impulsiveness to read the newer, more
comic, interpretations of the character: Laura Cowie, who played the part for Tree in 1911 and
Barker in 1914 was praised for her fresh 'kittenish' reading in 1911 and for being 'particularly
good in her vixenish mood' (HTC cutting; *Era*, 11 February). By the late twenties the transformation was complete and Hermias were condemned for 'lacking the spitfire quality without
which no Hermia can count for much' (VW cutting) at the Old Vic in 1926, or combining 'fire
and wit' with an inappropriate 'lachrymose touch' at Stratford in 1928 *Birmingham Daily
Mail*, 10 April). 'Spitfire', given extended currency as a result of the associations with the
fighter aeroplane of the same name, has remained a key epithet to describe successive
Hermias up to Emma Fielding's in 1994 (*Today*, 4 August). Some interpretations have been
accused of falsifying the character's social context: Zena Walker (for Devine), one of a group
of 'very modern youngsters', played her 'almost as if she were an American college girl'
(*Coventry Standard*, 26 March 1954); Priscilla Morgan was a suburban Athenian and 'a
whining little shrew of a maidservant' (*Sunday Times*, 7 June 1959), and, perhaps inevitably
in view of her previous roles, Rita Tushingham (for Tony Richardson) was 'sincere but heavy ... ,
trailing clouds from kitchen-sink amid the gloom of the wood near Athens' (*Plays and
Players*, March 1962). Despite changes in overall approaches to the play, however, contemporary Hermias still appear to be operating in very similar territory to Laura Cowie: Amanda
Harris was 'fiery' for Alexander (*Daily Telegraph*, 9 July 1986); Amanda Bellamy was 'pert,
squeaky, simpering' for Caird (*Guardian*, 13 April 1989) and Francine Morgan in Branagh's
staging was 'an endearing spitfire' (*Evening Standard*, 22 August 1990).

56–7   Benson cut these thematically resonant references to eyes.

58   Here Kean's Hermia advanced and knelt to Theseus; Barker's kissed his hand (promptbooks).

I know not by what power I am made bold,
Nor how it may concern my modesty 60
In such a presence here to plead my thoughts;
But I beseech your grace that I may know
The worst that may befall me in this case,
If I refuse to wed Demetrius.
THESEUS Either to die the death, or to abjure 65
For ever the society of men.
Therefore, fair Hermia, question your desires,
Know of your youth, examine well your blood,
Whether, if you yield not to your father's choice,
You can endure the livery of a nun, 70
For aye to be in shady cloister mewed,
To live a barren sister all your life,
Chanting faint hymns to the cold fruitless moon.
Thrice blessèd they that master so their blood
To undergo such maiden pilgrimage; 75
But earthlier happy is the rose distilled
Than that which, withering on the virgin thorn,
Grows, lives, and dies in single blessedness.
HERMIA So will I grow, so live, so die, my lord,
Ere I will yield my virgin patent up 80
Unto his lordship, whose unwishèd yoke
My soul consents not to give sovereignty.
THESEUS Take time to pause, and by the next new moon,
The sealing-day betwixt my love and me

60 Cut by Kean, presumably on grounds of modesty.
65 Kean's Hermia responded to 'death' with an action of fear; Benson's crowd sighed and
   moved; Daly's expressed terror; Barker's cast were instructed 'All play to this'; Benthall's
   Hermia collapsed on the floor, causing a general stir (promptbooks).
67–82 Problematic lines in the nineteenth century on pious and/or anachronistic grounds, and
   therefore cut and modified by all directors except Benson. Atkins cut 74–8.
78 Benson's crowd reacted with a movement (promptbook).
80 Daly's Hermia had a 'maiden heart and vow'.
81 Sarah Brooke for Tree in 1900 and Athene Seyler for Dean stressed 'lord' rather than 'his' in
   'unto his lordship' (Crosse, *Diary* II, p. [113] and IX, p. 46); One of Tree's promptbooks reads
   'Ere I will yield unto his lordship', which might justify a stress on 'Lord'. Devine's Hermia
   emphasised her position by pointing at Demetrius (promptbook).
82 At the end of this line Brook had a long pause before Hippolyta got up, thus motivating
   Theseus' next speech (promptbook).

For everlasting bond of fellowship,   85
Upon that day either prepare to die
For disobedience to your father's will,
Or else to wed Demetrius, as he would,
Or on Diana's altar to protest
For aye austerity and single life.   90
DEMETRIUS Relent, sweet Hermia; and, Lysander, yield
    Thy crazèd title to my certain right.
LYSANDER You have her father's love, Demetrius;
    Let me have Hermia's – do you marry him.
EGEUS Scornful Lysander, true, he hath my love,   95
    And what is mine my love shall render him;
    And she is mine, and all my right of her
    I do estate unto Demetrius.
LYSANDER I am, my lord, as well-derived as he,
    As well-possessed: my love is more than his,   100
    My fortunes every way as fairly ranked,

---

85   Cut by Kean.

90   Lysander took Hermia upstage here in Kean's production and some squires and Amazons also moved, perhaps in anticipation of a disturbance, since Kean also cut 91–8, moving directly to Lysander's defiance (promptbook).

91, 93   Lysander and Demetrius seldom excite much individual critical attention: when the lovers were played straight they were little more than walking gentlemen, usually dignified by such epithets as sound, stalwart, satisfactory, manly or earnest. Even in more comic treatments, they often receive tepid praise and attract little critical attention: in Fagan's 1920 production, they were 'satisfactory without any very striking qualities' (*Athenaeum*, 17 December 1920); Agate thought that 'Lysander and Demetrius are perhaps not more dissimilar than Rosencrantz and Guildenstern, but as two handsome peas in a pod Messrs Leon Quartermaine and Frank Vosper [in Dean's staging] were all that could be desired' (*Chronicles*, p. 42): for Daniels they were 'wet, public schoolboy lovers' (*Guardian*, in *LTR* 1982). Demetrius usually occupies a narrow spectrum around the 1926 Old Vic's 'reasonable man forced into awkward situations through no fault of his own' (VW cutting), while Lysander is more of an impetuous romantic, though with more variations such as Albert Finney's 1959 'teddy boy' (*News Chronicle*, 3 June), Karl Johnson's 'priggishly ardent young man' for Bryden (*Observer*, in *LTR* 1982), Paul Greenwood's 'wimp who fancies himself as a real man but can't quite bring it off' (*Sunday Today*, 13 July 1986), or Stephen Simm's 'sulking homme fatale' for Caird (*Guardian* 13 April 1989).

93–4   Tree had the crowd murmur, Egeus exclaim angrily, Demetrius and Lysander put their hands on their swords, soldiers and Amazons move, but they were all stilled when the Duke raised his hand (promptbook).

95–8   Saker and Tree joined Kean in cutting Egeus' speech, further reducing an already small part.

If not with vantage, as Demetrius';
And, which is more than all these boasts can be,
I am beloved of beauteous Hermia.
Why should not I then prosecute my right?   105
Demetrius, I'll avouch it to his head,
Made love to Nedar's daughter, Helena,
And won her soul; and she, sweet lady, dotes,
Devoutly dotes, dotes in idolatry,
Upon this spotted and inconstant man.   110
THESEUS I must confess that I have heard so much,
And with Demetrius thought to have spoke thereof;
But, being overfull of self-affairs,
My mind did lose it. But Demetrius, come,
And come, Egeus. You shall go with me;   115
I have some private schooling for you both.
For you, fair Hermia, look you arm yourself
To fit your fancies to your father's will;
Or else the law of Athens yields you up
(Which by no means we may extenuate)   120
To death, or to a vow of single life.
Come, my Hippolyta; what cheer, my love?

102–4 Kean, a fussy editor, cut 102 and conflated 103–4 by removing 'than all these boasts can be' and 'beauteous', Saker and Daly also cut 102, thus making the men unquestionably equally wealthy and reducing their individuality.

107 In Caird's staging, Egeus' reaction showed he didn't know about Helena, and Hermia used the opportunity to break away from Demetrius.

109 One of the cuts suggested by Bowdler that was not taken up in the theatre.

111–27 Theseus' exit speech with its dual commands to Egeus and Demetrius was often tidied up in the nineteenth century: Vestris took 116–22 after 127, bringing both the instructions to Demetrius and Egeus together, and removed 'What cheer, my love?' (as did Daly), Kean and Daly saved Theseus from accusations of inconsistency by removing 120; Saker softened Hermia's potential fates by cutting 119–127; Reynolds, Kean, and Atkins cut 122–7, presumably because it repeats Theseus' earlier command.

113 Caird's Theseus was angry at Hippolyta here.

121 For Brook, everyone bowed their head in acknowledgment of Theseus' command and a pause ensued before he addressed Hippolyta (promptbook).

122 Benson's crowd all left with Theseus and his retinue here, the final line of his version of the scene, looking round at Hermia. In 1900 Tree's Hippolyta expressed her sympathy for Hermia by helping her up from her kneeling position in front of Theseus, in 1911 she 'turns and smiles' at her as she leaves (promptbooks). In Bridges Adams's Athenian productions, he had Egeus exit 'after Hermia has caught his toga. He puts it away from her' while

Demetrius and Egeus, go along;
I must employ you in some business
Against our nuptial, and confer with you   125
Of something nearly that concerns yourselves.
EGEUS With duty and desire we follow you.

Exeunt all but Lysander and Hermia

LYSANDER How now, my love? Why is your cheek so pale?
How chance the roses there do fade so fast?
HERMIA Belike for want of rain, which I could well   130
Beteem them from the tempest of my eyes.
LYSANDER Ay me! For aught that I could ever read,
Could ever hear by tale or history,
The course of true love never did run smooth;
But either it was different in blood –   135
HERMIA O cross! too high to be enthralled to low.
LYSANDER Or else misgraffèd in respect of years –
HERMIA O spite! too old to be engaged to young.
LYSANDER Or else it stood upon the choice of friends –
HERMIA O hell, to choose love by another's eyes!   140

Demetrius threatens Lysander before he exits (promptbook). Theseus and Hippolyta paused at their respective doors before exiting in Brook's production (promptbook); the moment was a further indication of Hippolyta's unhappiness with the situation. In Bryden's production, 'casting a black Hippolyta (Marsha Hunt) ... produced some hints of pre-marital resentment - Theseus' "what cheer my love" (1.1.122) was nervously delivered as she stalked prematurely off stage in a state of high dudgeon. But it was not developed into a deliberate portrait of marriage as conquest and enslavement' (Shrimpton, 'Shakespeare', *SS* 37, p. 169). Alexander had Hippolyta cross to Theseus, break the head off a rose and give it to him before her exit, clearly indicating her view of his handling of the situation; his Lysander made as if to punch Demetrius and they circled one another before Egeus and Demetrius left (promptbook). Caird's Hippolyta initially did not react to Theseus, then slowly followed him, indicating her solidarity with Hermia by patting her arm. Noble's Theseus fished unconvincingly for a reason to get Egeus and Demetrius off; Egeus threw Hermia down and Hippolyta flounced off in distress.

128 Daly's Hermia sank on a convenient couch when everyone but Lysander left; Hermia and Lysander sat 'with heads together' for Barker (promptbooks). Calthrop played the rest of the scene against curtains drawn across after Theseus' exit so that Quince's shop could be set up upstage (Crosse, *Diary* VIII, p. 99). In keeping with the period setting, Alexander's Lysander gave Hermia a cigarette (promptbook).

128-31 Cut by Vestris; Kean cut 129.

135-140 Reynolds, Vestris (who cut Hermia's interjections), Phelps (who cut the exchange all the

LYSANDER Or, if there were a sympathy in choice,
War, death, or sickness did lay siege to it,
Making it momentany as a sound,
Swift as a shadow, short as any dream,
Brief as the lightning in the collied night,   145
That in a spleen unfolds both heaven and earth,
And, ere a man hath power to say 'Behold!',
The jaws of darkness do devour it up.
So quick bright things come to confusion.
HERMIA If then true lovers have been ever crossed   150
It stands as an edict in destiny.
Then let us teach our trial patience,
Because it is a customary cross,
As due to love as thoughts, and dreams, and sighs,
Wishes, and tears – poor fancy's followers.   155
LYSANDER A good persuasion. Therefore hear me, Hermia:
I have a widow aunt, a dowager,
Of great revenue, and she hath no child.
From Athens is her house remote seven leagues;
And she respects me as her only son.   160
There, gentle Hermia, may I marry thee;
And to that place the sharp Athenian law
Cannot pursue us. If thou lov'st me, then
Steal forth thy father's house tomorrow night,
And in the wood, a league without the town   165
(Where I did meet thee once with Helena
To do observance to a morn of May),
There will I stay for thee.
HERMIA   My good Lysander,
I swear to thee by Cupid's strongest bow,
By his best arrow with the golden head,   170

way to 149), and other nineteenth-century directors objected to these antiphonal lines as did
Bowdler. Atkins reduced the antiphony by cutting 137–8.

145-9 Cut in one of Tree's promptbooks, and by Atkins and Devine. An unusual cut since twentieth-
century directors usually cut only in areas which have been traditionally subject to changes,
and then more sparingly.

151 Cut by Kean, probably on pious grounds, and followed by Saker.

153-5 Hermia's generalising did not find favour with Vestris, Kean, Saker and Benson.

157-68 Vestris cut 'a dowager' and 'and she hath no child' and reversed the order of 160 and 161;
Kean also cut 'a dowager' but cut 160 and 167 as well as the potentially subversive 'thy
father's house' and, more obscurely, 'a league without the town'.

169-78 Phelps cut the possibly theatrically obscure 169–74, which perhaps undermine the purity of

By the simplicity of Venus' doves,
By that which knitteth souls and prospers loves,
And by that fire which burned the Carthage queen
When the false Trojan under sail was seen,
By all the vows that ever men have broke   175
(In number more than ever women spoke),
In that same place thou hast appointed me,
Tomorrow truly will I meet with thee.
LYSANDER Keep promise, love. Look, here comes Helena.

Enter HELENA

HERMIA God speed, fair Helena! Whither away?   180
HELENA Call you me fair? That 'fair' again unsay.

Hermia's oath; Kean, Saker, Daly all cut 170, possibly seeing a phallic reference? Kean, Daly, Saker and Benthall removed the couplet about Dido, and Saker extended his cut to 176. Reynolds ended his scene here with a song constructed from 171–2 and 175–6, with 177–8 as a refrain for each couplet.

179 Kean's Lysander took Hermia upstage in anticipation of Helena's entrance 'in thought' (promptbook). Daniels had his Helena start to exit again when she saw Hermia and Lysander. Lysander and Hermia were on the point of kissing in Alexander's staging when Lysander saw Helena. Lepage's Helena 'gazes through the bedsprings to watch Lysander and Hermia kissing' (*Evening Standard*, 10 July 1992).

180 Tree cut the end of the line, making Helena respond directly to Hermia's description of her, rather than her question to her.

181 The nineteenth century was not impressed with Helena: in 1816 Miss Foote 'gave all the interest to Helena, that character is susceptible of' (TM cutting); Vestris's Miss Cooper was 'full of touching pathos, simplicity, and beauty' (*Theatrical Journal*, 5 December 1840); and, for Kean, Miss Heath 'left nothing to be desired, except, perhaps, a trifle more vivacity' (*Era*, 19 October 1856). Phelps made an attempt to play the part comically and was casti-gated by Henry Morley, who thought that the character was 'an exquisite abstraction, a pitiful and moving picture of a gentle maid forlorn, playfully developed, as becomes the fantastic texture of the poem, but not at all meant to excite mirth' (in Rowell, *Dramatic Criticism*, p. 104). Similarly Shaw, reacting to Benson's 1889 production, commented that 'the soul of that damsel was weak' (*Shaw on Shakespeare*, p. 133). Lachrymose and queru-lous Helenas remain a feature of most productions, including Reinhardt's film, but attitudes have slowly changed with those qualities becoming sources of comedy rather than of pathos. In 1921 the common view, albeit expressed extremely, was, it is 'a most thankless role. There is a jarring note of unwomanliness about the character that creates prejudice against her rather than pity' (Stratford *Herald*, 6 May 1921). However, in 1924 Marie Ney at the Old Vic ('almost a complete break with the stocky, half-hearted traditional way of playing

> Demetrius loves your fair: O happy fair!
> Your eyes are lodestars, and your tongue's sweet air
> More tuneable than lark to shepherd's ear
> When wheat is green, when hawthorn buds appear.   185
> Sickness is catching. O, were favour so,
> Yours would I catch, fair Hermia, ere I go;
> My ear should catch your voice, my eye your eye,
> My tongue should catch your tongue's sweet melody.
> Were the world mine, Demetrius being bated,   190
> The rest I'd give to be to you translated.

the part', *Era*, 19 November) and Edith Evans at Drury Lane ('five-foot-ten, or thereabouts, of clucking, hen-witted gaby floundering for a shoulder upon which to lay her distracted head' (Agate, *Chronicles*, p. 42)) changed the traditional readings of the role, playing for comedy with an increased vigour which rapidly replaced the old approach, even if critics remained sceptical and apparently unprepared for such readings into the fifties. Although the *Birmingham News* thought that Dorothy Black (clownish in a white and grey dress, red wig, and rosy face) was 'a graceless hussy' (9 June 1934), the Stratford *Herald* noted 'Never before have I been made to realise how irritating a person was Helena, and never before have I so appreciated the inherent comedy of the character' (8 June). Reactions to Joyce Bland in 1937 were similar: she attempted 'to clown the part of Helena. If this reading could be made consistent, one would not grumble, but Helena in her love sickness is a serious woman, albeit a tiresome one' (*Yorkshire Post*, 30 March). According to the *Evening Standard* (27 January 1945), Marian Spencer played Helena for Coghill 'as if the whole thing was a Lonsdale comedy', which was not meant as praise, while Barbara Jefford's 1954 ' dizzy blonde'(*Daily Mail*, 24 March) still seemed like a 'new reading of a Helena not so much lachrymose as wittily petulant' (*South Wales Argus*, 24 March).

Although Coral Browne, in Benthall's 1957 version, was 'philosophic ... not merely sad-dened at her own unloved condition, but ... curious to know the mysterious secrets of attraction' (*Sunday Times*, 29 December), Hall set a trend for ever more athletic readings of the lovers (Vanessa Redgrave was 'admirably lachrymose and flouncing' in 1959, *Leamington Courier*, 5 June), which continues to be reflected in approaches to Helena: Marilyn Galsworthy (for Barton) was 'an apparently helpless ingenue later disclosed as an infinitely resourceful mantrap' (*Times*, 9 May 1977); Alexander's Helena, Joely Richardson, angry and lachrymose from the beginning, mixed anger with sentiment in her initial exchanges with Hermia before disintegrating 'from a courtly lady to a mud-spattered woman wrestling with all comers' (*Sunday Today*, 13 July 1986). Caird indicated Helena's disenchantment with the courtly world by dressing her in Doc Martens; his Hermia picked up the scattered gauds during this speeech. Noble's Helena, Hayden Gwynne, was 'a knight's faithful moll' (*Today*, 4 August 1994).

182–91   Kean cut all these lines from Helena's speech, Benson began his cuts at 183, Vestris and

O, teach me how you look, and with what art
You sway the motion of Demetrius' heart.
HERMIA I frown upon him; yet he loves me still.
HELENA O that your frowns would teach my smiles such skill!   195
HERMIA I give him curses; yet he gives me love.
HELENA O that my prayers could such affection move!
HERMIA The more I hate, the more he follows me.
HELENA The more I love, the more he hateth me.
HERMIA His folly, Helena, is no fault of mine.   200
HELENA None but your beauty; would that fault were mine!
HERMIA Take comfort: he no more shall see my face;
  Lysander and myself will fly this place.
  Before the time I did Lysander see,
  Seemed Athens as a paradise to me.   205
  O then, what graces in my love do dwell,
  That he hath turned a heaven unto a hell?
LYSANDER Helen, to you our minds we will unfold:
  Tomorrow night, when Phoebe doth behold
  Her silver visage in the watery glass,   210
  Decking with liquid pearl the bladed grass
  (A time that lovers' flights doth still conceal),
  Through Athens' gates have we devised to steal.
HERMIA And in the wood, where often you and I
  Upon faint primrose beds were wont to lie,   215
  Emptying our bosoms of their counsel sweet,
  There my Lysander and myself shall meet,
  And thence from Athens turn away our eyes

Saker at 186, Tree at 190, but all cut to 191. Daly, whose star Ada Rehan played Helena, kept all the speech, except for 190–1, which he rendered as 'were the world mine, it would I give / To be to you transformed', which removes a rhyme, deals with the obscurity of 'bated' and omits a reference to translation which is, therefore, reserved for Bottom's experience and not allowed to relate verbally to the lovers' experiences of transmutation.

196–7 This stichomythia did not find favour with Bowdler, who was followed by Kean, Saker, Benson and Tree.

200–1 A cut by Kean, Saker and Tree which seems arbitrary.

204–7 Cut by Bowdler, presumably on religious grounds, followed by nineteenth-century directors, and by Atkins, Hall, Langham.

214–23 Kean's Hermia placed her right arm round Helena's neck and took her left hand with her own left hand at the beginning of the speech, went to Lysander at 217 and embraced both Helena and Lysander (promptbook).

To seek new friends and stranger companies.
Farewell, sweet playfellow; pray thou for us,   220
And good luck grant thee thy Demetrius.
Keep word, Lysander; we must starve our sight
From lovers' food till morrow deep midnight.
LYSANDER I will, my Hermia.

                                                        Exit Hermia
                        Helena, adieu!
As you on him, Demetrius dote on you.   *Exit Lysander*   225
HELENA How happy some o'er other some can be!
Through Athens I am thought as fair as she.
But what of that? Demetrius thinks not so;
He will not know what all but he do know.
And as he errs, doting on Hermia's eyes,   230
So I, admiring of his qualities.
Things base and vile, holding no quantity,
Love can transpose to form and dignity.
Love looks not with the eyes, but with the mind,
And therefore is winged Cupid painted blind.   235
Nor hath love's mind of any judgement taste;
Wings, and no eyes, figure unheedy haste;
And therefore is love said to be a child
Because in choice he is so oft beguiled.
As waggish boys in game themselves forswear,   240
So the boy Love is perjured everywhere;
For, ere Demetrius looked on Hermia's eyne,
He hailed down oaths that he was only mine,
And when this hail some heat from Hermia felt,
So he dissolved, and showers of oaths did melt.   245
I will go tell him of fair Hermia's flight:
Then to the wood will he, tomorrow night,
Pursue her; and for this intelligence,
If I have thanks it is a dear expense;
But herein mean I to enrich my pain,   250
To have his sight thither, and back again.   *Exit*

219   Egeus and Demetrius returned in Langham's staging, giving Hermia a rather redundant
      motive for her exit (promptbook).
220   Alexander's Hermia embraced Helena at 'playfellow' (promptbook).
221–2 Hermia stopped Lysander's attempted kiss here in Alexander's staging (promptbook).
224   Tree cut 'I will, my Hermia.'
226–51 Helena's concluding speech has often been shortened: Vestris followed Bowdler in cutting

244–5, Phelps cut 240–5; Kean 232–3, Saker 230–3 and 235–45, Benson 236–41 and 244–5, Tree 236–9 and 244–5. Atkins lost 230–9, Devine 244–5, Hall 236–9, Langham 232–9. Saker ended with a 'Dance of Youths and Maidens' (playbill). Daly ended his act here, giving the curtain speech to his star Ada Rehan who was leaning on a tripod, although he still cut 230–3 and 240–1 (promptbook). Dean 'arouses our expectations by presenting her alone, in front of a curtain, to speak the long "How happy some o'er other some can be" soliloquy and then, while she speaks it, he sets his stage hands behind the curtain diabolically bump-bumping scenery about' (Farjeon, *Scene*, p. 41).

242–3   Although the old plural 'eyne' is obsolete, and the rhyme potentially obscure, no-one has changed these lines, and they are too important to the plot to be omitted.

A MIDSUMMER NIGHT'S DREAM

ACT I, SCENE 2

This scene has never been heavily cut, an accurate indication of the relative importance of the Mechanicals in nineteenth-century stagings. Played against the same architectural setting as 1.1. in the Renaissance theatre, the actors' clothing and dialogue would have set the scene. In proscenium arch stagings which use realistic Athenian and wood sets, this scene is usually placed far downstage so that complicated scene changes can be conducted behind the set. The Hatton Garden preparation copy suggested 'the baudy house' as a location for this scene. Vestris had 'A room in Quince's Cottage'. Phelps had a workshop 'divided by a pier and heavy beam; through the opening in the left hand compartment a glimpse was caught of the open sky and the trees of a suburban garden' (Moyr Smith, *Dream*, p. xiii); Kean's furniture and tools were supposedly 'Copied from Discoveries at Herculaneum' (playbill), although his stage manager's workbook reveals that many of the props had already been used in *Winter's Tale* (Tree cannibalised his *Dream* mise-en-scène for his *Winter's Tale*, a clear indication of the intellectual space the two plays occupied in the theatre). Ryder, Kean's Theseus, also had a Herculanean Quince's workshop at the Queen's in 1870 (playbill). Benson had 'a thatch-covered shed with a backing of Cyclopean work on the left-hand side; on the right we get a distant view of the palace of Theseus' (Moyr Smith, *Dream*, p. xv), an appropriate visual confirmation of the textual interrelationship of artisans and court. Barker used salmon-pink curtains with steel-blue masses to represent the roofs of the city here. Fagan had 'a quaintly rough shanty of three sloping walls of a biscuit-coloured wash with a few crude capering figures drawn upon them' (*Era*, 8 December 1920).

In 1954 Devine, who used a permanent wood setting, had Quince entering 'with house flat which he opens, opens bench, takes bell off wall & hits it', summoning the other Mechanicals (promptbook). This interesting metatheatrical moment attracted no comment. Hall placed Quince's shop in an inner area formed by the junction of the two staircases of his permanent set. There were only five chairs in Alexander's rehearsal-room set so Starveling missed out. In Lepage's staging the ubiquitous bed 'becomes their tiny shelter. They sit huddled round a brazier, a delightful mongrel in tow' (*Daily Telegraph*, 13 July 1992). Noble's modern dress Mechanicals entered in torrential rain.

Well into this century, in Athenian and Renaissance productions alike, the Mechanicals generally were all-purpose 'English yokels' (Williams, *Four Years*, p. 52), wearing rustic tunics with belts, tights and sandals which, as in Bridges Adams's 1934 staging, 'proclaim their roughness in clothes of natural colours' (*Leamington Courier*, 8 June). In Brook's production 'the artisans meet in string vests and braces, workers planning a play in their lunch-break' (*Daily Telegraph*, 14 September 1970). Victorian and contemporary stagings have generally dressed them in appropriate versions of respectable working-men's clothing: for Daniels, 'Bottom and his colleagues are not rude mechanicals, but bowler-hatted trades-men' (*Sunday Times*, 19 July 1981), Alexander's were 'an earnest suburban bunch in tweeds and pullovers' (*Jewish Chronicle*, 25 July 1986). Branagh differentiated between 'the grease-stained and tattooed roughness of Gerard Horan's beer-bellied bellows-mender' and Edward Jewesbury's 'dapper tailor' (*Financial Times*, 11 August 1990).

ACT I, SCENE 2

Enter QUINCE the Carpenter, and SNUG the Joiner, and BOTTOM the
Weaver, and FLUTE the Bellows-mender, and SNOUT the Tinker and
STARVELING the Tailor

QUINCE Is all our company here?

0 SD Tree and Bridges Adams had Quince appropriately discovered sawing wood. Tree's scene
      began with an elaborate entrance for Bottom in which all the others, except Snout, shook
      hands with him, establishing an animosity which was played up throughout the Mechanicals
      scenes as a general lack of trust between the actors (promptbooks). The key to Alexander's
      Stratford staging lay in an unscripted encounter between Hippolyta, discovered sitting in the
      half-light in the rehearsal-room set, and Bottom entering for his rehearsal. Their silent
      exchange of appraising glances was the motor for the subsequent action.

1   Quince, often old and often wearing spectacles (Sprague and Trewin, *Shakespeare's Plays*,
      p. 86), is usually anxious, fussy, harassed, timid, melancholy, keen not to offend Bottom, but
      quietly persistent, an interpretation that has remained remarkably consistent from Tree's
      production, when Quince was 'terribly anxious, and much harassed by the difficulties of his
      position' (*Era*, 13 January 1900) to Caird's, whose Quince was 'neurotic, sensitive' (*Daily
      Telegraph*, 13 April 1989), and Philip Voss's 'benign, bespectacled schoolmaster' in Noble's
      (Carole Woddis, *What's On*, 10 August 1994). In Dunlop's modern dress version,Bernard
      Bresslaw was 'a first World War vintage carpenter, with a slipping set of teeth, a secreted
      whisky bottle and a touching solemnity' (*Daily Mail*, 27 September 1967). Brook doubled
      Quince and Egeus (see discussion at 1.1.20); his Quince, Philip Locke, was an 'aficionado of
      amateur theatricals whose passion overcomes his natural diffidence' (*Leamington Courier*,
      4 September 1970). The role has sometimes been used to parody specific directors: Alan
      Badel in Guthrie's 1951 production had an Irish accent and was 'charmingly anxious and pre-
      occupied' causing the *Sketch* to ask 'Can this be Tyrone Guthrie's idea of a producer?' (16
      January 1952): David Haig in 1986 resembled John Dexter. In a similar vein, Kenneth
      Branagh played Quince in his own production as 'an officious dramatic society bore with
      ridiculously grandiose ambitions', initially clad in 'a nerd's uniform of double-breasted
      blazer and cravat' (*Independent*, 15 August 1990), but failed to impress those critics who dis-
      liked his overall efforts as a director. The Comedy Theatre of Bucharest's Romanian lan-
      guage version, seen in London in 1991, was notable for trebling Oberon, Theseus and Quince
      in an exploration of Romanian tyranny (see *LTR* and Peter Holland's account in *SS* 45).

BOTTOM You were best to call them generally, man by man, according
     to the scrip.
QUINCE Here is the scroll of every man's name which is thought fit
     through all Athens to play in our interlude before the Duke and   5
     the Duchess on his wedding day at night.
BOTTOM First, good Peter Quince, say what the play treats on; then
     read the names of the actors; and so grow to a point.

2   Bottom has been regarded as the nearest *A Midsummer Night's Dream* offers to a star role
     and the opportunities it gave to Samuel Phelps in the nineteenth century and Ralph
     Richardson in the twentieth century are discussed in the introduction. As the *Evening
     Standard* once noted, 'there is a powerful tradition that Bottom should be a fat man – huge,
     resplendent, overbearing, a colossal bladder of a man floating on the wind of his own self-
     importance' (22 July 1936). Most Bottoms have answered this physical description from
     Liston in 1816 to Desmond Barrit in 1994, via Stratford's Roy Byford in the 1920s and 1930s,
     who was noted for playing Falstaff without need of padding. Many have had the postulated
     mental characteristics: Frank Matthews was full of 'pompous conceit and profound stolidity'
     for Kean (*Times*, 12 February 1859); Beerbohm Tree had his 'masterful conceit, his invincible
     stupidity, and his irrepressible energy' (*Era*, 13 January 1900); Wolfit's was 'a jolly, cheerful
     conceit perhaps not quite stolid enough' (Crosse, *Diary* XVII, p. 145); Charles Laughton was
     'so conceited, so common, so illiterate, and yet so self-assured that he holds his own with
     fairies, dukes and workmates' (Stratford *Herald*, 5 June 1959). Benson usually had Bottoms
     who were 'robust, genial, and cheery' in the mode of George Weir (Stratford *Herald*, 1 May
     1903), but in 1915, A. E. George 'played it as an attractive boy, which detracted from the
     rough comedy of the scenes, and was out of harmony with the other clowns' (Constance
     Benson, *Mainly Players*, p. 283). Henry Baynton, who played Bottom in his own touring pro-
     ductions, tried something similar, writing to Clarkson the wig-maker that he was going to
     play Bottom 'on new lines ... as a youth' (Baynton letter, 4 January 1925). Even lean Bottoms,
     such as Baliol Holloway's much repeated characterisation, reflected 'that worthy's overrid-
     ing egotism and serious self-conceit' (Stratford *Herald*, 6 May 1921) and his 'narrowness of
     vision, an envy of those in higher places, and a haunting and perpetual suspicion that all
     other weavers in Athens are jealous of his skill and out to "do him down"' (*Evening
     Standard*, 22 July 1936). Exponents of Bottom have also been castigated, like Daly's James
     Lewis, for missing 'the stolid, obstinate, self-sufficient temperament of Bottom altogether'
     (Shaw, *Nineties*, I, p. 181), or, like Paul Rogers for Guthrie in 1951, his 'expansive nature and
     the bumptiousness' (*Guardian*, 28 December).
        Oscar Asche's conception of the part as 'a big chubby boy, good-natured and simple-
     minded, quite unlike Mr Tree's somewhat dry, domineering concept of the part, or Mr G. R.
     Weir's curious abstracted treatment' (*Westminster Gazette*, 27 November 1905), was

recognised as innovatory. He was praised for 'a degree of naturalness and restraint not often observed in exponents of the part. He aims at no abnormal appearance in the country clown, at no grotesque ugliness of visage or body... Mr Asche gets his fun less out of any personal peculiarities or comic qualities of his weaver than from the farcical situation of the rustic wight turned actor' (HTC cutting, 30 November 1905). Unsurprisingly, Nigel Playfair, in Barker's production, did not compete with readings like Arthur Bourchier's 'village autocrat, huge of size, almost beyond measure noisy' (HTC cutting) in Tree's 1911 revival, offering instead 'a rather mild spoken but extremely genial Bottom' (*ILN*, 14 February 1914).

Since the Second World War, interpretations of Bottom have varied much more from production to production as his mental, if not usually his physical, constitution, has been reassessed: in Benthall's 1949 staging, John Slater was 'a respectable working man with a very big voice but too small an opinion of himself' (*Birmingham Post*, 25 April); Anthony Quayle was nervous in 1954 – his 'sudden bursts of self-assertion spring from a rich agony of apprehension' (*Observer*, 28 March); Douglas Campbell was 'innocent, ingenuous' for Langham (*Financial Times*, 21 December 1960). Paul Hardwick, who took over from Laughton in Hall's 1962 revival, was 'a Bottom whose pomposity is always a step in the direction of wanting to do the best for everybody' (*Guardian*, 18 April); for Daniels, Geoffrey Hutchings was a 'splendid aldermanic Bottom, an innocent well-meaning worthy, with an endearingly misplaced self-confidence' (*Daily Mail* in *LTR* 1982); and Alexander's Pete Postlethwaite was 'the amateur dramatic society bore' (*Jewish Chronicle*, 25 July 1986). Even more comically appalling was Caird's David Troughton, 'a red-cheeked high-energy Bottom' (*Listener*, 27 April 1989) who had 'studied every professional trick down to wall-pressing Marcel Marceau mime' (*Guardian*, 5 December 1989). Richard Briers, in a generally low-key performance for Branagh, had 'the shuffling, shoulder-shrugging mannerisms of a small time conman' (*Evening Standard*, 22 August 1990) and Timothy Spall's 'Brando-smitten narcissist' for Lepage was also 'your seventies macho man with medallion, platform shoes and naff American drawl' (*Independent on Sunday*, 12 July 1992; *Tribune*, 17 July)).

Professional comedians such as the music-hall artist Jay Laurier at Stratford in 1938 and 1942, Stanley Holloway in 1954, Frankie Howerd in 1957, and Roy Hudd (at Regent's Park in 1991) have also played the part with some success: Howerd gave 'a glorious representation of that universal type, the over-confident amateur whom friends and relations have encouraged to believe himself a Roscius' (*Daily Telegraph*, 27 January 1958), 'a weaver who will go on being a weaver when the interlude is forgotten, and yet who will go on dreaming of that interlude, and perhaps too, of those mysterious intimations of an inspired asininity in the wood by moonshine' (*Times*, 27 December 1957).

Phelps's Bottom compulsively shuttled an imaginary bobbin from hand to hand. Jim Dale, in Dunlop's modern dress production, had a 'crash helmet and badge-laden jerkin' and insisted that his name was 'Botóme' (*Daily Mail, Times*; both 27 September 1967).

5–6   Kean's Duke and Duchess became the Prince and his Bride.

7–8   Kean cut from 'then read'.

QUINCE Marry, our play is 'The most lamentable comedy and most
  cruel death of Pyramus and Thisbe'.   10
BOTTOM A very good piece of work, I assure you, and a merry. Now,
  good Peter Quince, call forth your actors by the scroll. Masters,
  spread yourselves.
QUINCE Answer as I call you. Nick Bottom, the weaver?
BOTTOM Ready. Name what part I am for, and proceed.   15
QUINCE You, Nick Bottom, are set down for Pyramus.
BOTTOM What is Pyramus? A lover or a tyrant?
QUINCE A lover that kills himself, most gallant, for love.
BOTTOM That will ask some tears in the true performing of it. If I do
  it, let the audience look to their eyes: I will move storms, I will   20
  condole, in some measure. To the rest – yet my chief humour is
  for a tyrant. I could play Ercles rarely, or a part to tear a cat in,
  to make all split:
                  The raging rocks
                  And shivering shocks   25
                  Shall break the locks
                    Of prison gates,
                  And Phibbus' car
                  Shall shine from far,
                  And make and mar   30
                    The foolish Fates.
  This was lofty. Now name the rest of the players. – This is Ercles'
  vein, a tyrant's vein; a lover is more condoling.
QUINCE Francis Flute, the bellows-mender?
FLUTE Here, Peter Quince.   35

---

11   Brook's Bottom turned to the audience to make his comment on the quality of the play
      (promptbook).
12–13 Langham (who freely redistributed lines in the Mechanicals scenes) stopped Bottom usurp-
      ing Quince's directorial prerogatives too early by giving Bottom's last sentence to Quince.
16   Caird's Bottom jumped in joy at being given Pyramus, then had to ask who he was.
20–1 Kean, and Saker, cut 'I will ... rest'; Daly cut 'To the rest'.
24ff. Kean's Mechanicals applauded Bottom's speech.
32–3 Kean cut Bottom's speech from 'This is Ercles' vein' to the end.
35   Flute generally attracts little critical attention, although the contrast between the actor's
      physique and the part of Thisbe is usually played up: wavering falsettos and recalcitrant
      false bosoms in the pantomime dame tradition are a twentieth-century commonplace. One
      of the fullest accounts of the character is in the *Times* review of Vestris's staging: 'He had a
      lackadaisical look of innocent stupidity, objected to the part of Thisbe with a slight fret-
      fulness that at once subsided into a meek tolerance, and, utterly unable to originate a

QUINCE Flute, you must take Thisbe on you.

FLUTE What is Thisbe? A wandering knight?

QUINCE It is the lady that Pyramus must love.

FLUTE Nay, faith, let not me play a woman: I have a beard coming.

QUINCE That's all one: you shall play it in a mask, and you may speak   40
as small as you will.

BOTTOM And I may hide my face, let me play Thisbe too. I'll speak
in a monstrous little voice: 'Thisne, Thisne!' – 'Ah, Pyramus, my
lover dear; thy Thisbe dear, and lady dear.'

QUINCE No, no; you must play Pyramus; and Flute, you Thisbe.   45

BOTTOM Well, proceed.

QUINCE Robin Starveling, the tailor?

STARVELING Here, Peter Quince.

QUINCE Robin Starveling, you must play Thisbe's mother. Tom Snout,
the tinker?   50

thought in his own brain, allowed his countenance to be lit up at hearing another's bright
idea. He shared in the general joy and sorrow like one whose obtuse intellect apprehended
it the last, but whose good natured heart felt it the most' (*Times*, 17 November). Daniels's
production had 'a sharp perception of Flute's adolescent smuttiness' (*TLS*, 31 July 1981).

37   Alexander's Method disciple Flute put the stress on 'is'.

40   Kean left only 'That's all one.'

42–3   Kean omitted 'And I may hide my face.' Daly's Bottom trod on Flute's foot at 'let me play
Thisbe' and embraced him at 'Ah Pyramus' at which he proved to be 'very ticklish' (promptbook). Caird's Bottom put up his hand and came forward to offer to play Thisbe.

47   The name Starveling reflects the proverbial association of tailors with thinness and weakness
and would be suitable for a part played by John Sincklo, who played thin men in
Shakespeare's company (see Foakes's note to 0 SD). This ties in neatly with the tradition,
derived from Benson, that he is 'a very old man – who is also very deaf, and has considerable
difficulty in memorising his part' (Browne, *Dream*, p. 155). Bridges Adams had a nice gloss on
this reading in 1923, with a 'hopeless case who has to be tolerated because he makes the costumes cheaply' (*Stage*, 3 May). Starveling's deafness provided an opportunity for much comic
byplay but was never entirely accepted by critics and appeared less often after the Second
World War. O. B. Clarence began the practice of embroidering his name on a garment when
he was playing the part in Benson's company, H. O. Nicholson (who went on to play the part
for Barker and Fagan) continued the practice and Kay Souper was still using the same garment, now covered with the signatures of successive Starvelings at Stratford in 1937 (*Amateur
Theatre and Playwright's Journal*, June 1937). Bridges Adams had his Mechanicals all repeat
Starveling's name, presumably to indicate his deafness (promptbook).

49   Tree's deaf Starveling was disgusted at being allocated Thisbe's mother; Brook's was
delighted with his part (promptbooks). In Daniels's staging, Starveling crumbled and the
others sniggered when he was allocated Thisbe's mother.

SNOUT Here, Peter Quince.

QUINCE You, Pyramus' father; myself, Thisbe's father; Snug, the joiner, you the lion's part; and I hope here is a play fitted.

SNUG Have you the lion's part written? Pray you, if it be, give it me; for I am slow of study. 55

QUINCE You may do it extempore; for it is nothing but roaring.

BOTTOM Let me play the lion too. I will roar that I will do any man's heart good to hear me. I will roar that I will make the Duke say 'Let him roar again, let him roar again!'

QUINCE And you should do it too terribly, you would fright the 60 Duchess and the ladies that they would shriek; and that were enough to hang us all.

ALL That would hang us, every mother's son.

BOTTOM I grant you, friends, if you should fright the ladies out of their wits they would have no more discretion but to hang us; but I will 65 aggravate my voice so that I will roar you as gently as any sucking dove. I will roar you and 'twere any nightingale.

QUINCE You can play no part but Pyramus; for Pyramus is a sweet-faced man, a proper man as one shall see in a summer's day, a most lovely, gentlemanlike man: therefore you must needs play Pyramus. 70

BOTTOM Well, I will undertake it. What beard were I best to play it in?

QUINCE Why, what you will.

BOTTOM I will discharge it in either your straw-colour beard, your orange-tawny beard, your purple-in-grain beard, or your French- 75 crown-colour beard, your perfect yellow.

QUINCE Some of your French crowns have no hair at all, and then you will play bare-faced. But, masters, here are your parts, and I am to entreat you, request you, and desire you to con them by tomorrow night, and meet me in the palace wood, a mile without 80 the town, by moonlight; there will we rehearse, for if we meet in the city we shall be dogged with company, and our devices known. In the meantime I will draw a bill of properties, such as our play wants. I pray you, fail me not.

---

51 Snout also attracts little individual attention but he was 'the essence of grinning imbecility' in Asche's staging (*Era*, 2 December 1905). Crosse welcomed the 'stolid working-man trying to act, not a buffoon trying to be funny' in Tree's 1911 production (*Diary* V, p. 59). Dean made him 'keen as mustard, stuffed with amusement at the idea of playing in a play, and on the verge of laughter listening to Pyramus and Thisbe' (Farjeon, *Scene*, p. 44) and Guthrie made him a victim of a chronic stage fright in 1937. Bill Travers for Hall 'looked like a piece of Warwickshire cheese cake and sounds like a hesitant Labrador' (*Guardian*, 18 April 1962).

Daniels had 'a lugubrious Snout from Peter Ellis who might have stepped straight out of the Ragged Trousered Philanthropists' (*Guardian* 16 July 1981).

52 Reynolds's and Saker's Quinces also gave themselves the Prologue here. For Daniels, Snug's cough reminded Quince that he had forgotten about him.

54 Like Snout, most Snugs have made little individual impact. Asche's 'surly sulky Snug, who was represented as jealous of Bottom' in Benson's production (Crosse, *Diary* II, p. 110) became the accepted way of playing the part into the 1930s. Guthrie's 1937 staging had a Snug full of 'never-ending delight in being asked to play in a play at all' (*News Chronicle*, 27 December 1938).

59 Roaring contests between Snug and Bottom are common here: Snug 'gets on all fours' in Daly's production, presumably to contest Bottom's claim to be Lion (promptbook); Harry Caine, for Benson in 1911, showed Bottom's 'bombastic conceit... and his bullying tendency' in teaching the Lion how to roar and in 'pushing his comrades off the bench in Quince's workshop' (Stratford *Herald*, 28 July). For Bridges Adams the roaring contest ended when Snug choked (promptbook). Brook's Quince and Bottom roared 'in competition with Barry Stanton's huge and simple-minded Lion' (*Punch*, 15 September 1970). Caird's Bottom roared, but his Snug did not.

63 Daly cut 'That would hang us.' Benson gave the line, preceded by 'Aye', to Flute.

68 Bottom usually threatens to walk out here: Tree's Bottom attempted to leave when told he could only play Pyramus but was physically restrained by Flute and Quince; Barker's Quince turned away to Snug, but, on looking at Snug's face, which presumably indicated that Bottom was about to go, he turned back to Bottom and continued with his lines persuading him to stay; Bridges Adams had Bottom throwing down his part and being persuaded not to walk out; similarly, in Brook's production, Bottom walked out, and had to be wooed back by Quince's speech. In Daniels's production Quince took Bottom downstage with an arm round his shoulder to persuade him to stick with Pyramus (promptbooks).

71–8 Kean, Daly and Tree cut to 'But'; Benson cut from 77. Other directors, including Vestris, Atkins, Bridges Adams and Devine, have dealt with the theatrically obscure 'French crown' references by cutting Quince's response but leaving Bottom's as part of his list of beard colours. Bowdler, who presumably understood the reference to syphilis, cut both as did Phelps. Reynolds's Quince indicated that Bottom's own beard colour was red. Bottom had brought his false beards with him in Caird's production.

78 Quince misdistributed the parts in Tree's version and they were elaborately redistributed. Barker's similar version went thus: 'Quince gives parts to Flute Starv & Bottom. Flute hands one to Snout. Flute then finds he has got Starv's part & vice versa. They exchange. Starv's part being much smaller' (promptbook). Similarly, Barton's Quince 'absently hands him [Snug] the massive script intended for Pyramus'(*Observer*, 15 May 1977). Daniels had a small part for Snug, Caird had none.

80 In Daniels's staging, there was 'a nice moment of sheer consternation at the suggestion that they should learn their parts "by tomorrow night"' (Warren, 'Interpretations', p. 147).

BOTTOM We will meet, and there we may rehearse most obscenely and   85
     courageously. Take pains, be perfect: adieu!
QUINCE At the Duke's oak we meet.
BOTTOM Enough; hold, or cut bowstrings.

Exeunt

81 Caird's Bottom made an owl noise at 'moonlight'.
85 Even Bottom's malapropism does not survive Bowdler's attentions; Reynolds gave him part
    of Flute's sixpence a day speech from 4.2 and followed the speech with introductory dia-
    logue for an epilogue song derived from Colman's version. The general tenor of Reynolds's
    alterations is to make the amateur actors a group of blustering charlatans, well aware of
    their own inadequacies.
86 Saker gave 'Take pains ... ' to Quince; Tree gave Bottom 4.2.32–4 here.
88 Tree cut the final line and engineered a tableau of Bottom outside the cottage shaking hands
    with Quince through the window to end the act (promptbook). Caird's Snug exited practising
    his roar.

A MIDSUMMER NIGHT'S DREAM

ACT 2, SCENE I

Nineteenth-century productions vied with one another to produce ever more picturesquely realistic woodland scenes, illuminated by increasingly sophisticated recreations of moonlight, which transformed into Titania's bower and other parts of the woods for subsequent scenes via dioramic effects. Vestris set the standard: 'a translucid lake hemmed around with trees, with here and there a break in the woody ring, thro' which you gaze on some grassy spot where tiny elves keep up their midnight gambols, or shelving banks velvetted over with nature's softest greens, ... while above the star spangled sky shoots out its myriad lights, and the pale moon pours down her silver flood in a glittering hail on the water' (*Theatrical Journal*, 1 May 1841). Phelps filled the proscenium opening with a huge piece of gauze which remained in place until the exit of Oberon and Titania in 4.1, creating 'a misty transparency about the figures that gives them the appearance of flitting shadows' (Douglas Jerrold, in May Phelps, *Life*, p. 132); Phelps also had the moon physically pervade the play, using a diorama so that 'the moon was seen to rise, to shine between the boles of the trees, to be partially obscured by passing clouds, and then to swim, as it were, over and through the trees' (Moyr Smith, *Dream*, p. xiii). Even Benson's 1889 touring 'woodland glade by moonlight' had a 'particularly tender ... hazy copse in the background' with 'over-branching trees and foliage' (*Era* cutting) and a water-fall surrounded by water-lilies (Moyr Smith, *Dream*, p. xv). Tree's revivals represented the apogee of this tradition: Hawes Craven 'gives us a plantation on the slope of a hill, with a streamlet in the centre. Between the trunks of the trees, the sky is seen in glimpses; glow-worms sparkle in the bushes and the place is altogether moonshiny and mysterious', a rendition of 'typically English woodland scenery. Silver birches lift their slender stems to the skies, clouds of bluebells spread a mist of colour across the turf, while in the background a brook trickles down a mossy bank' (HTC cuttings, 1911).

Barker reacted against this by setting the wood scenes in green silk curtains, which made no attempt to recreate a real forest, although the overhanging 'giant wreath of flowers from which depends a light gauze canopy in which fire-flies and glow-worms flicker' (*Evening News*, quoted in Byrne, 'Fifty Years', p. 8) is not unfamiliar. While many post-war productions continued to use woodland scenes derived from the realistic tradition, Expressionistic influence as well as increased labour costs led to an increased reliance on lighting effects to create the wood, and to a stripping down of the actual wood presented. For example,

Thorndike and Warburton at the Old Vic had a wood of 'tall, spider-web trees, illumined with changing lights of varying colours' (VW cutting) and Fagan had 'a Wood near Athens, composed of four huge gnarled oaks, tremendous trunks and strange impressionist leaves' (*Era*, 8 December 1920); Atkins had something similar at Stratford in 1944, 'a delicate tracery of trees in silhouette against a pale sky' (*Birmingham Post*, 11 May). Calthrop relied heavily on lighting to establish the contrast between the wood and the court: 'The fairy scenes ... were given in an atmosphere of quiet duskiness, all very subdued. They depended very much on effects of lighting which were very well managed – quite unnatural but considering we had to do with fairies none the worse for that. When the fairies alone were on, the stage was shrouded in a dim blue light; as soon as any mortals came on the scene became lighter but not fully light except in the first and last acts, & in the hunting scene – to express broad daylight' (Crosse, *Diary* VIII, p. 97); Dean's 1924 Drury Lane Christmas attraction had a 'heavy, many-planed, elaborately built-up forest ... designed for the accommodation of masses of fairies' (Farjeon, *Scene*, p.42). Guthrie's 1937 pastiche Victorian production made an attempt to tackle the question of relative size with 'a transparent drop curtain on which painted flowers the height of the stage ... emphasise the minuteness of the fairy folk' (*Glasgow Herald*, 28 December), an attractive idea that did not come off well in practice because of the discrepancy between the supposed heights of mortals and fairies in the same scene.

At Stratford, Bridges Adams remained faithful to the realistic tradition in 1926 with 'a beautiful cool glade amid tall, nobly proportioned trees' (*Yorkshire Post*, 15 April) and 'an atmosphere of grotesque gloom' and 'a suggestion of things eerie, and even sinister' in 1928 (BSL cutting); when he moved to an 'Elizabethan' staging in 1932, in the new theatre, he still had a realistic wood with a cloven Duke's Oak and the rolling stage allowed the scene to move to another part of the forest without the usual lengthy waits.

For his Elizabethan staging, Gordon Craig gave Harcourt Williams 'a sketch of a horseshoe-shaped rostrum which he had seen in a production in Holland. Puck always rushed along this, creating the illusion that this was his dimension in space', while behind it 'we had a mountain of steps with great, heavy, bunched curtains which gave the effect of tree trunks, and for a background Paul [Smyth] painted an attractive wood-cloth with a silver sky' (*Four Years*, p. 53).

After the Second World War, more or less minimalist versions of realism prevailed: Benthall had a 'trunk-tortured' forest, lit by 'spangled starlight' in 1949 (*Birmingham Post*, 25 April); in 1951 Guthrie's set was just suggestive enough of 'a silvered thicket, moonlight in flood' (BSL cutting), although Ivor Brown thought a backcloth representing a Greek mountain resembled 'the Pennines under cloud' (*Observer*, 30 December); similarly, in Devine's 1954 staging, where the *Illustrated London News* saw 'tentative trees against the blue' (3 April)), the *Western Daily Express* thought that 'the Motley setting, permanent and flowerless, with its cold ornamental trees and shrubs and deep-blue sky, needed only a few fishes to suggest the sea bed. Here was an enchanted forest disenchanted' (25 March). Benthall's 1954 Old Vic export staging used 'a vast quantity of gauzy drops, woodland settings which seem to come straight from the old Alhambra, all drenched in aquamarine light' (*Financial Times*, 1 September), but he moved on in 1957 to 'the Greece of Claude with a generous daub of the chiaroscuro of Caravaggio for the night scenes' (*Plays and Players*, February 1958), although the *News Chronicle's* favoured painter was Fragonard (24 December 1957).

In Hall's Elizabethan staging 'the "solid" walls dissolved to reveal as deep and dark forest as the most dedicated romantic could wish' (*Glasgow Herald*, 3 June 1959), though the balcony formed by the junction of the staircases which remained 'as a rustic bridge in the enchanted wood' seemed to be so big that it 'somehow refuses to blend into the woodscape' (*Times*, 2 June 1959). Brook's permanent set changed only with the introduction of coiled wire trees flown in by fishing rods from the gallery and the use of trapezes for flying entrances. For Barton, John Napier had a 'petrifying forest where fire and smoke spout mysteriously from the ground' (*Guardian*, 9 May 1977), with 'trees springing up as if under an enchantment, a little mist and a leafy mould blanketing the ground, into which the spirits can sink, camouflaged by their colours' (*Listener*, 19 May 1977). In Daniels's staging, 'the lovers do not escape to a forest but a backstage Victorian world full of skips, spiral staircases, ladders, chairs, cut out clouds and reverse flats saying Act One Scene Three' (*Guardian*, 16 July 1981). Bill Dudley's sets for Alexander in 1986 evoked a childhood world of Arthur Rackham and Kate Greenaway. Sue Blane designed a kind of junkyard of the imagination for Caird: 'the spiral-staircase tree trunks wind up to branches cluttered with a kleptomaniac's fantasia of superannuated violins, chamber-pots, bed springs and even a crippled grand piano' (*Independent*, 13 April 1989). Lepage's mud-encircled pool of water also remained as a permanent fixture, coming into its own as both a muddied Nine Men's Morris and a reflection of the world of the unconscious. In Noble's forest scenes 'pulsing halogen bulbs and outsize umbrellas also form the forest on Antony Ward's stage, but its basic elements are four up-stage doors which convert neutral space into an area of enchantment and surprise' (Irving Wardle, *Independent on Sunday*, 7 August 1994). Other doors appeared apparently at random for lovers to chase round and through and for Oberon and Puck to perch on.

ACT 2, SCENE I

Enter a FAIRY at one door, and PUCK, or ROBIN GOODFELLOW
at another

0 SD   The original stage direction reflects Elizabethan staging practice, with the two characters
entering from doors in the tiring house façade. Benson's and Tree's versions of the opening
of this scene typify nineteenth-century approaches, which invariably involved balletic,
musical and spectacular effects. For Benson, 'the trees are fully made out, so that the fairies
may run behind and around them. As the curtain rises the stage is full of movement. All the
fairies are in motion, flitting about; they scatter as the singing fairy comes on' (Moyr Smith,
Dream, p. xv); Tree's 'Act Drop ascends in a "wood near the sea." In the distance, the waves
rise and fall under the rays of the moon. A summer storm is passing over – the thunder is
perhaps a little over loud – and the elves crouch and shelter in the shadows. But soon the
clouds pass away and the fairies emerge and dance in the moonlight. As they weave their
magic mazes flying fays [pass] across the sky in the distance' (*Era*, 22 April 1900). This may
have been intended as an enactment of the elemental consequences of Titania and
Oberon's quarrel or it may be an emblematic enactment of the mortals' troubles in the
wood but its impact is simply as a piece of irresistibly charming stagecraft, rather like the
much later 'streamer display' in Daniels's pastiche Victorian staging (*Financial Times*, 16 July
1981).

   The fairy who meets Puck here was often accurately described in nineteenth-century cast
lists as the First Singing Fairy, since she invariably sang her opening lines. Daly's First Fairy
disturbed Puck as she was picking flowers (promptbook). Tree began with an owl hooting
twice, followed by a Fairy Child entering and pulling the tail of one of the production's noto-
rious rabbits which it found by a tree. Asche's First Fairy in 1905 was too operatic: 'When …
the First Fairy is impersonated by a full-sized singer from Covent Garden who takes up her
position in the centre of the stage and executes shakes and trills while the action stands still,
all illusion is lost' (Dickins, *Forty Years*, p. 123). Barker's Peaseblossom danced on as First
Fairy and was surprised by Puck springing out; Bridges Adams had Puck catching the First
Fairy by her wings (promptbooks).

   By 1962, the balletic and spectacular had more than lost its charm, as reactions to Tony
Richardson's production demonstrate: 'Puck's first scene is almost a parody of bad directing.
The flying fairy effectively nullifies the first half and as soon as the little creature is safely
grounded he and Puck set about ruining the remaining speeches by tobogganing up and

down a hillock' (*Spectator*, 2 February 1962). So bad was the production that J. W. Lambert wondered if Richardson was 'paying a half-hearted tribute to the shade of Tree or Augustin Daly, as a single flying fairy was lowered uneasily from the flies, and swung unsteadily into the wings' (*Sunday Times*, 28 January).

Puck was a female part throughout the nineteenth century, often played by a child, such as the then eight-year-old Ellen Terry who played 'with restless elfish admiration, and an evident enjoyment of her own mischievous pranks' in Kean's production (Cole, *Kean*, p. 200). This emphasis on the character's impishness and mischievousness has been a recurrent feature of productions from Reynolds's adaptation, in which Miss Booth 'displayed the mischievous agility and good humour of Puck' (TM cutting), through 'the very incarnation of elfish mischief' in the form of Iris Hawkins for Fagan (*Referee*, 5 December 1920) to Barton's Leonard Preston, who was 'coarse, crude and impishly mischievous'(*Sunday Mercury*, 8 May 1977).

Puck's costume has often differentiated him from the other fairies. In 1855 Phelps's Puck wore an outsize head in the pantomime tradition: 'This grotesque touch, which reviewers said mingled well with the beauty of the setting, was undoubtedly added to underline the parallel between Puck and Bottom, drawing attention to the fact that Puck impinges upon the human world as Bottom enters the fairy world' (Allen, *Phelps*, p. 45). However, from the nineteenth century well into the twentieth, the dominant visual impression was of a some kind of earth spirit. Ellen Terry, Kean's Puck, wore 'a dark russet dress trimmed with blood red moss and lichen, with a garland made from the same material worn in her blonde, slightly tousled hair' (Fontane, *Aus England*, p. 49); Tree had his Puck 'clad in green, and barely distinguishable from the grass and bushes that surround him' (*Era*, 13 January 1900).

A change in interpretations of the character was visible in the contrast between Benson's and Tree's Pucks in 1900, when Kitty Loftus for Benson was 'an amusing sprite, mischievous and conscienceless, but without any touch of the devilish malice with which Miss Louie Freear invests him at Her Majesty's' (*Review of the Week*, 3 March). The trend towards using male Pucks after Granville Barker's production may have contributed to the tendency for twentieth-century Pucks to be more malicious than nineteenth-century ones. However, the part has remained one available to both genders, whether because of wartime manpower shortages or, more recently, the exigencies of touring (Branagh's 'Puck has had a sex change and speaks with a thick Ulster accent', *Independent*, 15 August 1990) or the availability of specialist skills (Lepage had an extraordinarily acrobatic androgynous Puck, Angela Laurier).

In 1914 Barker's male Puck, Donald Calthrop, had a red costume which differentiated him from the exotic 'ormolu' fairies, while Kirwan used Drayton's *Nimphidia* as the authority for Puck's 'rough coat of pearl grey and an equine-like headpiece' since he was 'likened to a mischievous little pony' in Elizabethan times (*Sunday Times*, 12 April 1914).

Arcane disputes about the correct earth colour could arise, as when Benson allowed Andrew Leigh to play Puck in 1920: 'I wanted to look ... all green from head to foot, green being the chosen colour of all the good people, and also one that would merge with the

PUCK How now, spirit; whither wander you?
FAIRY   Over hill, over dale,
                   Thorough bush, thorough briar,
              Over park, over pale,
                   Thorough flood, thorough fire;   5

forest background when Puck was at rest, and give the idea of invisibility. But Sir Frank
would have none of it. He had always had a brown Puck, and he spent a good half-hour one
morning lecturing me on folk-lore ... Green was sinister and Robin was a cheerful sprite'
('On Playing Puck', *The Old Vic Magazine*, February 1925). In 1924, however, Leigh was
'faun-like' (*Era*, 19 November) at the Old Vic, as was Hay Petrie at Drury Lane, with 'pointed
ears, goat beard, shaggy legs & so on: so his niggling little laugh was in keeping with this
appearance' (Crosse, *Diary* IX, p. 50). By 1937 at Stratford Leigh, following Barker, was 'no
familiar green imp, but a tousle-haired oaf in red jerkin'(*Star,* 30 March).

   Coghill's Puck was a 'a stray satyr who has got into Shakespeare's Athens while looking
for the real one' (*Daily Telegraph*, 26 January 1945). David O'Brien for Devine was 'a rough-
spoken bandy-legged creature of the woods, half-Panda, half-chameleon' (*Guardian*, 25
March 1954), with 'the barely concealed malevolences of a bow-legged subterranean
gnome' (*Leamington Courier*, 26 March); Ian Holm, for Hall, was 'an urchin, a ragamuffin,
with a street arab's pertness and pleasure in other people's disasters' (*Financial Times*, 3
June 1959). Tony Richardson's Puck was 'a shambling Cockney Caliban, who, wearing a
mud-coloured skin-suit covered in what appeared to be broad arrows, lumbered rheumati-
cally round at the furthest possible extreme from a "merry wanderer of the night"' (*Sunday
Times*, 28 January 1962); Jack Shepherd was 'a pleasantly sinister, long-legged Puck' for
Bryden (*Guardian*, in *LTR* 1982); Nicholas Woodeson's 'startling, grave mandarin-like Puck
has not a flicker of mischievous glee' (*Guardian*, 20 August 1987). For Caird in 1989 Richard
McCabe was a 'greedy, bug-eyed schoolboy Puck with cascading socks who flies around the
galaxy in a helicopter pilot's helmet with a rose clenched between his teeth' (*Daily Express*,
13 April). Wearing 'a white tutu as a belt around his blazer and baggy grey shorts' (*Financial
Times*, 13 April) in parodic tribute to older traditions, McCabe was a 'decadent lout of a Puck'
(*Listener*, 27 April) who related 'the sprite's vicious interventions to the liberty-taking public
school manners of alternative comedy' (*Financial Times*, 13 April).

1 Reynolds, typically, delayed Puck's entrance, giving the opening dialogue, with a Colman
   song, to two fairies. Vestris delayed Puck's entrance on a mushroom to 31, Kean's Puck first
   entered on a mushroom at 34, so Puck's first two speeches were given to a fairy; Benson cut 1.
     In Alexander's Stratford production, where the action in the wood was effectively Hippolyta's
   dream, fairies removed her outer clothing as a mark of her transformation into Titania.
   During these exchanges in Lepage's production 'a blue-faced fairy, streaked with muck,
   mimes sex with a Puck that... has evolved from crab to spider' (*Times*, 11 July 1992).

2 Brook divided the Fairy's lines among his four fairies. Daly cut 2–5.

I do wander everywhere
Swifter than the moon's sphere;
And I serve the Fairy Queen,
To dew her orbs upon the green.
The cowslips tall her pensioners be; 10
In their gold coats spots you see –
Those be rubies, fairy favours,
In those freckles live their savours.
   I must go seek some dewdrops here,
    And hang a pearl in every cowslip's ear. 15
Farewell, thou lob of spirits; I'll be gone.
Our Queen and all her elves come here anon.
PUCK The King doth keep his revels here tonight.
Take heed the Queen come not within his sight,
For Oberon is passing fell and wrath, 20
Because that she as her attendant hath
A lovely boy stol'n from an Indian king;
She never had so sweet a changeling,
And jealous Oberon would have the child
Knight of his train, to trace the forests wild. 25
But she perforce withholds the lovèd boy,
Crowns him with flowers, and makes him all her joy.
And now they never meet in grove or green,
By fountain clear or spangled starlight sheen,
But they do square, that all their elves for fear 30
Creep into acorn cups and hide them there.
FAIRY Either I mistake your shape and making quite,

10–15   Daly cut 10–13, Kean 12–15, Benson 12–13.

14–15   Zoe Caldwell's delivery of these lines for Hall excited much comment as an example of his methods: the *Birmingham Mail* commented on her 'expression of distaste as if it was a pretty corny mission' (3 June 1959), the Stratford *Herald* praised her 'delicious performance... as a worker fairy' bemoaning her lot (5 June), and the *Sunday Times* saw her 'weary complaint' as an example of the 'pretty wit' that occasionally figured in Hall's 'sending-up' of the play (7 June). In his 1962 revival, however, 'I missed the sardonic note' (*Birmingham Mail*, 18 April). Bryden's Edna Doré was 'a dewdrop-bearing drudge' (*Observer*, in *LTR* 1982).

16–17   Kean's delayed entrance for Puck meant changes here: 'lob of spirits' became 'dainty spirit' and 'her elves' became 'our elves'.

30   At 'their' in Caird's staging, Puck pointed to the Fairy who was standing behind him and 'she's amazed he knows where she is' (promptbook).

32–42   Directors sometimes take exception to the Fairy cataloguing Puck's attributes to Puck himself: one of Reynolds's fairies sees Puck offstage, thus enabling her to give some of the

Or else you are that shrewd and knavish sprite
Called Robin Goodfellow. Are not you he
That frights the maidens of the villagery, 35
Skim milk, and sometimes labour in the quern,
And bootless make the breathless housewife churn,
And sometime make the drink to bear no barm,
Mislead night-wanderers, laughing at their harm?
Those that 'Hobgoblin' call you, and 'Sweet Puck', 40
You do their work, and they shall have good luck.
Are not you he?

PUCK   Thou speakest aright;
I am that merry wanderer of the night.
I jest to Oberon, and make him smile
When I a fat and bean-fed horse beguile, 45
Neighing in likeness of a filly foal;
And sometime lurk I in a gossip's bowl
In very likeness of a roasted crab,
And when she drinks, against her lips I bob,
And on her withered dewlap pour the ale. 50
The wisest aunt, telling the saddest tale,
Sometime for threefoot stool mistaketh me;
Then slip I from her bum, down topples she,
And 'Tailor' cries, and falls into a cough;

'shrewd and knavish sprite speech', laboriously rendered into the third person. Kean, who had made some initial notes for his production in a Reynolds edition, has 'his' for 'your' in 32 and 'hither comes' for 'else you are' in 33, prior to Puck's entrance in 34. Kean's Puck began with 'Fairy'; Kean and Saker cut 36–7, Daly 36–40, Tree and Atkins cut from 35, Hall cut everything after 'Robin Goodfellow'.

43–57   Caird's Fairy screamed and crossed to clutch at Puck's leg like a groupie at 'wanderer of the night'; he knelt as if to kiss her on 'smile' before making a horse noise, put his hands 'down neck and onto her chest' at 'bob', took her onto his knee and dropped her to illustrate the story of the wisest aunt, and signed her autograph book at 'cough' (promptbook). 44–57 were difficult lines for nineteenth-century directors, replete with indecorous material: Vestris cut 45–6; Kean 45–6, 51, 54, 56–7; Saker cut 44–6, 48–9 and 56–7, Daly 45–6, 56 (but substituting 'swear' for 'loffe' in 55); Tree 51–4 and 56–7.

53   'bum' was unacceptable to Bowdler, Vestris and Phelps, who simply omitted it, and to Kean who substituted 'seat', Saker, who chose 'and', and Daly who replaced 'her bum' with 'beneath'.

54   Brook's Puck bent down and the fairies made a 'split' noise (promptbook). Vestris, Kean, Saker, Daly, Tree, cut the line, which is both obscure and, in nineteenth–century terms, indecorous.

And then the whole choir hold their hips and loffe,   55
And waxen in their mirth, and neeze, and swear
A merrier hour was never wasted there.
But room, Fairy: here comes Oberon.
FAIRY   And here my mistress. Would that he were gone!

Enter OBERON *the King of Fairies, at one door, with his train; and*
TITANIA, *the Queen, at another with hers*

55   Benson had a laugh and echo at the end of the line, repeated at the end of 57.
59 SD The original stage direction reflects Elizabethan staging practice with Oberon and Titania
       entering through doors in the tiring house façade. Subsequent productions have tended to
       follow this arrangement, often leading to a centre stage confrontation between Oberon and
       Titania. Reynolds's Oberon and Titania entered in 'cars' with their trains. The size of the
       entourages has varied in relation to theatrical aesthetics and economics. William A. Ringler
       ('Actors') suggests that the trains in early productions might have included as few as four
       fairies in total, possibly played by the same actors who played the Mechanicals, as occurred
       in the Contact Theatre Company production seen at the Lilian Baylis in 1993. Obviously
       this strikes at any notion of dainty *corps de ballet* fairies. Adrian Noble also used his
       Mechanicals as fairies; Brook simply had four adult fairies. The majority of productions,
       however, have included a substantial percentage of children in the minor fairy roles; Benson
       sometimes had 'forty or fifty tiny children ... clothed only in fleshings, with tiny wings on
       their heads and backs' (Constance Benson, *Mainly Players*, p. 80). In Reinhardt's film, the
       Indian Boy has a substantial role, being entertained and deserted by flying fairies and sere-
       naded by a band of gnomes in the course of a long musical routine that precedes Titania's
       arrival. Kenneth Anger who played the Indian Boy was later to write the notorious
       Hollywood exposé *Hollywood Babylon*; there apears to be no direct causal relationship
       between the two events.
          The traditional approach to costuming the fairies is concisely summarised in a 1920s
       acting edition: 'Conventional fairies' dress will be required by Oberon and Titania and the
       latter's fairies. This is traditionally of white muslin, cut very simply, and with gauze wings
       attached behind the shoulders... Modern miniature electric flash-lamps can be used very
       effectively' (Browne, *Dream*, pp. 154–5). This is borne out by an effect in Asche's staging:
       'the elves, the fairies, and the sprites besprinkle the nocturnal veil with multi-coloured starlets
       emanating from tiny electric lamps' (*Sunday Times*, 26 November 1905). Vestris's fairies
       were in the *corps de ballet* tradition, costumed in variations on Greek themes, with Oberon's
       fairies identified by their yellow scarves and Titania's by their blue ones (Pattie, *Dream*).
       That tradition has remained powerful into this century, boosted by the myriads of 'gauzy'
       female fairies, including many children, in the 1935 film's very spectacular fairy ballets.
       These ballets mix traditional theatrical trick work, such as the fairies spiralling upwards
       round a tree into the sky or flying across one of the many ponds, with specifically filmic

techniques such as filming fairies through a spangled gauze. The pull of the traditional is powerful: W. A. Darlington responded to Guthrie's 1937 Victorian pastiche thus, 'in theory I do not greatly care for the idea of a fairy corps de ballet with red sashes across their shoulders, looking like young queen Victorias. In practice I found them quite delicious' (*Daily Telegraph*, 28 December 1937). Benthall's productions were firmly balletic (in 1949 he had 'tulle-draped ballerinas', *Birmingham Post*, 25 April). The tradition was still being parodied in Caird's 1989 costumes and the 1991 *Pocket Dream*, but there have been three other important strands: one approach has been to have the fairies blending into the scenery, at least since the time of Phelps; a second, since about 1914, has been to adopt Elizabethan/Jacobean designs, often derived from Inigo Jones; the third has been the more abstract or conceptual approach associated with Barker, Brook, Lepage and Noble.

Phelps initiated the idea of presenting the fairies as part of the landscape and some of Benson's fairies had costumes which allowed them to turn their backs when mortals came on and appear as ferns, lilies or beds of primroses (Moyr Smith, *Dream*, p. xv). Tree's were also clothed in natural woodland colours: 'the fairies spring from out bulrushes and shrubs dressed in flower petals or green or brown silk, their little garments and their wings reflecting in every case the colours of nature in woodland and country' (*Era*, 13 January 1900). The overall effect resembled a Noel Paton picture (HTC cutting). In a variation on this tradition, Guthrie's minor fairies in 1951, all male, unlike those in his 1937 pastiche Taglioni version, were like 'camouflaged modern soldiers engaged in jungle warfare' rather than 'the dainty little girls moving lightly' which the *Stage* (3 January 1952) thought they ought to be.

Patrick Kirwan appears to have been the first director of the *Dream* to go to Renaissance sources, using Michael Drayton's *Nimphidia* as the authority for his rank and file 'pearl grey shadows' of fairies, since, according to Drayton, they were the ghosts of little boys and girls (*Sunday Times*, 12 April 1914). Harcourt Williams's 1929/31 fairies, based on Inigo Jones designs, were 'a heavily-skirted and panniered brigade of dames in an elderly make-up with wigs of long rough grey hair and smudged and gilded faces' (*Morning Post*, 3 November 1931). Wolfit remembered them as being 'dressed in seaweed from head to foot' (Wolfit, *Interval*, p. 134). Bridges Adams used his Elizabethan fairies to good effect in 1932: they 'come upon a winding course, and they are grey and silver, like rare moths. Most of them gather around their Queen, but distant parties of them are seen higher up the slope, phosphorescent in the heart of the woodland' (Stratford *Herald*, 29 April).

Barker's treatment of the fairies was revolutionary. Contemporary reviewers detected eastern influences, seeing them as 'heavy little idols of gold with shiny yellow faces' (*Era*, 11 February 1914) or, like Desmond MacCarthy, thought they were made of ormolu. However, once the initial shock had subsided, 'the very characteristics which made them at first so outlandishly arresting now contribute to make them inconspicuous. They group themselves motionless about the stage, and the lovers move past and between them as casually as though they were stocks or stones' (MacCarthy in Rowell, *Dramatic Criticism*, p. 159). This different kind of blending into the scenery from the more naturalistic approach of the Phelps tradition may link back to some version of the Renaissance conventions for invisibility reflected in the 'robe for to go invisible ' in Henslowe's Diary, and has carried through into Brook's grey-clad minor fairies and Lepage's blue-faced fairies, 'slimy, slug-like creatures, crawling through the oozy mud' (*Daily Telegraph*, 13 July 1992).

Of course the three strands of dealing with the fairies have not been discrete and Barton's 'hairy fairies, bald fairies, Bacchic fairies with fruit salads on their heads and sinister fairies' (*Guardian*, 9 May 1977) were ever-present in the wood, 'freezing into stumps and exotic foliage when mortals approach, with bald elfin heads peeping through the branches and recumbent gnomes serving as footstools' (*Times*, 9 May). They were also controversial, as previous fairies based on Elizabethan originals had been, since once again few critics recog-nised their provenance: 'blue-haired, shock-haired, or with no hair at all, waving long finger nails like Struwwelpeter, or galumping grossly like Caliban, these eerie grotesques are a world away from Shakespeare's delicate elves and sprites' (*Daily Telegraph*, 9 May). Similarly, particularly in the inter-war years,it was sometimes the fairies' assimilation to moonlight, rather than the forest itself, which made the greatest impact: Fagan's 'general colour scheme is made up of the greens and blues of forest moonlight, and the whole effect is very much that of a Rackham drawing' (*Daily Telegraph*, 6 December 1920); Norman Wilkinson's second fairy designs, for Calthrop, were blue, in the Elizabethan manner, with 'pale light on white faces partly shadowed by large mops of hair' suggesting Beardsley (*Era*, 14 November 1923) and his third, also Elizabethan, impressed as ' fantasies in dark blues and greens' (*Leamington Courier*, 8 June 1934).

More recent productions have drawn on all three traditions: Daniels had 'large puppets manipulated amidst much swirling of hands and flowing of coloured chiffon, by athletic, dark-costumed actors' (*Guardian*, in *LTR* 1982); Bryden's grey-wigged fairies wore 'tattered doublets and gowns, most of them a bosky brown, green or brown–green in hue. They are partly woodland spirits, partly Elizabethan spectres, and are presumably meant to represent both nature and tradition' (*New Statesman* in *LTR* 1982); Branagh's were 'an unlovely mix-ture of Flower Power, pantomime and *Cats*' (*Sunday Telegraph*, 19 August 1990) conceived along conventional lines, subscribing mostly to the wild, grubby school of fairy acting' (*Independent*, 15 August 1990). Sometimes Oberon's followers have been differentiated from Titania's. In Benson's production Oberon's train carried musical instruments made of flowers and were 'of more masculine aspect than those of Titania; but this distinction is not unduly emphasised, as sexlessness seems to be the leading characteristic of all of the elfin band' (Moyr Smith, *Dream*, p. xv). For Calthrop, 'Titania's dark-clad train was a little like some troop of deep-sea girl-guides' (Agate, *Chronicles*, p. 39). Oberon's bat-winged fairies are masculine and sinister in the 1935 film; Wolfit gave Oberon's fairies 'bats' wings' costumes which sometimes were used as 'an unusual bower for the Fairy King himself' (*Stage*, 1 January 1942) and Benthall had 'a black-garbed cohort that waited on Oberon ... from a Fokine production' in 1949 (*Birmingham Post*, 25 April). In his 1957 staging, 'some of Titania's attendants are a shade too earthy, notwithstanding diaphanous costumes and

OBERON Ill met by moonlight, proud Titania!   60
TITANIA What, jealous Oberon? Fairies, skip hence.

liberal fairy make-up' (*Stage*, 27 December). Caird's female fairies were 'a ballet class in
some remedial wing of St Trinian's. Their fluffy white tutus are ironic reminders of the drippy
sweetness of bygone productions, but then you notice the punk rocker boots, the smudged,
gum-chewing, impassively bolshy faces' while his male fairies, 'apparelled in an odd combination of combinations and tailcoats seem to rely on human cast-offs. Even their little pointy
wings are strap-on' (*Independent*, 13 April 1989).

    The minor fairies were disembodied voices in David Conville's 1982 Regent's Park produc-
tion and at the Young Vic in 1986 (*LTR* 1982 and 1986).

60   Oberon was traditionally a female part until 1914 because of the amount of singing Victorian
Oberons undertook ('A good deal of Oberon's part has been set – quite unnecessarily – to
music' (*Daily Telegraph*, 6 December 1905)) and also because as Agate commented on Julia
Neilson in Tree's production 'the mere fact of her being a woman just differentiates it from
humanity' (*Pall Mall Gazette*, 11 January 1900). However, Benson, unusually for his period,
always used a male actor while Fagan had a female exponent of the part as late as 1920 and
the female understudy to a male Oberon at the Old Vic in 1924 saw the role as 'a sort of
principal boy's part of the classics' (VW cutting).

    Madame Vestris defined the role for the nineteenth century: 'there was a dignified grace
worthy of the King of fairy land, and as she stood with her glittering armour and fantastic
helmet on an eminence, with a blue-tinted wood gliding by her in the background, presenting different aspects of the same sylvan scenery, the effect was little short of supernatural.
Madame Vestris evidently understood the value of the effect to be produced by distance,
and by generally remaining as the marked out but remote figure on a dark ground, or shone
upon by some artificial light, a supernatural appearance was generally given to Oberon'
(*Times*, 17 November 1840).

    Little critical attention was paid to interpretation of the role even after 1900, until
Dunlop's doubling of it with Theseus began to open up new interpretative possibilities: in
1911 Evelyn d'Alroy was, remarkably, castigated for 'an excess of femininity in her rendering' of
the part for Tree (*ILN*, 22 April); the *Athenaeum* found 'a great deal of the temperament of a
minor Parisian poet in Oberon' but thought that Mary Grey in Fagan's staging 'makes him too
much of a kind father to his fairy people' (17 December 1920); Robert Harris in 1924 was 'like
a lolling schoolboy' with 'no wand to support my royal dignity' (Robert Harris, 'Two Oberons',
The Old Vic and Sadler's Wells Magazine, December 1931); Powys Thomas (for Devine) had
'an air of dark nobility as well as jealous pride' (*Plays and Players*, May 1954) and Alec
McCowen was 'a gentleman dancing-master' for Langham (*Observer*, 12 December 1960).
Derek Godfrey's scarab-like Oberon, in Benthall's 1957 staging, 'listened to the lovers' quarrels,
not with malice, not with mockery, but with a stern ironic interest as if choosing to play the
spirit of fairness in the wars of love that is so often missing in life' (*New Statesman*, 4 January

1958), a characteristic he shared with Bryden's Paul Scofield, 'an intent watcher and listener, for ever poring over the knotty conundrum of humankind' (*New Statesman*, in *LTR* 1982).

Vestris as Oberon wore a Greek helmet, a knee-length gathered blue tunic decorated with stars, and grieves, and carried a spear. Even in the 1920s something very similar was being recommended in an acting edition: 'Oberon's suit can be of gold or bright yellow tissue, ... Oberon can wear a Grecian helmet of inverted-basin shape with small wings attached at the sides and should carry a gilded spear' (Browne, *Dream*, p. 155). However, there has been no clear pattern in costuming Oberon. At one point, Benson had an Oberon costume of fleshings and green gauze with a head-mounted electric light, but this was abandoned when the battery concealed in Oberon's wings leaked over the actor (Trewin, *Benson*, p. 57). Tree also availed himself of new technology: his Oberon was 'clad in robes of glittering gold, and crowned and girded with miniature electric lights' (HTC cutting, 1900). Henry Baynton asked Clarkson the wig-maker for an Oberon wig of 'red gold colour with dew drop effects on the end of the hairs' in 1924 (Baynton letter, 2 June). Kirwan's *Nimphidia*-inspired Oberon was a kind of 'splendid iridescent beetle, with luminous jerkin of blue and green and shod with "ladybird's wings" – that is boots of scarlet, speckled with black – while on his head rises the horned crest of a beetle' (*Sunday Times*, 12 April 1914). Devine's Oberon, who was compared to an 'Aztec bird of illish omen' (*Punch*, 31 March 1954), looked very similar to Kirwan's. At Stratford in 1937 Oberon was 'majestic in diaphanous plus fours' (*Star*, 30 March) with a 'crown of cellophane' (*Yorkshire Post*, 30 March). Robert Helpmann in Guthrie's first production was 'required to look (from the front) like a pantomime octopus and (from the back) like a ballet bluebottle' (*News Chronicle*, 27 December 1938); for Benthall in 1954 he was a 'sinister Oberon haunting the wood on great dragonfly wings' (*Birmingham Post*, 1 September). Gielgud appeared in Coghill's production 'as a Roman centurion with breast-plate, short skirt and bare legs', a green face, and 'a tuft of green beard at the end of his chin' (*Evening Standard*, 27 January 1945). According to Hayman, he changed the whole concept of the part after the first night and tried to appear youthful and handsome (*Gielgud*, p. 147). Hall's Oberons wore Elizabethan dress with bare feet and were, like Caird's, 'Spock-eared' (*Guardian*, 5 December 1989), Alan Howard wore a purple caftan for Brook, while Patrick Stewart, for Barton, was 'a dusky faun, loin-clothed and combining the attributes of a Greek athlete and a Hindu temple dancer' (*Times*, 9 May 1977), Paul Scofield, for Bryden, was 'an eerie wizard with the aspect of a surprised cockatoo' (*Guardian*, in *LTR* 1982) and Mike Gwilym for Daniels (entering on a rising spiral staircase (promptbook)) was 'dressed ludicrously like a glam-rock singer in black lurex and gold' (*Guardian*, in *LTR* 1982).

61   Traditionally Titanias were expected to look pretty and regal in a suitably fairy-like way, and to sing and dance well, attracting attention only when they diverged from those norms. Typically, Maud Tree in her husband's 1900 production was noteworthy for 'her gossamer costume of rainbow tints', her successor in 1911 for her 'girlish ingenuousness, ... spiritual delicacy and refinement' (HTC cuttings). Even the indefatigably Elizabethan Patrick Kirwan appeared to capitulate to contemporary fashion: 'Titania is likened to a star, so over her

> I have forsworn his bed and company.
> OBERON Tarry, rash wanton! Am not I thy lord?
> TITANIA Then I must be thy lady. But I know
>   When thou hast stol'n away from Fairyland,   65
>   And in the shape of Corin sat all day
>   Playing on pipes of corn, and versing love
>   To amorous Phillida. Why art thou here
>   Come from the farthest step of India? –
>   But that, forsooth, the bouncing Amazon,   70
>   Your buskined mistress and your warrior love,
>   To Theseus must be wedded; and you come

snow-white robe will be cast a star-shaped mantle or tunic of silver, while silver star rays will crown her hair' (*Sunday Times*, 12 April 1914). Gwen Ffrangcon-Davies was 'imperious, petulant and pale as mist' (Farjeon, *Scene*, p. 44) at Drury Lane in 1924; Dorothy Francis for Bridges Adams had 'womanly grace and tenderness and passion, all in miniature, delicate as the gentlest breeze' (Stratford *Herald*, 29 April 1932), and Guthrie's Vivien Leigh 'glimmers through the forest like a star' with 'flashing sequins on her eyelids' (*Evening Standard*, *Daily Express,* both 28 December 1937). After the Second World War the part attracted more attention, though critics often judged new readings against an unstated traditional approach, until the fashion for doubling after 1967 invested the part with greater interest. For Coghill, Peggy Ashcroft wore 'a sort of utility garden-party outfit, with a green blouse and a three-quarter length skirt', looking like 'a young English dowager' on her way to an opera matinée (*Evening Standard*, 27 January); conversely Jill Balcon in Guthrie's 1951 version was 'handicapped by a costume and wig which suggested that she had fluttered in from a coven of witches in the Macbeth country' (*Observer*, 30 December). For Devine, Muriel Pavlow was 'not so much a fairy queen as a rather defiant little suburban wife' (*Birmingham Mail*, 24 March) whereas Langham's Gwen Watford erred in another direction, smacking 'less of the enchanted wood than of the royal garden party' (*Observer*, 12 December 1960). Judi Dench, for Hall in 1962, was memorably described as frisking and swooping like 'a Persian kitten turned maenad' (*New Statesman*, 27 April). Recent Titanias have followed Dench in being more active: Brook's Titania was 'a Beardsley snake-queen come to life' (*Times*, 11 June 1971) and Alexander's knocked Oberon down at their first meeting. For Noble, Stella Gonet was 'a giggling, sexy Titania in pink ostrich feathers' (Jane Edwardes, *Time Out*, 10 August 1994).

   In Barton's staging, 'when he threatens her the lights go down; when she defies him they go up again' (*Observer*, 15 May 1977); Alexander's Titania threw 'the wimpish Oberon to the ground with a flick of the wrist, angrily rejecting his sovereignty' (*Guardian*, 10 July 1986).

62–8   Cut by Kean and Saker; Tree cut only 62 with its reference to the marital bed; Phelps, Daly and Hall cut only Titania's accusations of pastoral infidelity (64–8).
72–3   Cut by Benson from 'and'; Kean changed 'their bed' to 'them both'.

To give their bed joy and prosperity.

OBERON How canst thou thus, for shame, Titania,
    Glance at my credit with Hippolyta,   75
    Knowing I know thy love to Theseus?
    Didst not thou lead him through the glimmering night
    From Perigenia, whom he ravishèd,
    And make him with fair Aegles break his faith,
    With Ariadne, and Antiopa?   80
TITANIA These are the forgeries of jealousy:
    And never since the middle summer's spring
    Met we on hill, in dale, forest, or mead,
    By pavèd fountain or by rushy brook,
    Or in the beachèd margent of the sea   85
    To dance our ringlets to the whistling wind,
    But with thy brawls thou hast disturbed our sport.
    Therefore the winds, piping to us in vain,
    As in revenge have sucked up from the sea
    Contagious fogs; which, falling in the land,   90
    Hath every pelting river made so proud
    That they have overborne their continents.
    The ox hath therefore stretched his yoke in vain,
    The ploughman lost his sweat, and the green corn
    Hath rotted ere his youth attained a beard.   95
    The fold stands empty in the drownèd field,
    And crows are fatted with the murrion flock;
    The nine-men's-morris is filled up with mud,
    And the quaint mazes in the wanton green
    For lack of tread are undistinguishable.   100
    The human mortals want their winter cheer;
    No night is now with hymn or carol blessed.
    Therefore the moon, the governess of floods,
    Pale in her anger, washes all the air,
    That rheumatic diseases do abound;   105

77–80   Hall cut Oberon's accusations of mythological improprieties, following Vestris, Phelps, Kean,
        Saker, Daly, Benson and Tree. Barker had Oberon's fairies nod their heads to give emphasis
        to his accusations and Titania's bow theirs (in shame?) at the end of the speech.

81–117 Many directors have been uneasy with this speech, presumably on grounds of length:
        Vestris (and Benson) cut 101–6:Kean and Saker removed 84–5 and everything after 88
        (Phelps, Daly and Hall followed the second cut); Tree took out 93–8, 101–2, and the end
        of 111–14; Atkins removed 93–102 and six and a half lines after 105, but at least he kept the
        moon in 103. All of Barker's fairies nodded at the end of Titania's speech, presumably in
        agreement (promptbook). Peggy Ashcroft apparently found her Indian Boy a great help here

And thorough this distemperature we see
The seasons alter; hoary-headed frosts
Fall in the fresh lap of the crimson rose,
And on old Hiems' thin and icy crown
An odorous chaplet of sweet summer buds 110
Is, as in mockery, set. The spring, the summer,
The childing autumn, angry winter change
Their wonted liveries, and the mazèd world
By their increase now knows not which is which.
And this same progeny of evils comes 115
From our debate, from our dissension.
We are their parents and original.

OBERON Do you amend it, then: it lies in you.
Why should Titania cross her Oberon?
I do but beg a little changeling boy 120
To be my henchman.

TITANIA   Set your heart at rest.
The fairy land buys not the child of me.
His mother was a votress of my order,
And in the spicèd Indian air by night
Full often hath she gossiped by my side, 125
And sat with me on Neptune's yellow sands
Marking th'embarkèd traders on the flood,
When we have laughed to see the sails conceive

in Coghill's production (Coghill letter). Alexander's Titania floored Oberon again at the beginning of her speech. In both Alexander's and Caird's stagings Titania's fairies, including a changeling (the Indian Boy), clustered round her during the 'forgeries of jealousy' speech, with one of Caird's 'crying quietly' according to the promptbook, although the *Independent* objected to Caird's 'bespectacled and pigtailed fairies snivel[ling] into the skirts of Clare Higgins's Titania as she hauntingly catalogues the havoc' (6 December 1989).

118   Phelps, Kean and Saker completed their surgery on Titania's speech by removing Oberon's first line in reply.

120   The changeling child (the Indian Boy) was a fixture in nineteenth-century productions: Benson used him as Titania's train bearer; Tree's Puck attempted to steal him. He appears not to have been physically present in most twentieth-century productions until resuscitated by Coghill (although he was a major presence in the Reinhardt film) and has made intermittent but largely unremarked appearances since. Daniels and Caird both had him, but Barton did not, despite Michael Billington's comment that Patrick Stewart combined 'muscular verse speaking with an ambisextrous lust that explains why he is so keen to get hold of "a little changeling boy"' (*Guardian*, 9 May 1977).

127–35   The Indian woman's pregnancy was a favourite target for nineteenth-century directors,

And grow big-bellied with the wanton wind;
Which she, with pretty and with swimming gait   130
Following (her womb then rich with my young squire),
Would imitate, and sail upon the land
To fetch me trifles, and return again
As from a voyage, rich with merchandise.
But she, being mortal, of that boy did die,   135
And for her sake do I rear up her boy;
And for her sake I will not part with him.
OBERON How long within this wood intend you stay?
TITANIA Perchance till after Theseus' wedding day.
If you will patiently dance in our round,   140
And see our moonlight revels, go with us:
If not, shun me, and I will spare your haunts.
OBERON Give me that boy, and I will go with thee.
TITANIA Not for thy fairy kingdom! Fairies, away.
We shall chide downright if I longer stay.   145
Exeunt [Titania and her train]
OBERON Well, go thy way. Thou shalt not from this grove
Till I torment thee for this injury.
My gentle Puck, come hither. Thou rememberest
Since once I sat upon a promontory,
And heard a mermaid on a dolphin's back   150
Uttering such dulcet and harmonious breath
That the rude sea grew civil at her song,
And certain stars shot madly from their spheres
To hear the sea-maid's music?

following Reynolds and Bowdler: Vestris cut only 128–9 and 131, but Phelps cut 128–35, Kean, Saker and Benson cut 127–33, and Daly and Tree 128–34. It continued to be cut in the mid twentieth century, probably still for reasons of propriety: Bridges Adams omitted 131, except 'Following'; Atkins cut 130–4.

135 Noble's Oberon 'gives a satisfied smile. Anything that causes her pain is fine by him' (Benedict Nightingale, *Times* 5 August 1994).

136 Cut by Saker to finish off his changes to this speech.

137 Reynolds inserted an exchange, in preparation for a later spectacular effect which established that the Indian Boy was 'Still hid in India, far, far from Oberon's power' (Reynolds, *Dream*, p. 18).

145 In Tree's production, as Oberon's train left each boy shook his finger at a girl in Titania's train, a whimsical device that Tree also used elsewhere (promptbook).

148 Daly's Oberon sat down to reminisce about the 'fair vestal' with Puck lying at his side (promptbook).

PUCK   I remember.
OBERON That very time I saw (but thou couldst not)   155
        Flying between the cold moon and the earth
        Cupid all armed: a certain aim he took
        At a fair vestal thronèd by the west,
        And loosed his loveshaft smartly from his bow
        As it should pierce a hundred thousand hearts;   160
        But I might see young Cupid's fiery shaft
        Quenched in the chaste beams of the watery moon;
        And the imperial votress passèd on
        In maiden meditation, fancy-free.
        Yet marked I where the bolt of Cupid fell: 165
        It fell upon a little western flower,
        Before, milk-white; now purple with love's wound:
        And maidens call it 'love-in-idleness'.
        Fetch me that flower, the herb I showed thee once;
        The juice of it on sleeping eyelids laid   170
        Will make or man or woman madly dote
        Upon the next live creature that it sees.
        Fetch me this herb, and be thou here again
        Ere the leviathan can swim a league.
PUCK   I'll put a girdle round about the earth   175
        In forty minutes!   [*Exit*]
OBERON   Having once this juice
        I'll watch Titania when she is asleep,
        And drop the liquor of it in her eyes:
        The next thing then she, waking, looks upon –
        Be it on lion, bear, or wolf, or bull,   180

155   In Barton's production, Patrick Stewart's Oberon had a 'patronising but protective' attitude
      to Puck in his delivery of *I* and *thou* (*Observer*, 15 May 1977).
169   Caird's Puck put on his wings here.
175–6 Shaw objected that Daly's Puck announced 'her ability to girdle the earth in forty minutes in
      the attitude of a professional skater, and then begins the journey awkwardly in a swing, which
      takes her in the opposite direction to that in which she indicated her intention of going', accom-
      panied by 'a ridiculous clash of cymbals in the orchestra' (*Nineties*, pp. 178, 179).
176   For Barker, Calthrop 'pronounces these words as a piece of fantastic bombast, and off he struts
      extravagantly kicking out his feet in a comic swagger' (MacCarthy, in Rowell, *Dramatic Criticism*,
      p. 160); Ian Holm found new humour for Hall in his delivery of 'I'll put a girdle round the earth in
      ... er...mmm ... er forty minutes' (Stratford *Herald*, 5 June 1959); Bryden's Puck 'finds the magic
      flower in the audience' (*Financial Times*, in *LTR* 1982); Lepage's Puck put her girdle about the
      earth in the form of 'a prolonged high-wire spin' (*Independent on Sunday*, 12 July 1992).
180–1 Cut by Kean and Saker. Kott pointed out the associations of these animals with sexual potency.

On meddling monkey, or on busy ape –
She shall pursue it with the soul of love.
And ere I take this charm from off her sight
(As I can take it with another herb)
I'll make her render up her page to me.   185
But who comes here? I am invisible,
And I will overhear their conference.

Enter DEMETRIUS, HELENA *following him*

DEMETRIUS I love thee not, therefore pursue me not.
Where is Lysander, and fair Hermia?
The one I'll slay, the other slayeth me.   190
Thou told'st me they were stol'n unto this wood,
And here am I, and wood within this wood
Because I cannot meet my Hermia.
Hence, get thee gone, and follow me no more.
HELENA You draw me, you hard-hearted adamant!   195
But yet you draw not iron, for my heart
Is true as steel. Leave you your power to draw,

186 Offstage calling of names has often been used to motivate Oberon's question. Directors
have treated his invisibility in differing ways: in the sixteenth century he may have used 'a
robe for to go invisible' such as the one Henslowe includes in his inventory of costumes. In
1895 Daly's fairies were equipped with battery operated electric lights: Archer particularly dis-
liked Oberon using this line as an opportunity 'to blaze forth like the Eddystone light' (Felheim,
Daly, pp. 244–5). Caird too had a special light to represent Oberon's invisibility in 1989.

187 Brook flew down coils of wire on fishing rods to serve as his trees here (promptbook).
Caird's Helena and Demetrius entered in dressing gowns.

188 Cut by Kean, perhaps because the following line advances the situation and perhaps
because it was too bald a statement?

190 Cut by Vestris, Phelps, Kean and Saker, presumably as too violent and passionate.

191 For Caird, Demetrius dragged Helena downstage by the neck here.

192–3 The obsolete pun on 'wood' makes these thematically significant lines theatrically obscure
and Vestris, Phelps (who cut 190–3), Kean, Saker, Daly (who removed 191–2), Bridges Adams
and Atkins all cut them, though the modern tendency is to leave them: Lepage's Demetrius
(like others) thumped his forehead to indicate his mental distress.

195–226 Recent productions have explored the comic potential of these lines in terms of masochism,
but they caused difficulties for earlier directors. Vestris removed 203–13, 222 and 225–6; Phelps
got rid of 207–26; 195–213 proved too much for Kean and Saker; Benson cut 205–13, Daly
208–9 and 211–26, Tree cut 197–8 and 208–13. Atkins, Bridges Adams and Devine lost 208–10.
Bowdler had recommended cutting 217-19 for reasons of propriety; Phelps (as part of a longer
cut), Kean, Saker, Daly (as part of a longer cut), Benson, Tree and Atkins all followed suit.

And I shall have no power to follow you.

DEMETRIUS Do I entice you? Do I speak you fair?
 Or rather do I not in plainest truth   200
 Tell you I do not, nor I cannot love you?

HELENA And even for that do I love you the more.
 I am your spaniel; and, Demetrius,
 The more you beat me I will fawn on you.
 Use me but as your spaniel: spurn me, strike me,   205
 Neglect me, lose me; only give me leave,
 Unworthy as I am, to follow you.
 What worser place can I beg in your love
 (And yet a place of high respect with me)
 Than to be usèd as you use your dog?   210

DEMETRIUS Tempt not too much the hatred of my spirit;
 For I am sick when I do look on thee.

HELENA And I am sick when I look not on you.

DEMETRIUS You do impeach your modesty too much,
 To leave the city and commit yourself   215
 Into the hands of one that loves you not;
 To trust the opportunity of night,
 And the ill counsel of a desert place,
 With the rich worth of your virginity.

HELENA Your virtue is my privilege: for that   220
 It is not night when I do see your face,
 Therefore I think I am not in the night;
 Nor doth this wood lack worlds of company,
 For you, in my respect, are all the world.
 Then how can it be said I am alone   225
 When all the world is here to look on me?

---

202   Helena crawled to Demetrius' leg in Caird's production, presumably illustrating her spaniel-like qualities literally.

205   Caird's masochistic Helena hit herself with Demetrius's hand at 'spurn'. Noble's Helena proceeded to conduct herself as a very energetic spaniel.

211   Daniels had Demetrius cross to Helena wagging his finger (promptbook).

214   Brook's Demetrius pulled Helena's skirt down over her knees (promptbook).

214-24   Alexander had Demetrius and Helena lying down, with Helena starting to wrap herself round Demetrius and thus impeding him when he tried to get away (promptbook).

220   At 'privilege' Daniels had Demetrius 'sit back and down "Tut. I give up"' (promptbook).

226-7   Daniels made his sitting Helena lean on Demetrius' shoulder and fall over when he broke away (promptbook).

DEMETRIUS I'll run from thee and hide me in the brakes,
        And leave thee to the mercy of wild beasts.
HELENA The wildest hath not such a heart as you.
        Run when you will: the story shall be changed;   230
        Apollo flies, and Daphne holds the chase,
        The dove pursues the griffin, the mild hind
        Makes speed to catch the tiger – bootless speed,
        When cowardice pursues, and valour flies!
DEMETRIUS I will not stay thy questions. Let me go;   235
        Or if thou follow me, do not believe
        But I shall do thee mischief in the wood.
HELENA Ay, in the temple, in the town, the field,
        You do me mischief. Fie, Demetrius,
        Your wrongs do set a scandal on my sex!   240
        We cannot fight for love, as men may do;
        We should be wooed, and were not made to woo.
                                            [*Exit Demetrius*]
        I'll follow thee, and make a heaven of hell,
        To die upon the hand I love so well.   *Exit*
OBERON Fare thee well, nymph. Ere he do leave this grove   245
        Thou shalt fly him, and he shall seek thy love.

                        Enter PUCK

227–34 Kean, Saker, Daly, Benson and Tree simply cut the whole of this exchange; Demetrius' lines
        more often survive in the twentieth century, but Helena's generalisations of her plight
        (230–4), seldom find much favour: Phelps and Hall cut all of it, Atkins, Bridges Adams and
        Devine 232–4. 'On a single line – "Apollo flies and Daphne holds the chase" – Brook builds a
        superbly comic pursuit of Demetrius by Helena, tackling him and pinning him to the ground
        to hear her love' (*Observer*, 13 June 1971). At 'heart as you', Caird's Helena knocked
        Demetrius over; at 'chase' in 231 she put her foot on him.
235   Demetrius made to escape at 'questions' in Daniels's staging, but Helena caught him by the
        hand (promptbook). Alexander had Demetrius grab Helena's neck and squeeze it at 'ques-
        tions' (promptbook).
238–42 Alexander's Helena rubbed her head against Demetrius at the beginning of her speech
        (promptbook). At 'made to woo', Alexander's Demetrius kissed Helena who fell into
        Oberon's arms and then Oberon gave her back her missing shoe, to her surprise. Caird's
        Helena shook her head and then kissed Demetrius, who fell over before making his exit.
        Cut by Saker; Kean cut 240–2, Tree 241–2.
243–4   As Daniels's Helena started to exit, Oberon caught at her cape and she returned for it
        (promptbook). Kean read 'I'll follow thee, and die upon the hand I love so well.'
246 SD Benson's Puck made a flying entrance here; Tree's made his 'by way of a flying leap from
        a pool of plashing water' (HTC cutting, 1900).

              Hast thou the flower there? Welcome, wanderer.
PUCK Ay, there it is.
OBERON   I pray thee give it me.
              I know a bank where the wild thyme blows,
              Where oxlips and the nodding violet grows,   250
              Quite overcanopied with luscious woodbine,
              With sweet musk-roses, and with eglantine:
              There sleeps Titania sometime of the night,
              Lulled in these flowers with dances and delight;
              And there the snake throws her enamelled skin,   255
              Weed wide enough to wrap a fairy in;
              And with the juice of this I'll streak her eyes,
              And make her full of hateful fantasies.
              Take thou some of it, and seek through this grove:
              A sweet Athenian lady is in love   260
              With a disdainful youth; anoint his eyes,
              But do it when the next thing he espies
              May be the lady. Thou shalt know the man
              By the Athenian garments he hath on.
              Effect it with some care, that he may prove   265
              More fond on her than she upon her love.
              And look thou meet me ere the first cock crow.
PUCK Fear not, my lord; your servant shall do so.

                                                          Exeunt

247-8 Crosse thought that 'it was not necessary that the magic flower should be luminous' in Tree's
       1911 staging (*Diary* V, p. 50). In Brook's production Puck passed 'Love-in-idleness' to Oberon
       in the form of a spinning plate which was transferred from one wand to another as they flew
       above the stage on trapezes in a scintillating display of physical dexterity.

  249 This speech has often been treated as a song: Vestris, who made it a duet between Oberon
       and the First Fairy, cut 250–2, 255–6, Phelps 255–6; Kean and Saker 251–2, 255–6, Daly only
       255–6. In Tree's 1900 staging, 'after speaking the lines to Puck, the Oberon sang them to
       himself as he strolled into the depths of the wood, but the effect of this was natural and
       charming' (Dickins, *Forty Years*, p. 94). Crosse castigated Asche for 'a good deal too much of
       the "Singing Fairies". The fact that the lines beginning "I know a bank" have been set to
       music does not, or should not, affect Shakespeare's intention that they should be spoken by
       Oberon at an important point in the development of the plot, and to bring on fairies to sing
       them when they are reached in the dialogue while Oberon retires aimlessly into the back-
       ground, is a rather foolish instance of allowing the accessories... to obscure instead of illus-
       trating Shakespeare. In Mr Tree's revival Oberon did at least sing the lines him (or rather
       her)self, which was a bit better' (*Diary* IV, pp. 34, 36). Farjeon found Dean at fault with his

cavalier treatment: 'half-an-hour or an hour later, Titania, who must have a song at all costs, sings the words we have already heard spoken. She, too, knows a bank' (*Scene*, p. 41).

257   In Caird's production Puck was asleep but woke at 'streak'.

264   Reynolds's Puck repeated 'By his Athenian garments' to prepare for his future mistake; Reynolds ended his act here with Oberon's invocation to his spirits, a fairy dance to an air taken from Colman, and a 'Quartetto and Chorus' derived from 5.1.399–400. Caird's Puck attempted to leave here.

266–8   Vestris cut 266–7, thus removing any doubts about Oberon's intention to make Demetrius more infatuated with Helena than she is with him. At the end of the scene she effected the scene change to 'another part of the Wood' with the aid of a diorama: 'Oberon, waving his wand, melts with the scene from our sight, and leaves a forest glade with its carpet of green and line of trees, whose overspreading branches entwined one over the other, over arched the earth and jealously guards the fairies' sleeping haunts from the rude gaze of the surrounding sky' (*Theatrical Journal*, 1 May 1841). Other nineteenth-century directors also used dioramas to make scene changes in the wood. Daly played his version of the lovers' scenes from 2.2. here before reverting to the fairy elements of 2.2. In 1911 Tree ended the scene with another ballet 'accompanied by some striking effects of lighting and a fall of spangles which looked like coloured snow', causing Crosse to wonder if they might be the strange snow Theseus refers to in 5.1 (*Diary* V, p. 51).

ACT 2, SCENE 2

Enter TITANIA, Queen of Fairies, with her train

TITANIA   Come, now a roundel and a fairy song,
Then for the third part of a minute, hence –
Some to kill cankers in the musk-rose buds,
Some war with reremice for their leathern wings
To make my small elves coats, and some keep back   5
The clamorous owl that nightly hoots and wonders
At our quaint spirits. Sing me now asleep;
Then to your offices, and let me rest.
Fairies sing.

0 SD   Traditionally editors have located this scene in another part of the forest. Most productions using a mimetic representation of a forest have changed locations here, often with the help of a diorama, as in Vestris's production, and music, latterly Mendelssohn. Reynolds, taking his scenic cue from the Mechanicals, had 'TITIANA's Bower, decorated with Flowers – In the Centre, the Duke's Oak' (*Dream*, p. 23). Vestris began this scene with a dance of fauns. Moyr Smith noted that Phelps had flowers arising or descending 'to disclose or conceal the fairy queen as occasion demanded' (*Dream*, p. xiii), a very similar procedure to Dean, whose bower closed and opened electrically. Kean's Oberon was criticised for standing 'before the scene waving his wand, as if he were exhibitor of the diorama' (Morley, in Rowell, *Dramatic Criticism*, p. 100). Daly played the fairy elements of 2.2 after his version of the lovers' scenes from 2.2. For Tree in 1911, Walter Hann 'shows us a glade with a moonlit river, with Turneresque masses of foliage and a dainty bank for Titania to sink to sleep on' (HTC cutting). Wolfit's Titania slept in the trunk of a tree, a device perhaps derived from the Duke's Oak at Stratford in 1932, where Wolfit's wife Rosalind Iden had played Titania. Benthall in 1954 had a 'pretty scene in which the fairies put Titania to sleep under a canopy of roses fetched out of space' (*Times*, 1 September). Hall set the bower in an inner stage formed by the junction of the two staircases of his permanent set, though the majority of the action was played downstage. Titania's bower in Brook's production was a flying concoction of scarlet feathers in stark contrast to the white box of the permanent set. Alexander's Titania 'curls up on a leaf like a Botticelli seashell' (*Guardian*, 10 July 1986). Noble's Titania slept in 'a giant upturned umbrella, a sickly Barbara Cartland-pink bower complete with phallic handle' (Carole Woddis, *What's On*, 10 August 1994).

1   Saker began with 'Come, a fairy song' and 'Sing me now asleep', omitting 2–7. Kean kept 1, but otherwise Saker was following his version.

[FIRST FAIRY]	You spotted snakes with double tongue,
	Thorny hedgehogs, be not seen. 10
	Newts and blindworms, do no wrong,
	Come not near our Fairy Queen.
[CHORUS]	Philomel with melody
	Sing in our sweet lullaby,
	Lulla, lulla, lullaby; lulla, lulla, lullaby. 15
	Never harm
	Nor spell nor charm
	Come our lovely lady nigh.
	So good night, with lullaby.
FIRST FAIRY	Weaving spiders, come not here; 20

9ff. The fairies in this scene have traditionally been cast on the basis of singing ability: in nine-teenth-century productions the lead singer here was often the fairy who met Puck in 2.1 (often called the First Singing Fairy), although Tree brought on his Oberon, the vocally accomplished Julia Neilson, to sing 'Ye spotted snakes', 'an absurdity which went a long way towards making nonsense of the Oberon/Titania story' (Crosse, *Fifty Years*, p. 45). Kean's Titania was lulled to sleep by the so-called shadow dance, a ballet of fairies dancing in the moonlight, to Morley's dismay: 'Elaborately to produce and present, as an especial attrac-tion, fairies of large size, casting shadows made as black and distinct as possible, and offering in dance to pick them up, as if even they also were solid, is as great a sacrifice of Shakespeare to the purposes of the ballet-master, as the view of Athens in its glory was a sacrifice of poetry to the scene-painter' (in Rowell, *Dramatic Criticism*, p. 101). Benson's ini-tial productions at Eastbourne and Stratford included a fight between a spider and a wasp, presumably in this scene, but it was soon abandoned because 'the spider's legs came in for such rough treatment that the insect had to be renewed each night' (Constance Benson, *Mainly Players*, p. 80). Crosse noted the fact that Atkins had his 1942 Titania sing herself to sleep as one more eccentricity among the odd ways of organising Titania's lullaby he had seen over the years (*Diary* XVIII, pp. 57, 59). Hall had a 'particularly diverting ... roundelay sung by Titania's attendants to a dulcimer accompaniment' (*Morning Advertiser*, 6 June 1959). Titania's lullaby in Brook's production was 'a Hare Krishna-type dirge' (*Leamington Courier*, 4 September 1970). Daniels had the Indian Boy present in this scene, sitting on Titania's lap for the second chorus of the song. Caird's staging offered an antidote to all pre-vious approaches to the scene: Titania's fairies were equipped with swatters and brooms and during the song one of them dropped a 'spider' on Titania who reacted with a scream: 'when Titania suggests a song, for instance, the troupe groans as if they were far too adult to waste time on such soppy stuff and one of them dissociates herself from it by coolly eating an enormous spider while singing. When they dance the tubbiest of them rummages with frowning concentration in the back of her frilly knickers' (*Independent*, 13 April 1989).

20–3 Phelps cut these references to unpleasant fauna.

<pre>
                        Hence, you longlegged spinners, hence!
                        Beetles black approach not near;
                        Worm nor snail, do no offence.
        [CHORUS]   Philomel with melody
                        Sing in our sweet lullaby,   25
                    Lulla, lulla, lullaby; lulla, lulla, lullaby.
                        Never harm
                        Nor spell nor charm
                        Come our lovely lady nigh.
                        So good night, with lullaby.   *Titania sleeps.* 30
    SECOND FAIRY
                        Hence, away! Now all is well;
                        One aloof stand sentinel!   [*Exeunt Fairies*]
            Enter OBERON; [*he squeezes the juice on Titania's eyes*]

        OBERON   What thou seest when thou dost wake,
                        Do it for thy true love take;
                        Love and languish for his sake.   35
                        Be it ounce or cat or bear,
                        Pard, or boar with bristled hair
                        In thy eye that shall appear
                        When thou wak'st, it is thy dear.
                        Wake when some vile thing is near!   [*Exit*] 40
                    Enter LYSANDER *and* HERMIA

    LYSANDER Fair love, you faint with wandering in the wood,
</pre>

31–2 Cut by Saker and Daly.

32 SD Benson had Titania's sentinel captured by boys of Oberon's train (promptbook); Fagan's Mustardseed, mounting guard proudly, deserted his post in panic at Oberon's approach (*Daily Telegraph*, 6 December 1920); Bridges Adams had the smallest fairy march up and down guarding Titania with a bulrush until Puck kidnapped her (promptbook). Hall had 'one of the smaller fairies, set to guard Titania as she sleeps, being coshed and carried off in the modern manner' (*Birmingham Mail*, 3 June 1959). In a National Youth Theatre production in 1964 Puck dealt with the sentinel by taking her off 'hand-in-hand and most suggestively, into the bushes' (*Daily Mail*, 1 September). Daniels had a pitched battle between Oberon and the puppet fairies in which Oberon grabbed a puppet's face in one hand with the puppeteer 'screaming and flailing' (promptbook). Caird's sentinel fairy swooned after Puck kissed her.

33 Vestris used a snatch of Beethoven to accompany Oberon's incantation.

41 Reynolds had a scene change to 'Another Part of the Wood' (*Dream*, p. 23) here, with 'Two Banks on RH' for the lovers' resting places and 'Stage a little dark' (promptbook). In Barton's staging, 'when mortals do invade, it is against a background of bald elfin heads peeping

> And, to speak truth, I have forgot our way.
> We'll rest us, Hermia, if you think it good,
> And tarry for the comfort of the day.
> HERMIA Be it so, Lysander; find you out a bed,   45
> For I upon this bank will rest my head.
> LYSANDER One turf shall serve as pillow for us both;
> One heart, one bed, two bosoms, and one troth.
> HERMIA Nay, good Lysander, for my sake, my dear,
> Lie further off yet; do not lie so near.   50
> LYSANDER O take the sense, sweet, of my innocence!
> Love takes the meaning in love's conference;
> I mean that my heart unto yours is knit,
> So that but one heart we can make of it:
> Two bosoms interchainèd with an oath,   55
> So then two bosoms and a single troth.
> Then by your side no bed-room me deny,
> For lying so, Hermia, I do not lie.
> HERMIA Lysander riddles very prettily.
> Now much beshrew my manners and my pride   60
> If Hermia meant to say Lysander lied.
> But, gentle friend, for love and courtesy
> Lie further off, in human modesty;
> Such separation as may well be said
> Becomes a virtuous bachelor and a maid,   65
> So far be distant, and good night, sweet friend;
> Thy love ne'er alter till thy sweet life end!

through the branches and recumbent gnomes serving as footstools' (*Times*, 9 May 1977). Daniels had Hermia and Lysander enter to thunder with a cloak over their heads (prompt-book). Caird's Hermia had 'a mass of hand luggage' (*Guardian*, 13 April 1989).

47–70   The eighteenth-century editor Francis Gentleman led the way in disapproving of these lines which 'should be omitted, for though founded in delicacy, they may raise warm ideas' (Bell, *Dream*, p. 159). Reynolds substituted a duet, Vestris removed all of them, Phelps let 47 and the first half of 49 stand before cutting everything up to the middle of 62, Kean and Saker cut from 47 to 'distant' in 66, Benson cut 50 to 'friend' in 62, 63 and to 'and' in 66 (which produces a scarcely viable reading); Daly removed 51–65, Tree lost 49–58 and 60–1. Twentieth-century directors keep them – the initial change in taste can be pinpointed fairly exactly since Barker, playing a full text, kept them and Kirwan was castigated by the *Morning Post* for cutting 'the beautiful line which immediately follows and rhymes with' 47 and 'Hermia's maidenly reply' which it regarded as 'essentials' (23 April 1914). Latterly the lines have been played for more overt comedy: in Devine's production, Zena Walker 'entreats Lysander to lie further off, but in a way that will ensure his closer attention in the morning'

LYSANDER Amen, amen, to that fair prayer say I,
    And then end life when I end loyalty!
    Here is my bed; sleep give thee all his rest.   70
HERMIA With half that wish the wisher's eyes be pressed.
       They sleep.

       Enter PUCK

PUCK   Through the forest have I gone,
      But Athenian found I none
      On whose eyes I might approve
      This flower's force in stirring love.   75
      Night and silence – Who is here?
      Weeds of Athens he doth wear:
      This is he my master said
      Despisèd the Athenian maid;
      And here the maiden, sleeping sound   80
      On the dank and dirty ground.
      Pretty soul, she durst not lie
      Near this lack-love, this kill-courtesy.
      Churl, upon thy eyes I throw
      All the power this charm doth owe.   85
      [*He squeezes the juice on Lysander's eyes.*]
      When thou wak'st let love forbid
      Sleep his seat on thy eyelid.
      So, awake when I am gone;

(*Coventry Standard*, 26 March 1954); Brook's Lysander made to cross to Hermia at 67, but was stopped by Cobweb (promptbook). Lepage's Lysander, lying down in the ubiquitous mud, got a laugh on 'Here is my bed' (*Times*, 11 July 1992).

71 In Benson's staging, 'When night darkens down, and Hermia falls asleep in the wood, the fairies glide out carrying glowworms of electric light. These glowworms shrink into darkness on the approach of a mortal' (Moyr Smith, *Dream*, p. xv). Caird's Hermia put on her face cream before blowing Lysander a kiss, while he settled down for the night under a news-paper (promptbook).

72–6 Kean and Daly both cut here to produce a more direct opening: Kean went straight from Puck's failure to find an Athenian to 'Night and silence', Daly began the speech with those words. Caird's Puck sent these lines up, chanting them from the New Penguin edition and throwing it away contemptuously before 'Night and silence'.

82–3 Cut by Kean, preserving his audience's modesty.

85 When Barton's Lysander was charmed, 'he writhes violently' (*Observer*, 15 May 1977).

88 Noble had this line directed in aggrieved tones to a Lysander who was attempting to make love to Puck.

> For I must now to Oberon.   *Exit*
>
> *Enter* DEMETRIUS *and* HELENA, *running*

HELENA Stay, though thou kill me, sweet Demetrius!   90
DEMETRIUS I charge thee, hence, and do not haunt me thus.
HELENA O wilt thou darkling leave me? Do not so!
DEMETRIUS Stay, on thy peril; I alone will go.   *Exit*
HELENA O, I am out of breath in this fond chase!
　　　The more my prayer, the lesser is my grace.   95
　　　Happy is Hermia, wheresoe'er she lies,
　　　For she hath blessèd and attractive eyes.
　　　How came her eyes so bright? Not with salt tears –
　　　If so, my eyes are oftener washed than hers.
　　　No, no, I am as ugly as a bear,   100
　　　For beasts that meet me run away for fear.
　　　Therefore no marvel though Demetrius
　　　Do as a monster fly my presence thus.
　　　What wicked and dissembling glass of mine
　　　Made me compare with Hermia's sphery eyne?   105
　　　But who is here? – Lysander, on the ground?
　　　Dead, or asleep? I see no blood, no wound.
　　　Lysander, if you live, good sir, awake!
LYSANDER [*Waking.*]
　　　And run through fire I will for thy sweet sake!
　　　Transparent Helena, nature shows art   110
　　　That through thy bosom makes me see thy heart.
　　　Where is Demetrius? O, how fit a word
　　　Is that vile name to perish on my sword!
HELENA Do not say so, Lysander, say not so.
　　　What though he love your Hermia? Lord, what though? 115
　　　Yet Hermia still loves you; then be content.
LYSANDER Content with Hermia? No; I do repent

90　In Noble's production, 'stay' was like a command to a dog.
93　Alexander's Demetrius threatened Helena with his fist (promptbook).
94–105　Helena's loquaciousness often led to cuts: Vestris, Kean, Saker, Daly and Tree removed
　　98–105; Phelps ended his cut with 103. Benson cut 101–3, Atkins 100–5, Devine 102–3.
109　Caird's Lysander initially pursued Helena on all fours.
110　'Transparent' sometimes leads modern directors to give Helena a gesture indicating her
　　modest apprehension that her bosom is visible. Langham's Helena 'must perforce look
　　behind her' (*Daily Mail*, 21 December 1960); Caird's crossed her hands over her chest.
117–28　Vestris cut 'I do repent', 118 and 120–6. Similarly, Lysander's unreasonable 'reasons' were cut

The tedious minutes I with her have spent.
Not Hermia, but Helena I love.
Who will not change a raven for a dove?   120
The will of man is by his reason swayed,
And reason says you are the worthier maid.
Things growing are not ripe until their season;
So I, being young, till now ripe not to reason.
And touching now the point of human skill,   125
Reason becomes the marshal to my will.
And leads me to your eyes, where I o'erlook
Love's stories written in love's richest book.

HELENA Wherefore was I to this keen mockery born?
When at your hands did I deserve this scorn?   130
Is't not enough, is't not enough, young man,
That I did never, no, nor never can
Deserve a sweet look from Demetrius' eye
But you must flout my insufficiency?
Good troth, you do me wrong, good sooth, you do,   135
In such disdainful manner me to woo!
But fare you well: perforce I must confess
I thought you lord of more true gentleness.
O, that a lady of one man refused
Should of another therefore be abused!   *Exit*   140

LYSANDER She sees not Hermia. Hermia, sleep thou there,
And never mayst thou come Lysander near.
For, as a surfeit of the sweetest things
The deepest loathing to the stomach brings,
Or as the heresies that men do leave   145
Are hated most of those they did deceive,
So thou, my surfeit and my heresy,

---

by Phelps, Kean, Saker, Daly (120–5) and Atkins (121–8); Benson cut 123–8 and Tree's cuts
ran from 123 to 126.

131–50   Nineteenth-century directors toned down the reversal and the strength of language here
through cutting. Vestris, who was not given to minor verbal rearrangements, altered 131–2
to read 'Is't not enough that I never did nor can', and 147–9 to 'So thou, my heresy, of all be
hated, but most of me! And henceforth be my delight' and cut 136, 139–40 and 143–4. Phelps
cut 143–7; Kean, Saker, Daly (who also cut 131–4) and Benson removed 143–8; Tree cut
139–40 and 143–7.

137   Daniels gave emphasis to Helena's change of tack by having her tie up her bonnet.

138–40   Helena's complaint in Caird's staging owed something to Lysander working his way up
her leg with kisses and biting her leg and bottom.

> Of all be hated, but the most of me!
> And, all my powers, address your love and might
> To honour Helen, and to be her knight.   *Exit*   150
> HERMIA [*Waking.*]
> Help me, Lysander, help me! Do thy best
> To pluck this crawling serpent from my breast!
> Ay me, for pity! What a dream was here!
> Lysander, look how I do quake with fear –
> Methought a serpent ate my heart away,   155
> And you sat smiling at his cruel prey.
> Lysander! What, removed? Lysander, lord!
> What, out of hearing? Gone? No sound, no word?
> Alack, where are you? Speak and if you hear.
> Speak, of all loves! I swoon almost with fear.   160
> No? Then I well perceive you are not nigh.
> Either death or you I'll find immediately.   *Exit*

151   Reynolds's Hermia had a song on waking in which she calls on the 'harbingers of morning'
      who are indulging in a 'Bird Symphony' to 'cease your song and take your flight' because
      'while your tuneful notes thus vibrate through the wood, in vain I call upon my lost, lost love'
      (*Dream*, p. 27). In Alexander's staging, Hermia 'does snake acting with rucksack' (prompt-
      book). Noble's Hermia, lying on top of one of the doors that had retracted into the stage
      floor, appeared to levitate before waking from her dream.

157   Ada Ferrar, for Benson, was praised for 'the something very near tragedy of her awakening
      alone and no Lysander by' (Stratford *Herald*, 22 April 1903).

158   Cut by Kean, who had to change the last word in 157 to 'dear' in order to maintain the rhyme
      scheme.

160–2 Vestris, who added an exit cry of 'Lysander, Lord Lysander', cut 160–2; Saker cut 160; Daly
      cut 161–2. Tree went one better than Vestris, accompanying Hermia's shouts with birds and
      music in the orchestra. In Brook's production, 'the forest terrors which drive off the forsaken
      Hermia turn ... into the sounds of the approaching mechanicals' (*Observer*, 13 June 1971).
      In Alexander's staging Hermia took Lysander's rucksack off with her, Caird's Hermia remem-
      bered to take her coat and bag off with her.

Enter the Clowns [, BOTTOM, QUINCE, SNOUT, STARVELING, SNUG
and FLUTE. TITANIA remains on stage, asleep]

BOTTOM Are we all met?

QUINCE Pat, pat; and here's a marvellous convenient place for our
rehearsal. This green plot shall be our stage, this hawthorn brake
our tiring-house, and we will do it in action as we will do it before
the Duke.   5

BOTTOM Peter Quince!

QUINCE What sayest thou, bully Bottom?

BOTTOM There are things in this comedy of Pyramus and Thisbe that
will never please. First, Pyramus must draw a sword to kill himself,
which the ladies cannot abide. How answer you that?   10

SNOUT By'r lakin, a parlous fear!

STARVELING I believe we must leave the killing out, when all is done.

BOTTOM Not a whit; I have a device to make all well. Write me a
prologue, and let the prologue seem to say we will do no harm with

---

0 SD   Although the scene was sometimes played in yet another part of the forest, most stagings
using realistic wood scenes placed it close to Titania's sleeping place. At Stratford in 1926,
the Mechanicals were seen 'winding along a roundabout path and eventually arriving at the
place of rehearsal by sliding down a mossy bank' (BSL cutting). Dunlop's modern dress
Mechanicals were 'first seen in the forest rolling drunk, delighted over their singing of
"Strolling"' (*Plays and Players*, December 1967). In Daniels's staging, the rain which had
been continuous in the woods stopped and the Mechanicals were able to put their umbrellas
down. Throughout the scene Caird's Starveling was busily occupied with costumes, handing
Flute a skirt and measuring Snout. Noble's Starveling tried on the dress he was scheduled to
wear as Thisbe's mother. Like Brook, Bryden had his fairies 'mingle with the mechanicals in
rehearsal like watching shadows' (*Guardian*, in *LTR* 1982).

2   Irving Wardle objected that the laugh Lepage's Quince got on this line 'arriving in a mos-
quito-infested swamp' was against the text (*Independent on Sunday*, 12 July 1992), although
something similar presumably occurred in the original production as Quince went on to suggest that the actual tiring house was a hawthorn brake that could serve as a tiring house.

13–20   Kean had nothing to do with prologues or metrical niceties, cutting direct to concern about
the Lion; Saker and Daly cut all the discussion of the metrics of the proposed prologue.

our swords, and that Pyramus is not killed indeed; and for the more 15
better assurance, tell them that I, Pyramus, am not Pyramus, but
Bottom the weaver: this will put them out of fear.

QUINCE Well, we will have such a prologue; and it shall be written in
eight and six.

BOTTOM No, make it two more: let it be written in eight and eight. 20

SNOUT Will not the ladies be afeard of the lion?

STARVELING I fear it, I promise you.

BOTTOM Masters, you ought to consider with yourself, to bring in (God
shield us!) a lion among ladies is a most dreadful thing; for there
is not a more fearful wildfowl than your lion living; and we ought 25
to look to't.

SNOUT Therefore another prologue must tell he is not a lion.

BOTTOM Nay, you must name his name, and half his face must be seen
through the lion's neck, and he himself must speak through, saying
thus, or to the same defect: 'Ladies', or 'Fair ladies, I would wish 30
you', or 'I would request you', or 'I would entreat you, not to fear,
not to tremble: my life for yours. If you think I come hither as
a lion, it were pity of my life. No, I am no such thing; I am a man,
as other men are' – and there indeed let him name his name, and
tell them plainly he is Snug the joiner. 35

QUINCE Well, it shall be so. But there is two hard things: that is, to
bring the moonlight into a chamber; for, you know, Pyramus and
Thisbe meet by moonlight.

SNUG Doth the moon shine that night we play our play?

20 At the end of the line, after a pause, Caird's Snug had '3 jump roars', thus motivating
the next line, which was also followed by a pause and another roar and jump (promptbook).

21 In Reynolds's version, the problem of the ladies' fear of the Lion was raised by Bottom, but
would, in his words be 'quantified by my delicate colouring' (*Dream*, p. 29).

22 Spoken by Snug in Benson's and Tree's versions. Snug is otherwise silent in this scene,
unless he speaks 39 (which is given to Snout in F2, where Qq and F simply have the abbrevi-
ation Sn.) or 51 (where Q2 and F have Sn). See also the discussion at 51.

23–4 Kean and Saker omitted 'God shield us', presumably on religious grounds.

27 Kean left out 'Therefore'.

28ff. Bottom, in Caird's staging, directed Snug during this speech, moving him about as he made
suggestions, which Quince wrote down.

31–2 Kean reduced Bottom's attempts at delicacy by removing 'or, "I would request you", or
"I would entreat you"' and '"my life for yours"'.

39–45 Vestris made Bottom less excitable by the removal of 40–1 and she and her company were
censured by *John Bull* for attempting 'to render Shakespeare correct by omitting what these
gentry conceive to be an anachronism' (21 November 1840); Kean cut 39–45, removing the

BOTTOM A calendar, a calendar! Look in the almanac – find out 40
moonshine, find out moonshine!
QUINCE Yes, it doth shine that night.
BOTTOM Why, then may you leave a casement of the great chamber
window, where we play, open, and the moon may shine in at the
casement. 45
QUINCE Ay; or else one must come in with a bush of thorns and a
lantern, and say he comes to disfigure, or to present the person of
Moonshine. Then there is another thing: we must have a wall in
the great chamber; for Pyramus and Thisbe, says the story, did talk
through the chink of a wall. 50
SNOUT You can never bring in a wall. What say you, Bottom?
BOTTOM Some man or other must present Wall; and let him have some
plaster, or some loam, or some rough-cast about him to signify Wall;
or let him hold his fingers thus, and through that cranny shall
Pyramus and Thisbe whisper. 55
QUINCE If that may be, then all is well. Come, sit down every mother's
son, and rehearse your parts. Pyramus, you begin. When you have
spoken your speech, enter into that brake, and so everyone
according to his cue.

Enter PUCK

PUCK What hempen homespuns have we swaggering here 60
So near the cradle of the Fairy Queen?
What, a play toward? I'll be an auditor,
An actor too perhaps, if I see cause.

debate about alternative methods of presenting Moonshine. Brook's Moth threw down the
almanac from the gallery (promptbook).
46–8 Kean gave these lines to Bottom, cutting 'Ay; or else' and reverting to Quince at 'Then'.
51 Kean and Benson gave the line to Snug. This attribution is potentially more comic since the
joiner would, presumably, have been responsible for constructing the stage wall. Q1 has the
unambiguous speech prefix 'Sno.' but Q2 and F have 'Sn.' (See also 22 above and Foakes's
notes to 39 and 51).
52 When Bottom resolved the problem of how to present Wall in Reynolds's version he was
'smiling contemptuously' (*Dream*, p. 29).
53 Kean corrected 'loam' to 'lime'.
60–3 Cut by Kean, whose Puck intervened silently. Tree's Puck 'tickles Quin with wand; ditto Bot,
then Snout, Starv, & Snug. Then Snout again who thinking it is Star pushes him over. Star
yells. Quin says: "Sit down[.]" Puck tickles Bot's legs 3 times, he thinking it is a fly tries to
catch it[.] Puck buzzes, all rise and try to catch it. then Quin goes on with book'; Bridges
Adams's Puck made Snout, Snug and Starveling sneeze by touching them on the shoulder;

QUINCE Speak, Pyramus! Thisbe, stand forth!

BOTTOM (*as Pyramus*)
        Thisbe, the flowers of odious savours sweet –   65

QUINCE Odours – 'odorous'!

BOTTOM (*as Pyramus*)   ...odours savours sweet.
        So hath thy breath, my dearest Thisbe dear.
        But hark, a voice! Stay thou but here awhile,
        And by and by I will to thee appear.   *Exit* 70

PUCK A stranger Pyramus than e'er played here.   [*Exit*]

FLUTE Must I speak now?

QUINCE Ay, marry must you; for you must understand he goes but to
    see a noise that he heard, and is to come again.

FLUTE (*as Thisbe*)
        Most radiant Pyramus, most lilywhite of hue,   75
          Of colour like the red rose on triumphant briar,
        Most brisky juvenal, and eke most lovely Jew,
          As true as truest horse that yet would never tire,
        I'll meet thee, Pyramus, at Ninny's tomb –

QUINCE 'Ninus' tomb', man! – Why, you must not speak that yet; that   80
    you answer to Pyramus. You speak all your part at once, cues and
    all. Pyramus, enter – your cue is past. It is 'never tire'.

FLUTE O –
    (*as Thisbe*)
    As true as truest horse, that yet would never tire.

    Enter PUCK, *and* BOTTOM *with the ass head on*

Brook's Puck checked Quince's promptbook and stepped on Bottom's foot (promptbooks).
Daniels had Puck enter through the bottom of a theatrical skip (promptbook). Alexander's
Puck took Quince's script, handing it back once he had found out what was going on.

66   Daly's Bottom had a fit of prima donna nerves when corrected by Quince and had to be
      coaxed to resume by Snug and Snout (promptbook).

71   Cut by Kean.

75   Tree's (deaf) Starveling thought Flute's assumed voice was a bird singing (promptbook).
      Daniels's Flute was one of many who had trouble with his female voice: Quince had to say
      the lines with him in an appropriate way and rearrange him from a 'butch' pose to a more
      'feminine' one (promptbook).

84 SD The wording of the F SD (which has Piramus for Bottom) indicates the use of a prop ass head in
      the original production. The nature of the ass head can be crucial to an actor's ability to play
      Bottom's translated scenes effectively, as one of Phelps's letters to his wife from a touring
      engagement shows: 'I am very glad I have brought the Donkeys head, for though they have a
      new one it is not good – it is a most <u>impudent</u> looking ass instead of the <u>stupid</u> sleek thing it

should be for Bottom – it looks impossible that it should <u>sleep</u> – I should be dreadfully annoyed if I had to wear it' (letter dated 21 April 1867, now in HTC). Although conventional (realistic) ass heads had working ears and mouths by 1833 when Bunn's promptbook notes here 'the ears of the Ass made to move', many of them caused problems for their wearers: Asche, for example, made 'as much as possible of Bottom in the episode of Titania's spell and infatuation, but here the ass's head deprives the actor of the effects of his facial play' (HTC cutting, 30 November 1905) and John Slater in Benthall's 1949 production was 'utterly extinguished by the ass's head' (*Times*, 25 April). Alfred Clark in Fagan's production was notable precisely for his skill in manipulating the strings in his mask, and for avoiding 'the disaster that befalls most Bottoms, who are simply engulfed in their head as in a cavern' (*Athenaeum*, 17 December 1920). Perhaps unsurprisingly, the music-hall trained comedians coped well with their ass heads: Jay Laurier had one 'which winked a wicked eye, cocked its ears, and brayed' (*News Chronicle*, 8 April 1942); Stanley Holloway 'was able to synchronise speech and braying with teeth movements and ear wiggling' (*Little Bit o' Luck*, p. 302) and Frankie Howerd 'made excellent use of the ass's head, cocking his ears and rolling the eyes to great effect' (*Education*, 10 January 1958).

In order to tackle the problems posed by the traditional ass head, directors in the twentieth century have tried more skeletal alternatives, often involving some kind of skull cap with ass's ears: Harcourt Williams devised a light mask for Ralph Richardson in 1931 which left his eyes visible and 'added greatly to his power of expression as the donkey' (*Four Years*, p. 128). Paul Rogers ran into trouble with his non-traditional head in Guthrie's 1951 staging: 'his "translation" is, anyhow, muffed by his being deprived of the traditional ass's head and fitted out merely with an expressionistic straw bonnet which does not disguise him at all' (*Guardian*, 28 December). In Hall's production, Charles Laughton was not given a full ass head, just 'immense flapping ears' (*Birmingham Post*, 2 June 1959), which enabled him to use his face in the translation scenes to great effect and without critical disapproval. Perhaps the most surprising aspect of Tony Richardson's much-disliked production was the ass head: 'Jocelyn Herbert had designed a superb ass's head, complete with mobile eyes and a pair of most expressive twitching ears. A jaunty half-face mask can make the scene of Bottom's "translation" seem slightly whimsical, but this huge and lugubrious head raises it to something much sadder and more macabre – comparable in tone to Cocteau's *Beauty and the Beast*' (*Spectator*, 2 February 1962). Brook gave his Bottom a clown-like nose, a cap with ears, and hoofs: Barton's had long ears and furry gloves, Daniels's was conventional but 'for once genuinely frightening' (*Guardian*, 16 July 1981). In Branagh's production, Richard Briers's 'transformation into an ass seemed to be merely a medical problem of large, malformed ears' (*Evening Standard*, 22 August 1990). Puck in Alexander's staging stripped off Bottom's shirt and gave him a fur balaclava with ears. Probably the most striking of all translations was Timothy Spall's in Lepage's production: Angela Laurier as Puck 'twines her legs around his neck with her feet sticking out looking like ass's ears' (*Financial Times*, 11 July 1992). Noble's Bottom, Desmond Barrit, habitually wore an old-fashioned motorbike crash helmet which became the frame for his ass's ears and he was given false teeth as the ass.

BOTTOM (*as Pyramus*)
       If I were fair, fair Thisbe, I were only thine.   85
QUINCE O monstrous! O strange! We are haunted! Pray, masters, fly,
   masters! Help!
         Exeunt Quince, Snug, Flute, Snout and Starveling
PUCK   I'll follow you: I'll lead you about a round,
       Through bog, through bush, through brake, through briar;
       Sometime a horse I'll be, sometime a hound,   90
        A hog, a headless bear, sometime a fire,
      And neigh, and bark, and grunt, and roar, and burn,
      Like horse, hound, hog, bear, fire at every turn.   *Exit*
BOTTOM Why do they run away? This is a knavery of them to make
   me afeard.   95

Enter SNOUT

SNOUT O Bottom, thou art changed. What do I see on thee?
BOTTOM What do you see? You see an ass head of your own, do you?
                          [*Exit Snout*]

Enter QUINCE

QUINCE Bless thee, Bottom, bless thee! Thou art translated!   *Exit*

85   At 'only thine' in Alexander's staging, 'All clock B' (promptbook).
88–93 Vestris, Kean, Tree and Atkins cut all these lines to give a scene which concentrated on
      Bottom, and the Mechanicals' reactions to him, minimising Puck's role; Phelps, Benson and
      Daly cut 90–3. Kean's rejection of the lines may well reflect his choice of the eight-year-old
      Ellen Terry to play Puck. Barker's Puck chased, pinched, and tripped the Mechanicals. In
      Reinhardt's film, special camerawork transformed Puck rather literal-mindedly into hog,
      bear and fire. In the post-translation fracas in Daniels's staging, Puck threw boas from the
      skip at various Mechanicals and spun an umbrella wildly (promptbooks).
96–7 Kean and Saker gilded the lily, adding 'An ass's head' to Snout's line; Atkins, who presum-
      ably disliked Bottom's metatheatrical reference to his own condition, cut both lines. In
      Daniels's staging Snug 'takes refuge in the property basket during the transformation scene,
      emerging when he thinks everyone else has gone to find himself staring straight into
      Bottom's braying muzzle' (*Times*, 16 July 1981); Alexander's Snout had come back for his hat.
98   Barker's Quince was attempting to recover the property basket when he met Bottom again;
      Langham, typically, added a cry for help to motivate Quince's exit (promptbooks).
      Alexander's Quince had come back for his briefcase.

BOTTOM I see their knavery. This is to make an ass of me, to fright
    me, if they could; but I will not stir from this place, do what they   100
    can. I will walk up and down here, and will sing, that they shall
    hear I am not afraid.
    [*Sings.*] The ousel cock so black of hue,
             With orange-tawny bill,
             The throstle with his note so true,   105
             The wren with little quill –
TITANIA [*Waking.*] What angel wakes me from my flowery bed?

BOTTOM [*Sings.*]
             The finch, the sparrow, and the lark,
             The plainsong cuckoo grey,
             Whose note full many a man doth mark   110
             And dares not answer nay –
    for indeed, who would set his wit to so foolish a bird? Who would
    give a bird the lie, though he cry 'cuckoo' never so?
TITANIA I pray thee, gentle mortal, sing again;
             Mine ear is much enamoured of thy note.   115
             So is mine eye enthrallèd to thy shape,
             And thy fair virtue's force perforce doth move me
             On the first view to say, to swear, I love thee.

107   In the Reinhardt film, the Indian Boy is very clearly deserted by Titania because she has
       acquired a more substantial object of her affection in the shape of the translated Bottom.

111   Bottom's 'nay' is an open invitation for the actor to elongate it into a neigh. The *Birmingham
       Post* praised Alfred Clark, in Fagan's production, for his laugh that became a bray
       (6 December 1920).

112–13   Vestris created a sharper contrast between Bottom's singing and Titania's response to it by
       omitting these somewhat obscure lines – as later did Kean, Saker, Daly, Tree, Atkins, Bridges
       Adams, Benthall, Devine and Hall.

114   There are two schools of thought about how Bottom should react to Titania: in 1911 Crosse
       thought that Bourchier's 'alarm when Titania first accosts him was out of place, and he did
       not take his new position calmly as a matter of course, as the true Bottom does' (*Diary* V,
       p. 57), whereas Wolfit, though 'perhaps not quite stolid enough' in 1941, 'showed he under-
       stood the character by not appearing alarmed when Titania first addresses him. He rightly
       took her advances as a matter of course.' (*Diary* XVII, p. 145). In Daniels's staging, 'Geoffrey
       Hutchings presents a Lancashire Bottom complete with waistcoat and watch-chain, living up
       to his work-mates' high opinion, splendidly in control of the situation with Juliet Stevenson's
       Titania' (*Times*, 16 July 1981). Not only was he not very surprised by Titania's advances, but
       'he played with the fairies as if they were his own kids' (*Financial Times*, in *LTR* 1982).

118   Caird's fairies started to giggle here, but were stopped by Titania.

BOTTOM Methinks, mistress, you should have little reason for that. And
    yet, to say the truth, reason and love keep little company together   120
    nowadays; the more the pity that some honest neighbours will not
    make them friends. Nay, I can gleek upon occasion.
TITANIA Thou art as wise as thou art beautiful.
BOTTOM Not so neither; but if I had wit enough to get out of this wood,
    I have enough to serve mine own turn.   125
TITANIA Out of this wood do not desire to go:
    Thou shalt remain here, whether thou wilt or no.
    I am a spirit of no common rate;
    The summer still doth tend upon my state,
    And I do love thee. Therefore go with me.   130
    I'll give thee fairies to attend on thee,
    And they shall fetch thee jewels from the deep,
    And sing, while thou on pressèd flowers dost sleep;
    And I will purge thy mortal grossness so
    That thou shalt like an airy spirit go.   135
    Peaseblossom, Cobweb, Moth, and Mustardseed!

119   In Reynolds's version, Bottom's reaction to Titania's declaration of love is an escape attempt, which provides a stronger motivation for her subsequent reaction than the Shakespearean lines.

121–2   Vestris, Daly and Hall omitted the last part of 122 with its obscure 'gleek'; Kean cut from 'the more'.

123   Alexander's Titania 'falls breathily for Bottom crying [the line] in tones of rapt wonderment' (*Guardian*, 10 July 1986).

126   In Hall's revival Judi Dench was 'formidable' and when she spoke the line Bottom 'blenches. This, he realises, is no lady. As he withdraws with her, you sense the old Bottom-brain seething with dumb questions. Should he speak again? And just how does one lie with a fairy?' (*New Statesman*, 27 April 1962). Caird's Titania 'zapped' Bottom and the fairies mimed pulling him back on a rope, tying him to the bedstead that served as a bower. Spall, for Lepage, was 'a sad figure, more frightened than puzzled by his transformation, more in danger of going mad than into ecstacy' (*Financial Times*, 11 July 1992).

127   Daniels had Bottom trip and fall to the ground at 'wilt or no' (promptbook).

128   Cut by Kean, followed as usual by Saker, possibly as sacrilegious?

130   Laughton 'moved with bewildered courtesy into the arms of Titania', 'his braying and undisguised lust for Titania... are gems of wit' (*Evening Standard*, 3 June, Stratford *Herald*, 5 June 1959). At 'love thee' Brook's Titania jumped on Bottom with her legs around his waist (promptbook).

132–5   Cut by Kean (and Saker); Atkins cut 134–5. Perhaps Titania is close to sacrilege again?

136   When Titania called for the fairies in Bunn's 1833 version, Bottom reacted thus: 'There the

Enter four Fairies.

PEASEBLOSSOM Ready.
COBWEB And I.
MOTH And I.
MUSTARDSEED And I.   140
ALL Where shall we go?
TITANIA Be kind and courteous to this gentleman:
    Hop in his walks and gambol in his eyes;
    Feed him with apricocks and dewberries,
    With purple grapes, green figs, and mulberries;   145
    The honey-bags steal from the humble-bees,
    And for night-tapers crop their waxen thighs,
    And light them at the fiery glow-worms' eyes
    To have my love to bed, and to arise;
    And pluck the wings from painted butterflies   150
    To fan the moonbeams from his sleeping eyes.
    Nod to him, elves, and do him courtesies.
PEASEBLOSSOM Hail, mortal!
COBWEB Hail!
MOTH Hail!   155
MUSTARDSEED Hail!
BOTTOM I cry your worships mercy, heartily. I beseech your **worship's**
    name.
COBWEB Cobweb.
BOTTOM I shall desire you of more acquaintance, good Master **Cobweb**;   160
    if I cut my finger I shall make bold with you. Your name, honest
    gentleman?
PEASEBLOSSOM Peaseblossom.

large ears move and he reclines his head on her shoulder' (promptbook). **Hall's fairies here**
were dressed in costumes appropriate to their names. Noble's included the **other Mechanicals**
as the named fairies, adding a further dimension to the intermingling of **the worlds** of
Athens and the wood.
140 Barker's Bottom was given to bursts of sneezing as the result of his contact **with**
    Mustardseed (promptbook).
142 When the fairies saw Bottom in Alexander's staging, they ran behind Titania **to hide**.
144–51 These lines, a powerful reminder of the inevitable discrepancy between the **imagined** size
    of the fairies and their actual size, were cut by Kean; Saker cut from 147, **Atkins from 145**.
157–73 Kean cut the obscure references to squash and peascod and performed similar **surgery** on
    the ox-beef joke, ending 169 with 'you' (for 'your') and picking 171 up at 'I **promise you**'. Tree
    cut everything.

BOTTOM I pray you commend me to Mistress Squash, your mother, and to Master Peascod, your father. Good Master Peaseblossom, 165
    I shall desire you of more acquaintance, too. – Your name, I beseech you, sir?

MUSTARDSEED Mustardseed.

BOTTOM Good Master Mustardseed, I know your patience well. That same cowardly, giant-like ox-beef hath devoured many a gentleman 170
    of your house. I promise you, your kindred hath made my eyes water ere now. I desire you of more acquaintance, good Master Mustardseed.

TITANIA Come, wait upon him. Lead him to my bower.
    The moon methinks looks with a watery eye, 175
  And when she weeps, weeps every little flower,
    Lamenting some enforcèd chastity.
    Tie up my lover's tongue; bring him silently.

                                         Exeunt

175–8   Cut by Daly; Kean cut 176–7. At 'heartily' Alexander's Cobweb fell over and Bottom picked her up.

177   Reynolds's scene ended, inevitably, with a dance for the fairies and Bottom; Vestris too had her fairies dance and lead Bottom and Titania off, albeit to the accompaniment of Weber's *Preciosa*. Benson had a garland dance and tableau of Bottom and Titania; Tree had his fairies pointing at Bottom to end the act with an emphasis on his translation ; Atkins's Bottom neighed to give a stronger motivation to Titania's exit line (promptbooks). In Reinhardt's film, James Cagney's Bottom, insouciant with Titania, is treated to a full-scale parody wedding ceremony. Hall had a sprinkling of rose petals 'on the couch where Titania and Bottom lay, golden light seeming to linger enchantedly on the falling petals even when darkness was complete and the hush held the audience silent' (*Glasgow Herald*, 3 June 1959). Brook's first half ended with a triumphal parodic wedding procession with paper plates and streamers being thrown as Bottom was chaired off with an erect phallus created by an actor's arm between his legs (promptbook), while 'Oberon swings across on a trapeze to the roar of Mendelssohn's Wedding March'; it was 'an occasion for real sexual revels and not a joke against an outclassed clodpole' (*Times*, 28 August 1970).

ACT 3, SCENE 2

Enter OBERON, *King of Fairies*

OBERON I wonder if Titania be awaked;
        Then what it was that next came in her eye,
        Which she must dote on, in extremity.

Enter PUCK

        Here comes my messenger. How now, mad spirit?
        What night-rule now about this haunted grove?   5
PUCK My mistress with a monster is in love.
        Near to her close and consecrated bower,
        While she was in her dull and sleeping hour,
        A crew of patches, rude mechanicals,
        That work for bread upon Athenian stalls,   10
        Were met together to rehearse a play
        Intended for great Theseus' nuptial day.
        The shallowest thick-skin of that barren sort,
        Who Pyramus presented, in their sport
        Forsook his scene and entered in a brake,   15

---

0 SD   Vestris set this scene in yet another part of the wood, with a distant view of a lake; Fagan's unchanging wood was criticised by the *Daily Telegraph* (6 December 1920) for confining action which 'in the original supposes three different settings' to one place. In Brook's staging, 'I have never seen a more nightmarish presentation of a forest than the animation of those springs [coils of wire on fishing rods flown in by fairies on the catwalks] into reptilian coils trapping Hermia and snaking out over the audience's heads' (*Times*, 11 June 1971).

1–4   Daly began with Oberon's greeting to Puck, cutting his soliloquy. Caird had Oberon putting back on his strap-on 'little pointy wings ... with the prosaic weariness of someone slipping his dentures back in of a morning' (*Independent*, 13 April 1989).

6–32   In the eighteenth century, Francis Gentleman put a case for cutting here which has been followed by many directors: 'Though Puck's narration possesses spirit, ease, and painting, yet as it only recites what is already known, and not with uncommon force or humour, we think the scene would begin better with Oberon's speech, supposing he had heard all from his attendant spirit before they appear' (Bell, *Dream*, p. 169). The scene usually follows an interval, after the

When I did him at this advantage take:
An ass's nole I fixèd on his head.
Anon his Thisbe must be answerèd,
And forth my mimic comes. When they him spy –
As wild geese that the creeping fowler eye,   20
Or russet-pated choughs, many in sort,
Rising and cawing at the gun's report,
Sever themselves and madly sweep the sky –
So at his sight away his fellows fly,
And at our stamp here o'er and o'er one falls;   25
He 'Murder!' cries, and help from Athens calls.
Their sense thus weak, lost with their fears thus strong,
Made senseless things begin to do them wrong,
For briars and thorns at their apparel snatch,
Some sleeves, some hats; from yielders all things catch.   30
I led them on in this distracted fear,
And left sweet Pyramus translated there;
When in that moment, so it came to pass,
Titania waked, and straightway loved an ass.

OBERON This falls out better than I could devise.   35
But hast thou yet latched the Athenian's eyes
With the love juice, as I did bid thee do?

PUCK I took him sleeping – that is finished too –
And the Athenian woman by his side,
That when he waked, of force she must be eyed.   40

Enter DEMETRIUS *and* HERMIA

OBERON Stand close: this is the same Athenian.
PUCK This is the woman, but not this the man.
DEMETRIUS O, why rebuke you him that loves you so?

first part in two-part productions, after the second act in three-act stagings, so the speech serves
a useful recapitulatory function which may have saved it from even more frequent and deeper
cutting. Vestris cut 21–2 and 24–32, Phelps 20–30, Kean (and Saker) 15–16, 18–23, 25–32, Benson
20–3, Daly 20–3, 27–30 and Tree 18–23 and 25–32. Twentieth-century directors have been more
sparing in their alterations: Atkins and Hall cut 20–3, Bridges Adams, Devine, Hall and Langham
25–30. Atkins also cut from 27 to 30. Alexander began with a tableau illustrating Puck's account
of the action so far, with characters unfreezing as their descriptions were given, so that
Demetrius and Hermia came to life at 40. In Caird's staging, Puck pulled at Oberon's clothes
during his long speech, stealing his scarf which he gave back at 'from yielders'.

35   Caird's Puck was visibly relieved that Oberon was happy.

42   In Caird's production Puck slunk off when he realised his mistake.

43ff.   The lovers' quarrels were very heavily cut and often rearranged in this, the most heavily cut

Lay breath so bitter on your bitter foe.
HERMIA Now I but chide; but I should use thee worse,   45
For thou, I fear, hast given me cause to curse.
If thou hast slain Lysander in his sleep,
Being o'er shoes in blood, plunge in the deep,
And kill me too.
The sun was not so true unto the day   50
As he to me. Would he have stol'n away
From sleeping Hermia? I'll believe as soon
This whole earth may be bored, and that the moon
May through the centre creep, and so displease
Her brother's noontide with th'Antipodes.   55
It cannot be but thou hast murdered him:
So should a murderer look; so dead, so grim.
DEMETRIUS So should the murdered look, and so should I,
Pierced through the heart with your stern cruelty;
Yet you, the murderer, look as bright, as clear,   60
As yonder Venus in her glimmering sphere.

scene in nineteenth-century stagings of the *Dream*. Sometimes whole exchanges were removed, sometimes there were substantial cuts in longer speeches. Vestris and Phelps, who each cut around 20 per cent of the play overall, cut around 30 per cent of this scene; Kean, who cut about 40 per cent elsewhere, removed some 60 per cent here. Their approach was applauded by most critics who found the scenes tedious and the lovers hard to tell apart. For this reason, the German novelist Theodor Fontane welcomed Kean's colour coding of the lovers: 'Lysander, dressed in light brown, belongs to Hermia, who wears light blue, and Demetrius, dressed in light blue, belongs to Helena, who wears light brown' (*Aus England*, p. 48). Daly's third act, for example, was 'judiciously compressed, so that the spectator might not see too much of the perplexed and wrangling lovers' (Winter, *Shrines*, p. 173). While an uncut version might have been less tedious, it would almost certainly have been unacceptable on grounds of decorum. After 1900, partly under Benson's influence, the lovers were increasingly often played for comedy: Crosse, for example, objected to 'rather too much farce and horse-play' in their scenes when he saw Benson's production in 1900 (Diary II, p. 110) and Lily Brayton and Frances Dillon 'put remarkable fire into the quarrelling scene' for Asche in 1905 (*Sketch*, 6 December). Reinhardt filmed many of the lovers' quarrels as simultaneous dialogues, thereby reducing their 'tedium' but also keeping some of their flavour. Guthrie's 1937 pastiche Victorian *Dream* was probably at its least Victorian in the presentation of the lovers, since he played the quarrel 'with an admirable mixture of shrewishness and full-blooded fun' (*Daily Express*, 28 December 1937), in a manner reminiscent of 'a French farce adapted for the English stage' (*London Mercury*, February 1938).

Benthall's 1949 lovers represented the contemporary state of the art: 'the Hermia, Penelope Munday, reacts to the turn of fortune with fierce zest and Clement McCallin's

Lysander is just the boy for this girl – flamboyant in word and movement. Peter Norris keeps Demetrius more on the solid ways of convention and makes him a bit of a prig. Diana Wynyard as Helena, pursues this worthy object with twittering insistence which is still glamorous in clamour' (*Stage*, 25 April).

In 1951 Guthrie was being castigated for spoiling 'some of the most delicious comedy ever written by intruding tumbles and rompings' (*Guardian*, 28 December) and old critical reservations lingered throughout the 1950s: for Devine 'the two pairs of lovers began conventionally enough, but they played their changes of allegiance and pursuits through the wood and counterpointed accusations and cross-accusations with such verve that before long the audience warmed to them' (*Leamington Courier*, 26 March 1954); Langham's lovers, 'so often tedious, are called upon to provide ruthlessly savage slapstick' (*Daily Mail*, 21 December 1960). The lovers are now not only firmly comic, but ever more athletic: Daniels's Hermia 'graduates from Jane Austen-like demureness to raucous man-beating energy and passion in the vigorously animated sequences in the second half' (*Guardian*, in *LTR* 1982); Alexander's was 'quick to seize her defecting lover by the ankles like a grim terrier' (*Guardian*, 20 August 1987); Caird's Helena went in for judo throws. It is difficult to see how much further this line can be developed after reaching its zenith (or nadir) with the literally muddied lovers lapping the slithery and slimy banks of Lepage's shallow lake in semi-naked delirium. The important point is to present them, as Noble did, not only with a 'razor-sharp comic drive' but also as 'youngsters who suffer their way to maturity' (John Peter, *Sunday Times*, 7 August 1994).

44–6 Cut by Tree. In Daniels's staging, to see Jane Carr's 'real distress at the sudden desertion of her Lysander is to know both the pain of her wound and the uproariousness of hurt dignity let fly. She had begun the evening looking like some Dresden china figurine. By this time the tiny creature had transformed herself into a demented troll, who almost pulls the place apart in her temper' (*Daily Mail*, 17 July 1981).

46 After a version of this in Reynolds, Demetrius replies with seven lines from Helena's discarded 'call you me fair' speech from 1.1, three spoken and four as an air (derived from Colman), before the exchange modulates into a duet which pieces together some of the rejected lines: 'These looks, these tears, these tender sighs, / Are these, in murd'rers found? / 'Tis I'm the victim, and your eyes, / Your scorn, has caus'd the wound' (*Dream*, p. 35).

48 Cut by Vestris, Kean (who, typically, remembered to make 49 more grammatical by changing 'And' to 'Then') and Daly.

49 Daniels had Demetrius take Hermia's dagger (which she had found among the backstage props on the set) and put it in the skip. In Caird's staging, Hermia offered Demetrius her body so he could kill her, but he hugged her instead.

50–5 Cut by Phelps, switching direct from killing to murder and removing Hermia's generalisations. Vestris, Daly, Benson, Tree, Atkins and Hall (who, like Vestris and other nineteenth-century directors, kept 'From sleeping Hermia' in 1959, but removed it in his revivals) cut 52–5.

57–67 Cut by Vestris, broadly followed by Phelps.

61 In Caird's staging, Demetrius kissed Hermia's cheeks at 'sphere'.

HERMIA What's this to my Lysander? Where is he?
    Ah, good Demetrius, wilt thou give him me?
DEMETRIUS I had rather give his carcass to my hounds.
HERMIA Out, dog! Out, cur! Thou driv'st me past the bounds   65
    Of maiden's patience. Hast thou slain him then?
    Henceforth be never numbered among men.
    O, once tell true; tell true, even for my sake:
    Durst thou have looked upon him being awake?
    And hast thou killed him sleeping? O, brave touch!   70
    Could not a worm, an adder do so much?
    An adder did it; for with doubler tongue
    Than thine, thou serpent, never adder stung.
DEMETRIUS You spend your passion on a misprised mood.
    I am not guilty of Lysander's blood,   75
    Nor is he dead, for aught that I can tell.
HERMIA I pray thee, tell me then that he is well.
DEMETRIUS And if I could, what should I get therefor?
HERMIA A privilege, never to see me more;
    And from thy hated presence part I so.   80
    See me no more, whether he be dead or no.   *Exit*
DEMETRIUS There is no following her in this fierce vein;
    Here therefore for a while I will remain.
    So sorrow's heaviness doth heavier grow
    For debt that bankrupt sleep doth sorrow owe,   85
    Which now in some slight measure it will pay,
    If for his tender here I make some stay.
        [*He*] *lies down* [*and sleeps*].

65   Hermia threw cases at Demetrius on 'dog' and 'cur' in Caird's production.
66   Langham gave Demetrius a laugh at the end of the line (promptbook).
68–73   Cut by Kean, Daly, Tree; Hall cut 72–3. Daniels had Hermia knock Demetrius over and then grind his hand on the ground at 'tell true' (promptbook).
77   Daniels's Hermia switched tactics here, stroking Demetrius' hair in blandishment (promptbook).
79–81   Daniels had his Hermia revert to her previous tactics, pulling Demetrius' hair and pushing him onto his knees, throwing him on his face at 'part I so' and kicking the suitcase as she exited (promptbook). Alexander's Hermia still had both rucksacks when she exited. Vestris's Hermia substituted 'Or death or him I'll find immediately' (an altered version of 2.2.162) as her exit line.
82–7   Phelps placed these lines after Puck's exit at 101.
84   Benson's Oberon 'uses his power to weigh Demetrius down with sleep, and again, to summon such of the lovers whose presence is desired' (HTC cutting, 24 February 1900).
86–7   A rather obscure line cut by Vestris, Kean, Saker, Benson, Tree and Bridges Adams.

OBERON What hast thou done? Thou hast mistaken quite,
    And laid the love juice on some true love's sight.
    Of thy misprision must perforce ensue   90
    Some true love turned, and not a false turned true.
PUCK Then fate o'errules, that, one man holding troth,
    A million fail, confounding oath on oath.
OBERON About the wood go swifter than the wind,
    And Helena of Athens look thou find.   95
    All fancy-sick she is and pale of cheer
    With sighs of love, that costs the fresh blood dear.
    By some illusion see thou bring her here;
    I'll charm his eyes against she do appear.
PUCK I go, I go, look how I go!   100
    Swifter than arrow from the Tartar's bow.   *Exit*
OBERON   [*Squeezing the juice on Demetrius' eyes.*]
    Flower of this purple dye,
    Hit with Cupid's archery,
    Sink in apple of his eye.
    When his love he doth espy,   105
    Let her shine as gloriously
    As the Venus of the sky.
    When thou wak'st, if she be by,
    Beg of her for remedy.

       Enter PUCK

PUCK   Captain of our fairy band,   110
    Helena is here at hand,
    And the youth mistook by me,
    Pleading for a lover's fee.

88 After Demetrius had finished, there was a five-second pause in Barker's production, before
  Oberon hit Puck with his sceptre; Puck then jumped down to the lower stage and sat facing
  Oberon, rubbing himself (promptbook). Noble's Oberon stepped on Puck's foot to trap him
  as he attempted to escape.

90–3 Cut by Vestris, Kean, Saker, Daly, Benson, Tree, Atkins, Benthall, Devine, Hall; Phelps and
  Bridges Adams cut only Puck's lines. The resulting versions are smoother, less generalised
  and make Puck less cheeky.

91 In Daniels's staging, Oberon took Puck by the neck here (promptbook).

96–7 Descriptive amplifications cut by Vestris, Phelps, Kean, Saker, Benson, Tree.

100 Alexander's Puck was petulant here.

101 Vestris's Puck made a flying exit here, probably using a dummy double. Bryden's Puck
  adopted 'a ludicrous Cupid-style pose when departing' (*Financial Times*, in *LTR* 1982).

	Shall we their fond pageant see?
	Lord, what fools these mortals be!
OBERON	Stand aside. The noise they make
	Will cause Demetrius to awake.
PUCK	Then will two at once woo one –
	That must needs be sport alone;
	And those things do best please me
	That befall prepost'rously.

Enter LYSANDER *and* HELENA

LYSANDER Why should you think that I should woo in scorn?
        Scorn and derision never come in tears.
        Look when I vow, I weep; and vows so born,
            In their nativity all truth appears.   125
        How can these things in me seem scorn to you,
        Bearing the badge of faith to prove them true?
HELENA You do advance your cunning more and more.
            When truth kills truth, O devilish-holy fray!
        These vows are Hermia's. Will you give her o'er?   130
            Weigh oath with oath, and you will nothing weigh;
        Your vows to her and me, put in two scales,
        Will even weigh, and both as light as tales.
LYSANDER I had no judgement when to her I swore.
HELENA Nor none, in my mind, now you give her o'er.   135

---

114   Crosse noted that Greet's Oberon at Tunbridge Wells in 1899 responded unnecessarily to this rhetorical question by nodding and grinning 'like a china image' (*Diary* II, p. 88).

116–21 Lines anticipating staged action which were cut by Daly; Kean and Saker cut from 118.

121   Caird's Puck gave Helena an angry face and Lysander a crying one.

122–36 Heavily cut in nineteenth-century stagings because of contemporary attitudes towards the propriety or otherwise of the lovers' scenes. Vestris removed 124–9, 131–3, and 135; Phelps cut after 'weep' in 124, 125, 129–35; Kean, Saker, Daly and Tree cut 126–7, 129 and 131–3, creating a new couplet rhyme. Benson cut 123–7, 129, 131–4; Atkins cut 126–7. Atkins's Lysander in 1950 varied 'his manly style with Hermia to an affected love-sick tone when under the influence of the charm he turns to Helena' (Crosse, *Diary* XX, p. 13). For Daniels, Lysander backed on, trying to delay Helena (promptbook). Caird's Lysander wept copiously, taking a handkerchief out of Helena's pyjamas on 'appears'.

130   Caird's Helena took back her handkerchief here.

132–3   Cut by Atkins, who often removed lines that had even remote metatheatrical resonances.

135   Cut by Daly, which tidies up the rhyme scheme and removes a repetition of 'o'er'.

LYSANDER Demetrius loves her, and he loves not you.
DEMETRIUS (*Waking*.)

> O Helen, goddess, nymph, perfect, divine!
> To what, my love, shall I compare thine eyne?
> Crystal is muddy! O, how ripe in show
> Thy lips, those kissing cherries, tempting grow!   140
> That pure congealèd white, high Taurus' snow,
> Fanned with the eastern wind, turns to a crow
> When thou hold'st up thy hand. O, let me kiss
> This princess of pure white, this seal of bliss!

HELENA O spite! O Hell! I see you all are bent   145

> To set against me for your merriment.
> If you were civil, and knew courtesy,
> You would not do me thus much injury.
> Can you not hate me, as I know you do,
> But you must join in souls to mock me too?   150
> If you were men, as men you are in show,
> You would not use a gentle lady so,
> To vow, and swear, and superpraise my parts,
> When I am sure you hate me with your hearts.
> You both are rivals, and love Hermia;   155
> And now both rivals to mock Helena.
> A trim exploit, a manly enterprise,
> To conjure tears up in a poor maid's eyes
> With your derision! None of noble sort
> Would so offend a virgin, and extort   160
> A poor soul's patience, all to make you sport.

LYSANDER You are unkind, Demetrius: be not so,

137 For Caird, Puck had to direct the waking Demetrius towards Helena rather than Lysander.

139–44 Demetrius' waking hyperbole has often been reduced: Vestris and Kean cut from his waking couplet direct to Helena's response. Other directors have given her more to respond to: Phelps's Demetrius had the lines and, presumably, the actions to go with the end of 143 and 144, though the specific verbal reference to her hand had been deleted; Saker, rather ungrammatically, cut to 142, Daly from 141. Hall cut 141–2.

145–61 Helena's long speech was punctuated in Langham's production by interjected protestations from Lysander and Demetrius. Its opening words were problematic for Kean, who read 'O spiteful fate', and Daly, who read 'O fury'. Nineteenth-century directors, predictably, reduced the speech's vehemence by cutting: only 155–8 survived unscathed in all nineteenth-century versions. At 154 in Daniels's production, the men each took one of Helena's hands and followed her on their knees as she backed away (promptbook).

For you love Hermia – this you know I know –
And here with all good will, with all my heart,
In Hermia's love I yield you up my part;   165
And yours of Helena to me bequeath,
Whom I do love, and will do till my death.
HELENA Never did mockers waste more idle breath.
DEMETRIUS Lysander, keep thy Hermia; I will none.
If e'er I loved her, all that love is gone.   170
My heart to her but as guest-wise sojourned,
And now to Helen is it home returned,
There to remain.
LYSANDER   Helen, it is not so.
DEMETRIUS Disparage not the faith thou dost not know,
Lest to thy peril thou aby it dear.   175
Look where thy love comes: yonder is thy dear.

Enter HERMIA

HERMIA Dark night, that from the eye his function takes,
The ear more quick of apprehension makes;
Wherein it doth impair the seeing sense
It pays the hearing double recompense.   180
Thou art not by mine eye, Lysander, found;

163–4   Vestris's cut reduced the force of Lysander's volte-face.
168   Vestris cut Helena's choric near aside.
171   Cut by Tree, making Demetrius less obviously inconsistent.
174   Tree's Lysander and Demetrius hold out their hands to embrace Helena, but she exits and
         they fall into one another's arms; Demetrius then pushes Lysander away and pursues
         Helena off (promptbook). Although this is a good piece of business as a physical manifesta-
         tion of emotional entanglement, it also gets Demetrius and Helena offstage before Hermia's
         entrance, so that the truncated exchange between Hermia and Lysander is conducted in pri-
         vate. Atkins also had Lysander and Demetrius falling into one another's arms as they
         attempt to embrace Helena (promptbook).
175   Langham's Hermia was heard offstage, calling for Lysander at the end of Demetrius' line.
         At the end of 176 his Lysander said 'Oh!' and Demetrus 'Ah!' (promptbook).
177–80   Hermia's contextualising and generalising has not found much favour with directors, who
         have preferred to cut direct to 181 (Phelps, Kean, Saker, Benson, Tree, Atkins, Bridges Adams,
         Devine, Hall) or omitted 179–80 (Daly, Benthall, Langham); Vestris omitted 177–180 and
         reconstructed 181–3 as 'O Lysander why unkindly didst thou leave me so?'. Reynolds, who
         had cut heavily, rephrased and rearranged up to this point, ended the scene with partial
         appearances for some of Hermia's 'thief of love' speeches and both women exiting together

Mine ear, I thank it, brought me to thy sound.
But why unkindly didst thou leave me so?
LYSANDER Why should he stay whom love doth press to go?
HERMIA What love could press Lysander from my side? 185
LYSANDER Lysander's love, that would not let him bide,
    Fair Helena – who more engilds the night
    Than all yon fiery oes and eyes of light.
    [*To Hermia*] Why seek'st thou me? Could not this make
        thee know
    The hate I bare thee made me leave thee so? 190
HERMIA You speak not as you think; it cannot be.
HELENA Lo, she is one of this confederacy!
    Now I perceive they have conjoined all three
    To fashion this false sport in spite of me.
    Injurious Hermia, most ungrateful maid, 195
    Have you conspired, have you with these contrived
    To bait me with this foul derision?
    Is all the counsel that we two have shared,
    The sisters' vows, the hours that we have spent
    When we have chid the hasty-footed time 200

to try to prevent Lysander and Demetrius fighting. Helena and Hermia do not reappear until the dénouement, nor do they speak another of Shakespeare's lines. The quarrel in this scene lasts for over three hundred lines in Shakespeare; Reynolds dispatches it in forty, sacrificing any nuances of character or situation development to what passes for narrative flow.

182   Caird's Hermia put down her bags here.

187–8   Phelps removed everything except 'Fair Helena'.

189–90   Cut by Vestris, Kean and Benson, once again reducing Lysander's emotional hyperbole.

192–218   Pope marked 198–210 with the asterisks he used to distinguish the best lines in Shakespeare (these are the only lines he marked in the *Dream*) and recent critics have pointed to the speech's thematic value. However, the theatre's verdict has been harsher and the later parts of the speech have often been filleted. Vestris was relatively conservative in losing only 211–14. Although Kean, Saker and Daly omitted 193–4 (Daly actually beginning at 195), once again reducing the amount of comment on the situation, the main target has been the recollections of Hermia and Helena's shared childhood. There are two main approaches to 203–14: Benson cut everything; Kean started the trend to cut all the sampler and song section (203–8) and the heraldic references (212–14, cut well into the twentieth century). Saker, Daly and Tree followed Kean's editing; Bridges Adams followed Benson. The end of the speech also suffered into the 1950s, with Devine following Phelps and other nineteenth-century directors in cutting the last three passionate and generalising lines. Atkins made the longest cuts in the speech, removing 198–214 and 217–19.

For parting us – O, is all forgot?
All schooldays' friendship, childhood innocence?
We, Hermia, like two artificial gods
Have with our needles created both one flower,
Both on one sampler, sitting on one cushion,   205
Both warbling of one song, both in one key,
As if our hands, our sides, voices, and minds
Had been incorporate. So we grew together
Like to a double cherry, seeming parted,
But yet an union in partition,   210
Two lovely berries moulded on one stem;
So with two seeming bodies but one heart,
Two of the first, like coats in heraldry,
Due but to one, and crownèd with one crest.
And will you rent our ancient love asunder,   215
To join with men in scorning your poor friend?
It is not friendly, 'tis not maidenly.
Our sex, as well as I, may chide you for it,
Though I alone do feel the injury.
HERMIA I am amazèd at your passionate words.   220
        I scorn you not; it seems that you scorn me.
HELENA Have you not set Lysander, as in scorn,
        To follow me, and praise my eyes and face?
        And made your other love, Demetrius,
        Who even but now did spurn me with his foot,   225
        To call me goddess, nymph, divine and rare,
        Precious, celestial? Wherefore speaks he this
        To her he hates? And wherefore doth Lysander
        Deny your love, so rich within his soul,
        And tender me, forsooth, affection,   230

For Devine, Barbara Jefford was 'like a plaintive woodpigeon' (*Truth*, 2 April 1954); Coral Browne, in Benthall's 1957 production, was constantly surprising herself, proclaiming 'both in one key' with 'her eyes wide, and in them the light of new and intricate discovery' (*ILN*, 4 January 1958) and had only 'To pause surprised at the line, "both warbling of one song, both in one key," for the house to crumple in helpless laughter' (*Birmingham Post*, 27 December).

217–42 One of Kean's and Saker's most sweeping cuts, removing wholesale one of the direct confrontations between the two women.

225 Cut by Tree.

227–35 The end of Helena's speech has been subject to heavy cutting: Phelps cut everything after 'hates?' in 228; Benson also cut from 'hates' but left 231 and 234–5 where he changed 'But'

But by your setting on, by your consent?
What though I be not so in grace as you,
So hung upon with love, so fortunate,
But miserable most, to love unloved:
This you should pity rather than despise.   235
HERMIA I understand not what you mean by this.
HELENA Ay, do! Persever, counterfeit sad looks,
Make mouths upon me when I turn my back,
Wink each at other, hold the sweet jest up.
This sport, well carried, shall be chronicled.   240
If you have any pity, grace, or manners,
You would not make me such an argument.
But fare ye well. 'Tis partly my own fault,
Which death or absence soon shall remedy.
LYSANDER Stay, gentle Helena: hear my excuse,   245
My love, my life, my soul, fair Helena!
HELENA O, excellent!
HERMIA [*To Lysander*] Sweet, do not scorn her so.
DEMETRIUS If she cannot entreat, I can compel.
LYSANDER Thou canst compel no more than she entreat;
Thy threats have no more strength than her weak prayers.   250
Helen, I love thee, by my life, I do:

to 'Ah' and 'This' to 'Me'; Tree and Atkins omitted everything after 'celestial'; Hall left 232–3 and 235. Kean and Saker included it in their much longer cut from 217 to 242.

238   Cut by Benson.

239–44   Another of Helena's generalising speeches to suffer from nineteenth-century directors: Phelps cut 239–40; Kean's and Saker's cut from 217 ended with 242; Benson cut 240–2; Tree cut 239–44. Devine (wary of the metatheatrical?) cut 240.

244   Emma Thompson, Branagh's Helena, was effective here: 'overcome by a sense that only her death can remedy the tangled situation, she embarks on a melodramatic swoon, but suddenly arrests the action and jerks back up again at the thought that her "absence" might do the trick just as well' (*Independent*, 15 August 1990).

246   Barker's Lysander kissed Helena's hand four times during this line. Bridges Adams had both Lysander and Demetrius try to embrace Helena who ducked out of their way so that they fell into one another's arms (promptbooks). See line 174 for other versions of this business.

247–50   The first exchange of threats between the two men was cut by Vestris, Phelps, Kean, Saker, Benson, Tree. Hall cut 248–50.

251   In Barton's staging, 'When Lysander and Demetrius fight over her, she sits down to view the contest, munching an apple from her picnic basket' (*Tatler*, July/August 1977); Daniels's Helena had her hands over her ears here (promptbook).

> I swear by that which I will lose for thee
> To prove him false that says I love thee not.
> DEMETRIUS I say I love thee more than he can do.
> LYSANDER If thou say so, withdraw, and prove it too. 255
> DEMETRIUS Quick, come.
> HERMIA   Lysander, whereto tends all this?
> LYSANDER Away, you Ethiop!
> DEMETRIUS   No, no, sir,
> Seem to break loose, take on as you would follow,
> But yet come not. You are a tame man, go.
> LYSANDER Hang off, thou cat, thou burr! Vile thing, let loose, 260
> Or I will shake thee from me like a serpent.
> HERMIA Why are you grown so rude? What change is this,
> Sweet love?
> LYSANDER   Thy love? – out, tawny Tartar, out;
> Out, loathed medicine! O hated potion, hence!
> HERMIA Do you not jest?
> HELENA   Yes, sooth, and so do you. 265
> LYSANDER Demetrius, I will keep my word with thee.
> DEMETRIUS I would I had your bond, for I perceive
> A weak bond holds you. I'll not trust your word.
> LYSANDER What? Should I hurt her, strike her, kill her dead?
> Although I hate her, I'll not harm her so. 270
> HERMIA What? Can you do me greater harm than hate?

252–3   Grammatically complex, and cut by Kean, Benson.

256ff.   For reasons of decorum, Kean and Saker cut the bulk of the rest of the scene down to 335, filtering some fourteen of the rejected lines in after 344.

257–80   Vestris initiated the nineteenth-century approach to these indecorous lines with swingeing cuts which left 257–72 as 'LYSANDER Away, I hate thee. HERMIA Hate me? Wherefore?'. Phelps kept only the first half of 257, Lysander and Hermia's exchange in 263–5, and 272–8 and the last part of 280; Daly omitted 257–9, cutting 272 after 'me' to the end of 274; Benson took out Demetrius' lines in 257–9, (leaving the direct address to Lysander), 261, 263–4, 266 to 'Wherefore' in 272, 274 and the first half of 275; Tree cut all of 257–9, 264 and everything from Helena's words in 265 to 'Be certain' in 280; Devine cut 266–79. In Daniels's staging at 259–60 the men were 'squaring up according to the Marquess of Queensberry' (*Financial Times*, 16 July 1981) and Hermia jumped on Lysander's back, giving extra point to 'burr' (promptbook).

264   Bowdler objected to this line.

265   In Daniels's staging, Jane Carr is 'a tiny, rosebud-lipped spitfire who, having been dragged across the floor, whirled around like a top and trampled on by her lover cries "Do you not jest?"' (*Guardian*, 16 July 1981).

Hate me? Wherefore? O me, what news, my love?
Am not I Hermia? Are not you Lysander?
I am as fair now as I was erewhile.
Since night you loved me; yet since night you left me.   275
Why then, you left me – O, the gods forbid! –
In earnest, shall I say?
LYSANDER   Ay, by my life;
And never did desire to see thee more.
Therefore be out of hope, of question, of doubt;
Be certain, nothing truer – 'tis no jest   280
That I do hate thee and love Helena.
HERMIA [*To Helena*]
O me, you juggler, you canker-blossom,
You thief of love! What, have you come by night
And stol'n my love's heart from him?
HELENA   Fine, i'faith!
Have you no modesty, no maiden shame,   285
No touch of bashfulness? What, will you tear
Impatient answers from my gentle tongue?
Fie, fie, you counterfeit, you puppet, you!
HERMIA 'Puppet'? Why so? – Ay, that way goes the game.
Now I perceive that she hath made compare   290
Between our statures; she hath urged her height,
And with her personage, her tall personage,
Her height, forsooth, she hath prevailed with him.
And are you grown so high in his esteem
Because I am so dwarfish and so low?   295

272 Langham's Hermia 'jumped on Lysander as if she were springing on a Palladium trampoline'
     (*Birmingham Post*, 21 December 1960).
281 Brook's Lysander hooked Hermia onto a trapeze from which she dangled until 295 (prompt-
     book). Vestris put Lysander's 336–7, followed by Hermia's 344, here and cut the first part of 282.
282 Daniels's Hermia pushed Helena twice on each name (promptbook).
284–305 Cut by Vestris from the beginning of Helena's speech; partly perhaps because her actresses
     did not match Shakespeare's physical description of the characters, more probably on
     grounds of decorum. Phelps cut 290–3, 295; Daly cut from 'no maiden shame' to 298, and
     from the end of 303 to 305; Benson cut to 298.
288 'I shall long remember the moment [in Devine's staging] when, rising on tiptoe to unexpected
     height, she [Barbara Jefford] looked down into the radiant upturned face of tiny Miss [Zena]
     Walker, and said with finality, "You puppet, you"' (*Western Daily Express*, 25 March 1954).
289 For Daniels, Jane Carr, 'mocked for her littleness, ... becomes a demure guided missile
     devastating whole areas with a glance' (*Guardian*, 16 July 1981).

How low am I, thou painted maypole? Speak!
How low am I? I am not yet so low
But that my nails can reach unto thine eyes.
HELENA I pray you, though you mock me, gentlemen,
Let her not hurt me. I was never curst;   300
I have no gift at all in shrewishness.
I am a right maid for my cowardice;
Let her not strike me. You perhaps may think
Because she is something lower than myself
That I can match her.
HERMIA   Lower? Hark, again!   305
HELENA Good Hermia, do not be so bitter with me.
I evermore did love you, Hermia,
Did ever keep your counsels, never wronged you,
Save that in love unto Demetrius
I told him of your stealth unto this wood.   310
He followed you; for love I followed him,
But he hath chid me hence, and threatened me
To strike me, spurn me, nay, to kill me too.
And now, so you will let me quiet go,
To Athens will I bear my folly back,   315
And follow you no further. Let me go;
You see how simple and how fond I am.
HERMIA Why, get you gone! Who is't that hinders you?
HELENA A foolish heart that I leave here behind.
HERMIA What, with Lysander?
HELENA   With Demetrius.   320
LYSANDER Be not afraid; she shall not harm thee, Helena.

298   When Langham's Hermia, Judi Dench, 'dashed across the stage to try to get at Helena and
      scratch her eyes out she had the look of a nippy little fly-half making for the line, and but for
      the sure (though rather high) tackling of Lysander (John Stride) and Demetrius (Michael
      Meacham) she would have scored several times' (*Daily Telegraph*, 21 December 1960).
299–300   Daniels's men formed a rugby scrum to protect Helena from Hermia (promptbook).
300   Benson began to cut again at 'I was never curst' and continued right through to 320, preserv-
      ing narrative continuity at the expense of self-analysis and self-justification.
304   Cut by Phelps, together with 'Lower' in 305, and references to Hermia's height in 325–6,
      328–30, reflecting the stature of the actresses.
311–13   Cut by Vestris, Phelps, Tree, Atkins; Devine cut 312–13
316–44   Vestris cut from 'Let me go', keeping 'get you gone' followed by 446-7. The cut is in keeping
      with her other changes in this scene, toning down the vehemence of the quarrel and reduc-
      ing it to the minimum necessary to keep the plot moving.

DEMETRIUS No, sir. She shall not, though you take her part.
HELENA O, when she is angry she is keen and shrewd;
   She was a vixen when she went to school,
   And though she be but little, she is fierce.   325
HERMIA Little again? Nothing but low and little?
   Why will you suffer her to flout me thus?
   Let me come to her.
LYSANDER   Get you gone, you dwarf,
   You minimus of hindering knot-grass made,
   You bead, you acorn.
DEMETRIUS   You are too officious   330
   In her behalf that scorns your services.
   Let her alone: speak not of Helena,
   Take not her part; for if thou dost intend
   Never so little show of love to her,
   Thou shalt aby it.
LYSANDER   Now she holds me not –   335
   Now follow, if thou dur'st, to try whose right,
   Of thine or mine, is most in Helena.
DEMETRIUS Follow? Nay, I'll go with thee, cheek by jowl.
          Exeunt Lysander and Demetrius
HERMIA You, mistress, all this coil is 'long of you.
   Nay, go not back.

325–6   Cut by Daly; Benson cut 326. Decorum and the relevant actresses' actual stature probably explain the changes.

327   Caird's Hermia launched herself into the arms of Lysander and Demetrius here.

328–36   Daly cut Lysander's first speech and 331–2, Benson cut from 'you dwarf' to 'part' in 333; Tree cut Lysander's part of 335. Kean's and Saker's massive cut from 256 ended with 335. Once again the dispute is toned down by the changes, which may also partly reflect the physical stature of the actresses.

335–8   In Brook's production 'Hermia blocks Lysander's exit by hurling herself horizontally across the door, only to be left dangling spitting fire and thrashing her legs from the trapeze' (*Times*, 11 June 1971). In Caird's staging, Lysander made a false exit and kissed Helena, prompting Demetrius to return and kiss Helena and Lysander on 'cheek' and 'jowl' in 338.

338–42   Kean started his cut to 342 by leaving out 'cheek by jowl', Saker began at 339, Daly omitted 342–3.

339ff.   As the *TLS* noted, 'crinolines lend some additional comic business to the fight between Helena and Hermia' in Daniels's staging (31 July 1981): Hermia grabbed Helena's skirt at ''long of you', it came off, revealing the underpinning hoops, at 'company' and Helena then 'picks up hoops and shows long leg' at 'longer' (promptbook). At 341 in Alexander's

HELENA   I will not trust you, I,   340
    Nor longer stay in your curst company.
    Your hands than mine are quicker for a fray;
    My legs are longer, though, to run away!   *[Exit]*
HERMIA I am amazed, and know not what to say.   *Exit*
        Oberon and Puck come forward.
OBERON This is thy negligence. Still thou mistak'st,   345
    Or else committ'st thy knaveries wilfully.
PUCK Believe me, King of Shadows, I mistook.
    Did not you tell me I should know the man
    By the Athenian garments he had on?
    And so far blameless proves my enterprise   350
    That I have 'nointed an Athenian's eyes;
    And so far am I glad it so did sort,
    As this their jangling I esteem a sport.
OBERON Thou seest these lovers seek a place to fight:
    Hie therefore, Robin, overcast the night;   355
    The starry welkin cover thou anon
    With drooping fog as black as Acheron,
    And lead these testy rivals so astray
    As one come not within another's way.
    Like to Lysander sometime frame thy tongue,   360
    Then stir Demetrius up with bitter wrong,
    And sometime rail thou like Demetrius;
    And from each other look thou lead them thus,
    Till o'er their brows death-counterfeiting sleep
    With leaden legs and batty wings doth creep.   365
    Then crush this herb into Lysander's eye,

production, 'Hel bites Herm's hand and frees herself chased by Herm who grabs Hel's legs but misses' (promptbook).

344   Benson removed this choric line. In Caird's staging, Hermia received her bags from Puck and then did a 'take'.

345   Tree's Oberon threatened Puck with his spear; Atkins had Puck being pulled up short and taken by the ear; Oberon had his arm round Puck's neck in Daniels's staging (promptbooks).

347–53   Benson's Puck was mute; Kean and Saker minimised his defiance by removing 352–3. At 349 Caird had Puck give Oberon a 'cheesy grin – it's all your fault' (promptbook). Caird's Puck spoke 352–3 in the style of Olivier's Richard III.

356–7   Tree cut the amplification of Oberon's instruction.

360–3   Vestris, Kean and Saker removed the lines explaining Puck's tactics with Lysander and Demetrius; Atkins cut from 361.

366   Vestris had the herb crushed into 'the eyes of each', so the removal of the subsequent lines

Whose liquor hath this virtuous property,
To take from thence all error with his might,
And make his eyeballs roll with wonted sight.
When they next wake, all this derision 370
Shall seem a dream and fruitless vision,
And back to Athens shall the lovers wend
With league whose date till death shall never end.
Whiles I in this affair do thee employ
I'll to my Queen and beg her Indian boy; 375
And then I will her charmèd eye release
From monster's view, and all things shall be peace.
PUCK My fairy lord, this must be done with haste,
For night's swift dragons cut the clouds full fast,
And yonder shines Aurora's harbinger, 380
At whose approach ghosts wandering here and there

helped to preserve naturalistic probability.

367–9 Cut by Vestris (and Atkins); Kean and Saker cut 368–9. Presumably the gloss on how the charm will work was deemed unnecessary.

370–5 These lines which anticipate the dénouement have sometimes been omitted. Vestris (and Atkins) cut 372–3; Daly cut 370–3; Hall cut 372–5.

372–395 Another substantial cut of descriptive material by Kean (to a reconstructed 394) and Saker.

377–462 Reynolds ended his act by replacing Shakespeare's lines with a scene designed not only to end his act spectacularly, but also to give insight into why Oberon wants the Indian Boy. It seems not impossible that the homoerotic elements in the presentation of the Indian Boy detected later by Jan Kott may have struck some chords with Reynolds to judge by Oberon's explanation: 'Not, not so much from love of him, as her, / I court this contest, – I'd put her to the trial – / If she refuse, I know her love is on the wane, – / But, if she yield! – Ah! that she may! and still –'. At this point clouds descend and open and a fairy appears to tell Oberon that Titania is sending the Indian Boy. Oberon, very properly in the light of this revelation, decides to uncharm the Fairy Queen. The clouds ascend, the sea is discovered with a fairy palace in the distance and the act concludes with 'TITANIA's *galley and other gallies in full sail.– Dance – during which, Indian Boy is brought forward*' and the chorus 'Pierce the air with sounds of joy! / Hail Titania's treasur'd Boy!' (*Dream*, pp. 40–1).

377–81 In Guthrie's 1937 staging, Puck's 'spasm of fear when he talks of the ghosts was well conceived and excuted' (Crosse, *Diary* XVII, p. 51); Barton's showed 'real dread' (*Observer*, 15 May 1977). As Caird's Oberon made to exit Puck grabbed his leg in fear, climbing onto his lap at 'harbinger' and then sliding down and clinging like a child. Daniels also stressed Puck's fear, but less elaborately (promptbook).

378–93 Cut by Vestris (from 377), who reconstructed some of the lines as a song at the beginning of 4.1, and by Phelps and Tree.

> Troop home to churchyards. Damnèd spirits all,
> That in crossways and floods have burial,
> Already to their wormy beds are gone.
> For fear lest day should look their shames upon,   385
> They wilfully themselves exile from light,
> And must for aye consort with black-browed night.

OBERON But we are spirits of another sort.
> I with the morning's love have oft made sport,
> And like a forester the groves may tread   390
> Even till the eastern gate, all fiery-red,
> Opening on Neptune with fair blessèd beams,
> Turns into yellow gold his salt green streams.
> But notwithstanding, haste, make no delay;
> We may effect this business yet ere day.   [*Exit*] 395

PUCK   Up and down, up and down,
> I will lead them up and down;
> I am feared in field and town.
> Goblin, lead them up and down.
> Here comes one.   400

Enter LYSANDER

386–7   Cut by Langham.

388   In Benthall's 1957 version, 'the darkness that descends upon the glades and distant tumbled hills is singularly beautiful. Stealing upon the spirit like the first touch of longed-for slumber, it is at once palpable and transparent and the stars in the wide sky glitter with a supernatural brilliance' (*Sunday Times*, 29 December).

394   Phelps started at 'haste', Vestris began with 'About it Spirit'. Reynolds placed his very truncated version of this scene after the rehearsal/performance of 'Pyramus and Thisbe' which took place in his version of 4.1. Caird's Oberon looked at his watch here.

395   Vestris used gauzes to create the fog, as did Phelps; in addition to his proscenium-filling net, 'other thicknesses of gauze, partly painted, were used occasionally to deepen the misty effect' (Moyr Smith, *Dream*, p. xiii). Barker drew metatheatrical attention to the fairies' stage management of the lovers' quarrels here: 'Obe turns & exits quickly through curtains C followed by train[.] Puck then down C lower stage motions for lights to go down[,] then up to cloth, bends down & raises curtain as it ascends' (promptbook). Daniels used clouds and fog borders to create the mist here, in keeping with his Victorian toy theatre approach.

396–9   Vestris and Kean gave the lines to Oberon, putting them into the third person; Asche had an effective, if overdone, lighting effect of Puck 'as a kind of will o' the wisp misleading the rival lovers in the darkness' (Crosse, *Diary* IV, p. 36).

400   Cut by Vestris and Kean.

LYSANDER Where art thou, proud Demetrius? Speak thou now.
PUCK Here, villain, drawn and ready! Where art thou?
LYSANDER I will be with thee straight.
PUCK   Follow me then
        To plainer ground.

                        [*Exit Lysander*]

            Enter DEMETRIUS

DEMETRIUS   Lysander, speak again.
        Thou runaway, thou coward, art thou fled?   405
        Speak! In some bush? Where dost thou hide thy head?
PUCK Thou coward, art thou bragging to the stars,
        Telling the bushes that thou look'st for wars,
        And wilt not come? Come, recreant, come, thou child,
        I'll whip thee with a rod. He is defiled   410
        That draws a sword on thee.
DEMETRIUS   Yea, art thou there?
PUCK Follow my voice. We'll try no manhood here.

                           Exeunt

           Enter LYSANDER

LYSANDER He goes before me, and still dares me on;
        When I come where he calls, then he is gone.
        The villain is much lighter-heeled than I;   415
        I followed fast, but faster he did fly,
        That fallen am I in dark uneven way,
        And here will rest me. (*Lies down.*) Come, thou gentle day,

---

401   In Brook's production, 'when the hobgoblin Puck walks on stilts, his alarmed victims scurry through his legs' (*Daily Telegraph*, 14 September 1970).

403ff.   The lines spoken by Puck in the voices of Lysander and Demetrius are often, as in Phelps's and Langham's productions, spoken by the actors who play Lysander and Demetrius: in Caird's staging, Puck's Demetrius imitation was 'Military' and his Lysander 'Romantic' (promptbook). Tree had Cobweb watching from the brook in 1911 – his fairies tended to be present throughout the wood scenes.

408–11   Kean cut everything except 'And wilt not come?'

416–18   Vestris cut to 'me'; Kean and Saker cut from 417 and Kean reconstructed 418–19 as 'Once let gentle day show me her grey light'. Caird's Lysander repeated 416–17 like a gramophone record stuck in a groove.

418   The *Leamington Courier* thought that Hall's lovers 'might have been allowed a mossy bank or two for their slumbers in place of the hideously uncomfortable steps left over from the palace scene' (5 June 1959).

For if but once thou show me thy grey light
I'll find Demetrius and revenge this spite. [*Sleeps.*]   420

Enter PUCK *and* DEMETRIUS

PUCK Ho, ho, ho! Coward, why com'st thou not?
DEMETRIUS Abide me if thou dar'st, for well I wot
    Thou runn'st before me, shifting every place,
    And dar'st not stand nor look me in the face.
    Where art thou now?
PUCK   Come hither; I am here.   425
DEMETRIUS Nay then, thou mock'st me. Thou shalt buy this dear
    If ever I thy face by daylight see.
    Now, go thy way; faintness constraineth me
    To measure out my length on this cold bed.
    By day's approach look to be visited. [*Sleeps.*]   430

Enter HELENA

HELENA O weary night, O long and tedious night,
    Abate thy hours, shine comforts from the east,
    That I may back to Athens by daylight
    From these that my poor company detest;
    And sleep, that sometimes shuts up sorrow's eye,   435
    Steal me awhile from mine own company. (*Sleeps.*)
PUCK   Yet but three? Come one more,
    Two of both kinds makes up four.
    Here she comes, curst and sad.
    Cupid is a knavish lad   440
    Thus to make poor females mad.

Enter HERMIA

HERMIA Never so weary, never so in woe,
    Bedabbled with the dew, and torn with briars –

422-4 Tree cut Demetrius' speech, running Puck's end to end; Vestris kept a minimal presence for Demetrius, starting her cut after 'dar'st'.
430 Cut by Tree, presumably objecting to the tag rhyme.
431-45 Vestris cut Helena's speech; Kean and Saker cut everything; Daly had Helena enter last with a consequent rearrangement of lines.
437 Crosse noted in response to Atkins's 1942 Westminster Theatre staging that 'Puck's shepherding the lovers may now be taken as established business' (*Diary* XVIII, pp. 57, 59).
438 Caird's Puck had a lengthy pause before 'four' while he worked it out.

> I can no further crawl, no further go;
> My legs can keep no pace with my desires. 445
> Here will I rest me till the break of day.
> Heavens shield Lysander, if they mean a fray. [*Sleeps.*]

PUCK On the ground
Sleep sound.
I'll apply 450
To your eye,
Gentle lover, remedy.
[*Squeezes the juice on Lysander's eyes.*]
When thou wak'st,
Thou tak'st
True delight 455
In the sight
Of thy former lady's eye;
And the country proverb known,
That every man should take his own,
In your waking shall be shown. 460
Jack shall have Jill,
Naught shall go ill:
The man shall have his mare again, and all shall be well.
[*Exit Puck;*] *the lovers remain on stage, asleep*

445 Brook's Puck knelt to provide a resting place for Hermia and then carried her over to Lysander by 447 (promptbook).

447 Vestris's stage direction is 'Music – the mist clears off and discovers another part of the Forest – Dem, Lys, Hel and Her, asleep on separate banks – Puck and fairies forming a tableau – Puck advances and touches the eyes of each with the magic herb' (Pattie, *Dream*, p. 32), which means all four are under the influence of magic at the end, not just Demetrius. Greet (seen by Crosse at Tunbridge Wells in 1899) had Puck anoint both male lovers' eyes (*Diary* II, p. 88). Coghill's lovers lay down far apart 'but Puck made a gesture and they rolled together into their right pairs' (Coghill letter). Dunlop's Puck 'tickles Hermia's breasts before pouring his healing potion on to her eye-lids' (*Plays and Players*, December 1967). For Benson 'the fairies carrying lights and led by "Puck" crept one by one on the stage, and at the finish prostrated themselves before "Oberon," drowsily humming the last bars as a lullaby, before sinking into sleep' (Constance Benson, *Mainly Players*, p. 176).

461 Puck took off his wings here in Caird's staging. He made his exit to an ironic accompaniment of the 'Sugar Plum Fairy' music.

463 Vestris ended the scene with a dance, as did Kean, whose pantomimic transformation scene, as 'fairies, not airy beings of the colour of the greenwood, or the sky, or robed in misty

white, but glittering in the most brilliant dresses, with a crust of bullion about their legs, cause the curtain to fall on a splendid ballet' (Morley, in Rowell, *Dramatic Criticism*, p. 101).

463 SD F has the SD 'They sleep all the Act', which has sometimes been assumed to refer to the lovers sleeping and remaining on stage during an interval in some early revival of the play. However, it seems more likely that it refers to the need for the lovers to stay where they are when Puck leaves, in order to be ready to be woken in 4.1. Noble's 'lovers finally go to sleep magically supended in hammocks' (Jane Edwardes, *Time Out*, 10 August 1994); although the actual mechanics of slipping them into the hammocks were rather clumsy, it did have the benefit of clearing the stage for the next scene while leaving them visible to the audience.

ACT 4, SCENE I

Enter TITANIA, Queen of Fairies, and BOTTOM, and fairies
[including PEASEBLOSSOM, COBWEB and MUSTARDSEED;] and the
King OBERON behind them

TITANIA Come, sit thee down upon this flowery bed
    While I thy amiable cheeks do coy,
    And stick musk-roses in thy sleek smooth head,
    And kiss thy fair large ears, my gentle joy.
BOTTOM Where's Peaseblossom?   5
PEASEBLOSSOM Ready.
BOTTOM Scratch my head, Peaseblossom. Where's Mounsieur
    Cobweb?
COBWEB Ready.
BOTTOM Mounsieur Cobweb, good Mounsieur, get you your weapons   10
    in your hand, and kill me a red-hipped humble-bee on the top of
    a thistle; and, good Mounsieur, bring me the honey-bag. Do not
    fret yourself too much in the action, Mounsieur; and, good
    Mounsieur, have a care the honey-bag break not; I would be loath
    to have you overflown with a honey-bag, signior. Where's Moun-   15
    sieur Mustardseed?

0 SD Nineteenth-century directors usually followed Vestris in changing the scene to Titania's
    bower here, although the action is continuous, and the four lovers can still be on stage pro-
    viding a silent commentary on the onstage action until Bottom joins them in sleep. In the
    nineteenth century, Bottom's awakening (and in Kean's, Saker's and Benson's versions, 4.2)
    was played before returning to the forest scene of 3.2. for the arrival of Theseus and
    Hippolyta. Vestris and Saker began with a song constructed from lines omitted in 3.2. In 1981
    Daniels began with a ribbon dance, very much in keeping with his Victorian pretensions.
    Lepage's lovers were actually asleep under the bed Bottom and Titania used.
  1 Barton's Titania, 'loving an ass, tries a few enthusiastic "hee-haws" of her own' (*Observer*,
    15 May 1977); Caird began with Bottom in a tutu dancing with fairies wearing miniature ass
    heads in tribute to him..
7–22 Several nineteenth-century directors slimmed down Bottom's ponderous humour here:
    Kean and Saker (followed by Atkins) cut from 'Do not' to 'signior' (12–15) and Kean also
    omitted some of the 'Mounsieurs' and made other minor verbal changes; Daly cut 17–19;

MUSTARDSEED Ready.

BOTTOM Give me your neaf, Mounsieur Mustardseed. Pray you, leave
your courtesy, good Mounsieur.

MUSTARDSEED What's your will? 20

BOTTOM Nothing, good Mounsieur, but to help Cavalery Peaseblossom
to scratch. I must to the barber's, Mounsieur, for methinks I am
marvellous hairy about the face. And I am such a tender ass, if my
hair do but tickle me, I must scratch.

TITANIA What, wilt thou hear some music, my sweet love? 25

BOTTOM I have a reasonable good ear in music. Let's have the tongs
and the bones.

TITANIA Or say, sweet love, what thou desir'st to eat.

BOTTOM Truly, a peck of provender, I could munch your good dry oats.
Methinks I have a great desire to a bottle of hay. Good hay, sweet 30
hay hath no fellow.

TITANIA I have a venturous fairy that shall seek
The squirrel's hoard, and fetch thee new nuts.

BOTTOM I had rather have a handful or two of dried peas. But, I pray
you, let none of your people stir me; I have an exposition of sleep 35
come upon me.

TITANIA Sleep thou, and I will wind thee in my arms.
Fairies be gone, and be all ways away.   [*Exeunt Fairies*]
So doth the woodbine the sweet honeysuckle
Gently entwist; the female ivy so 40
Enrings the barky fingers of the elm.
O, how I love thee! How I dote on thee!
[*They sleep.*]

Enter PUCK. OBERON *comes forward*

OBERON Welcome, good Robin. Seest thou this sweet sight?

Tree cut to 'scratch' in 22. Some directors follow the early texts in keeping Cobweb in line 21, others substitute the correct name, Peaseblossom.

25–34   Kean cut 'my sweet love' and 26–7; Tree cut everything to 'peas'.

31   Moth gave hay to Bottom in Tree's production (promptbook).

37–42   Kean cut all these indecorous lines, except the innocuous 38, which Titania used to shoo the fairies off the bed in Caird's production. Caird's Titania and Bottom had a 'long french kiss' after 'elm' (promptbook) and in Lepage's staging, their coupling was 'noisily orgasmic' (*Daily Telegraph*, 13 July 1992) with 'comic outbursts of braying while those bedsprings are put to hard use' (*Evening Standard*, 10 July 1992).

43   Tree's Oberon had the Indian Boy on his right arm as visual confirmation of the changed situation; Langham also had him in this scene (promptbooks).

       Her dotage now I do begin to pity;
       For, meeting her of late behind the wood   45
       Seeking sweet favours for this hateful fool,
       I did upbraid her and fall out with her,
       For she his hairy temples then had rounded
       With coronet of fresh and fragrant flowers;
       And that same dew, which sometime on the buds   50
       Was wont to swell like round and orient pearls,
       Stood now within the pretty flowerets' eyes
       Like tears that did their own disgrace bewail.
       When I had at my pleasure taunted her,
       And she in mild terms begged my patience,   55
       I then did ask of her her changeling child,
       Which straight she gave me, and her fairy sent
       To bear him to my bower in Fairyland.
       And now I have the boy, I will undo
       This hateful imperfection of her eyes.   60
       And, gentle Puck, take this transformèd scalp
       From off the head of this Athenian swain,
       That, he awaking when the other do,
       May all to Athens back again repair,
       And think no more of this night's accidents   65
       But as the fierce vexation of a dream.
       But first I will release the Fairy Queen.
              [*Squeezing a herb on Titania's eyes.*]
       Be as thou wast wont to be;
       See as thou wast wont to see.
       Dian's bud o'er Cupid's flower   70
       Hath such force and blessèd power.
    Now, my Titania, wake you, my sweet Queen!

45–60   Hall cut the whole of this explanation of offstage developments but the main targets for
        other directors have been 47–54 and 61–7. Vestris, Kean and Saker all spared Oberon and
        Titania the ignominy of upbraiding and falling out (47) and were then joined by Tree,
        Bridges Adams and Atkins in cutting the evocative description of the flower-bedecked
        Bottom (48–53). Kean, Saker and Bridges Adams also took out Oberon's pleasure in taunt-
        ing Titania (54). Daly, and Langham (who had the Indian Boy on stage), cut the end of 57
        and the whole of 58.
  61–7   Cut by Kean, Saker and Atkins, presumably since it anticipates action we are yet to see
        and duplicates Oberon's effective instruction to Puck to remove the ass head.
   72   Titania awoke to the 'Reconciliation Serenade ... "Sweet Rose, fair flower"' in Saker's
        production (playbill).

TITANIA [*Starting up.*]
　　　My Oberon, what visions have I seen!
　　　Methought I was enamoured of an ass.
OBERON There lies your love.
TITANIA 　　　　　　　　　How came these things to pass?　　75
　　　O, how mine eyes do loathe his visage now!
OBERON Silence awhile: Robin, take off this head.
　　　Titania, music call, and strike more dead
　　　Than common sleep of all these five the sense.
TITANIA Music, ho, music such as charmeth sleep!　　　　80
　　　　　　　[*Soft music plays.*]
PUCK [*To Bottom, removing the ass's head*]
　　　Now when thou wak'st, with thine own fool's eyes peep.
OBERON Sound, music! Come, my Queen, take hands with me,
　　　And rock the ground whereon these sleepers be.
　　　　　　　[*They dance.*]
　　　Now thou and I are new in amity,
　　　And will tomorrow midnight solemnly　　　　　　85
　　　Dance in Duke Theseus' house triumphantly,
　　　And bless it to all fair prosperity.

73–5　In Barton's staging, Titania's 'revulsion when his true nature is revealed is not, for once, passed over' (*Observer*, 15 May 1977). Bryden's Titania was 'short on confused wonderment' in the negative view of the *Financial Times* whereas the *New Statesman* thought she was 'half-amused to discover the trick they have played on her' (both in *LTR*, 1982). When Caird's Titania woke up she screamed and then hit Oberon.

77　Vestris's Puck 'flies off with the head' here (Pattie, *Dream*).

78–81　Although Foakes sees the rural music at 27 and the double calls for music as thematic, and Foss advanced a complicated case about the calls here in his book *What the Author Meant*, the double call for music here has often been seen as problematic by directors. Cut by Vestris, Kean, Saker and Atkins; Daly and Benson left 81.

82–3　Vestris cut 'Sound, music' and 83, as did Kean, Saker, Benson; Daly played 82–9 after 91.

83　In Daniels's production, the doubling of Oberon and Titania with Theseus and Hippolyta 'led, as it always does, to contrivance: their dance of amity had to be greatly prolonged, using stand-ins towards the end of it, to enable them to change into elaborate Victorian riding costumes for their reappearance' (Warren, 'Interpretations', p. 147). For Caird, 'when [John] Carlisle's silken Oberon commands his tribe to rock the ground, the stage explodes in a post-punk mélange of *Come Dancing* and Prokofiev's *Romeo and Juliet* suite' (*Financial Times*, 13 April 1989), with Oberon and Titania indulging in more classical styles and the young fairies rocking in very contemporary ones.

85–9　These anticipatory lines were cut by Atkins; Vestris, Kean and Saker cut 88–9.

> There shall the pairs of faithful lovers be
> Wedded, with Theseus, all in jollity.

PUCK   Fairy King, attend, and mark: 90
        I do hear the morning lark.

OBERON Then, my Queen, in silence sad,
        Trip we after night's shade;
        We the globe can compass soon,
        Swifter than the wandering moon.   95

TITANIA Come, my lord, and in our flight
        Tell me how it came this night
        That I sleeping here was found
        With these mortals on the ground.

                        Exeunt Oberon, Titania and Puck

Wind horns. Enter THESEUS *with* HIPPOLYTA, EGEUS, *and all his*
train.

92–9 Cut by Daly; Tree cut 92–5.

99   Vestris, like Colman, Reynolds, Kean, Saker, Daly and Benson, placed Bottom's awakening
      here, thus prolonging suspense over the lovers' fate, and facilitating a change to another
      part of the forest. She cleared the stage thus: 'They mount the foot of sloping bank ...
      Portions of a Fairy bower rises on each side, meets over them and goes off up the bank with
      them – Lights up as the bower expands' (Pattie, *Dream*, p. 35). Vestris also initiated the prac-
      tice of a slow sunrise over the lake to precede Theseus and Hippolyta's entrance, replacing
      the moonlit mistakes with the clear light of day. Phelps managed the same effect by removing
      the gauze which had filled the proscenium throughout the wood scenes, and offering a lark
      song and sunrise effect: 'day dawned, and showed a ravine between pine-clad hills: horns
      were sounded, and Theseus, Hippolyta and their train entered from below, as if coming up
      the ravine' (Moyr Smith, *Dream*, p. xiii). Theseus' hunting party in Kean's production
      included four Heralds (one to wake each of the lovers), Squires, Amazons and Slaves (who
      carried a boar on a pole, even though Shakespeare's 'proposed hunting' was set aside). Daly
      brought on Philostrate with the hunting party who arrived in a barge; Shaw objected to
      Theseus, 'clad in the armour of Alcibiades and the red silk of Charley's Aunt' having to pick
      his way through the sleeping lovers, who were as conspicuous as the lions in Trafalgar
      Square, make all his hunting speeches and then exclaim 'But soft, what nymphs are these?'
      as though 'he could in any extremity of absence of mind have missed seeing them all along'
      (Shaw, *Nineties*, I, pp. 181, 180). Benson's Theseus, like Dunlop's in 1967, was accompanied
      by real, if reluctant, hounds. Bridges Adams managed his transition with 'the flight of the
      fairies on the approach of dawn, streaming over the hillside and but faintly glimpsed
      between the trees. This is followed by a distinct pause; the light of morning breaks, the
      music of a wide-awake humanity sounds the alarm, and Duke Theseus and his alabaster

THESEUS Go, one of you, find out the forester;   100
            For now our observation is performed,
            And since we have the vaward of the day,
            My love shall hear the music of my hounds.
            Uncouple in the western valley; let them go:
            Dispatch, I say, and find the forester.   105
                                    [*Exit an Attendant*]
            We will, fair Queen, up to the mountain's top,
            And mark the musical confusion
            Of hounds and echo in conjunction.
HIPPOLYTA I was with Hercules and Cadmus once,

knights-at-arms command the scene. The fairy world has vanished with the night' (Stratford *Herald*, 29 April 1932). This effect was still unusual enough to seem like a 'laudable innovation' to Crosse in 1949, when he saw it in Atkins's production at the St Martin's (*Diary* XX, p. 17). In 1954 Benthall had a 'long ballet before the fairies melted away in the daybreak' (*Birmingham Post*, 1 September). As Richardson's fairies vanished, 'their squealing fades into a music of horns heard distantly' (*Times*, 25 January 1962). Brook eschewed effects, 'forgoing business and gimmickry (a calculated risk) at the first hint of morning – forgoing even a change of light so that day comes through the words themselves, where the true magic has been all along' (*Listener*, 17 June 1971); Brook's Oberon and Titania (who were doubled with Theseus and Hippolyta) effected the change from one character to another here simply by putting on cloaks, yet even the veteran critic J. C. Trewin found this 'the most astonishing moment in a night of wonders' (*Birmingham Post*, 5 September 1970). In Daniels's staging 'another great moment is the masque-like reveille of Titania and Bottom in the Bower, the company spinning out as the orange dawn comes up and, Oberon's work done, descending quietly into the basket along with Bottom's gnarled and disconcerting donkey head' (*Financial Times*, 16 July 1981). The *TLS* noted that Daniels's Victorian staging meant that 'the hunting scene looks more convincing than usual when played in pinks and toppers' (31 July 1981). Alexander staged this scene in the loggia of a neoclassical hunting lodge, with the fairies laying the lovers down in a star formation.

In Reynolds's version, which had altered the preceding lines to reflect the fact that the lovers had not yet fought and slept, Bottom awoke and had a scene with his friends, then Theseus and Philostrate, who are in the woods hunting, discuss the plays that might be performed and Theseus intervenes in the rehearsal. The scene of the lovers' awakening does not appear, nor does Hippolyta, and there is no performance of 'Pyramus and Thisbe' in the last act.

100–5 Vestris cut 100–4; Kean and Saker cut 101, Kean also cut 'let them' and 105. Tree supplied the sound of the dogs in 1911 through a 'hound record', an early example of a recorded sound effect.

109 Hippolyta in Alexander's staging now had a different tone of voice, presumably reflecting her adventures as Titania.

When in a wood of Crete they bayed the bear   110
With hounds of Sparta: never did I hear
Such gallant chiding; for besides the groves,
The skies, the fountains, every region near
Seemed all one mutual cry. I never heard
So musical a discord, such sweet thunder.   115

THESEUS My hounds are bred out of the Spartan kind,
So flewed, so sanded; and their heads are hung
With ears that sweep away the morning dew;
Crook-kneed, and dewlapped like Thessalian bulls;
Slow in pursuit, but matched in mouth like bells,   120
Each under each. A cry more tuneable
Was never hallooed to nor cheered with horn
In Crete, in Sparta, nor in Thessaly.
Judge when you hear. But soft, what nymphs are these?

EGEUS My lord, this is my daughter here asleep,   125
And this Lysander; this Demetrius is,
This Helena, old Nedar's Helena.
I wonder of their being here together.

THESEUS No doubt they rose up early to observe
The rite of May, and hearing our intent   130
Came here in grace of our solemnity.
But speak, Egeus; is not this the day
That Hermia should give answer of her choice?

EGEUS It is, my lord.

THESEUS Go, bid the huntsmen wake them with their horns.   135
Shout within; wind horns; [the lovers] all start up.
Good morrow, friends. Saint Valentine is past;
Begin these woodbirds but to couple now?
[The lovers kneel.]

116ff.   Dean left out Theseus' description of his hounds (Crosse, *Diary* IV, p 44).

124   Caird marked the change in subject with some business in which Hippolyta hit Theseus
on the bottom and they laughed and kissed before Theseus saw the lovers.

127   Tree cut Helena's paternity.

129–32   Vestris cut to 'Egeus'; Kean's version of 129–32 follows 135, omitting on both modest and
anachronistic grounds the reference to early rising to do observance to the 'rite of May'.
Daniels had his lovers 'laid to sleep not in pairs but in a general heap, enabling Mike Gwilym
to wring even more wry humour than usual from '"No doubt" and "Good Morrow".'
(Warren, 'Interpretations', p. 147). Caird's Theseus directed 129 at the audience with irony.

136–7   Kean, followed by Saker, cut these further anachronistic lines; Daly cut 137.

LYSANDER Pardon, my lord.
THESEUS   I pray you all, stand up.
    I know you two are rival enemies:
    How comes this gentle concord in the world,   140
    That hatred is so far from jealousy
    To sleep by hate, and fear no enmity?
LYSANDER My lord, I shall reply amazedly,
    Half sleep, half waking; but as yet, I swear,
    I cannot truly say how I came here.   145
    But as I think (for truly would I speak)
    And now I do bethink me, so it is –
    I came with Hermia hither. Our intent
    Was to be gone from Athens, where we might
    Without the peril of the Athenian law –   150
EGEUS Enough, enough, my lord; you have enough –
    I beg the law, the law upon his head!
    They would have stol'n away, they would, Demetrius,
    Thereby to have defeated you and me,
    You of your wife, and me of my consent,   155
    Of my consent that she should be your wife.
DEMETRIUS My lord, fair Helen told me of their stealth,
    Of this their purpose hither to this wood;
    And I in fury hither followed them,
    Fair Helena in fancy following me.   160
    But, my good lord, I wot not by what power
    (But by some power it is), my love to Hermia,
    Melted as the snow, seems to me now

138   Demetrius and Lysander were hand in hand in Caird's production until 160.
143   In 1937 Guthrie apparently had Hippolyta serving 'the awakened lovers with brew from a bowl with a ladle' (Farjeon, *Scene*, p. 47).
144–7   Lysander's stumbling to wakefulness becomes much crisper in Vestris and Daly, who cut all these lines; Phelps similarly cut after 'think' in 146, Kean and Saker cut everything except 'But as I think'.
148–50   Atkins cut from the end of 148; Daly added a 'be' to 149 to tidy up the grammar.
155–60   Hall's cut here removes Egeus' characteristically fussy gloss on his defeat and Demetrius' explanation of events the audience has already seen. Vestris, Kean, Saker kept 157 and 159; Benson cut 155–6. For Daniels 'Simon Templeman made so much of Demetrius's lyrical speech about his rediscovered love for Helena that he moved Juliet Stevenson's Hippolyta to influence Theseus to overbear Egeus's will' (Warren, 'Interpretations', p. 147).
162–3   Vestris, Kean and Saker read 'my love to Hermia seems to me now'.
163–75   Demetrius's account of his problems was often toned down by cutting here: Vestris cut 165

As the remembrance of an idle gaud
Which in my childhood I did dote upon; 165
And all the faith, the virtue of my heart,
The object and the pleasure of mine eye,
Is only Helena. To her, my lord,
Was I betrothed ere I saw Hermia;
But like a sickness did I loathe this food. 170
But, as in health come to my natural taste,
Now I do wish it, love it, long for it,
And will for evermore be true to it.
THESEUS Fair lovers, you are fortunately met.
Of this discourse we more will hear anon. 175
Egeus, I will overbear your will;
For in the temple, by and by, with us
These couples shall eternally be knit.
And, for the morning now is something worn,
Our purposed hunting shall be set aside. 180
Away with us to Athens. Three and three,
We'll hold a feast in great solemnity.
Come, Hippolyta.
Exit Theseus with Hippolyta, Egeus, and his train
DEMETRIUS These things seem small and undistinguishable,
Like far-off mountains turnèd into clouds. 185

168 and from the middle of 168 to 173, Daly (and Hall) cut 170–3, Benson 170–1, Tree to 165 and from the middle of 168 to 175, Atkins cut to 173.

168 Langham's combative Egeus interjected 'My lord' in the middle of this line, and elsewhere.

173 Alexander's Egeus stepped forward but Theseus stopped him. Caird's Helena reacted by weeping.

176 Daniels and Caird had Egeus leave at the end of the line. Alexander's rejected Lysander's proffered handshake.

182 Caird's Hippolyta had a moment with Hermia before she left.

183 Daly had a barge to transport the hunting party back to Athens by a 'panoramic illusion' which was 'altogether a mistake' (Dickins, *Forty Years*, p. 178). Eric Adeney, as Harcourt Williams's Egeus, 'went out with Theseus protesting to the last', but for Wolfit he 'made the best of a bad job when Theseus overbore his will' (Crosse, *Diary* XII pp. 51, 53, and XVII, p. 147). Noble's Egeus left from a different exit from everyone else and did not reappear in 5.1.

184–96 Cut by Vestris, Kean and Saker (and Hall); Daly opened with Demetrius' words from 189 and cut 193; Benson gave the first part of 195 to all the lovers and cut 195–6 as did Tree who added a 'Yes we are awake'; Tree opened his exchanges with Helena's words from 187, cutting Demetrius and Hermia, and assigned Demetrius' statement in 190–1 to Lysander. Devine cut Demetrius' question in 189–90.

HERMIA Methinks I see these things with parted eye,
       When everything seems double.
HELENA   So methinks;
       And I have found Demetrius, like a jewel,
       Mine own, and not mine own.
DEMETRIUS   Are you sure
       That we are awake? It seems to me   190
       That yet we sleep, we dream. Do not you think
       The Duke was here, and bid us follow him?
HERMIA Yea, and my father.
HELENA   And Hippolyta.
LYSANDER And he did bid us follow to the temple.
DEMETRIUS Why, then, we are awake. Let's follow him,   195
       And by the way let us recount our dreams.

                                                    Exeunt lovers

                      Bottom wakes.

BOTTOM When my cue comes, call me, and I will answer. My next is
       'Most fair Pyramus'. Heigh ho! Peter Quince? Flute the bellows-
       mender? Snout the tinker? Starveling? God's my life! Stolen hence
       and left me asleep! I have had a most rare vision. I have had a dream,   200
       past the wit of man to say what dream it was. Man is but an ass
       if he go about to expound this dream. Methought I was – there is
       no man can tell what. Methought I was – and methought I had – but
       man is but a patched fool if he will offer to say what methought
       I had. The eye of man hath not heard, the ear of man hath not seen,   205
       man's hand is not able to taste, his tongue to conceive, nor his heart
       to report what my dream was! I will get Peter Quince to write a
       ballad of this dream; it shall be called 'Bottom's Dream', because
       it hath no bottom; and I will sing it in the latter end of a play, before
       the Duke. Peradventure, to make it the more gracious, I shall sing   210
       it at her death.   *Exit*

In Benson's 1903 production 'these solemn lines are burlesqued' with laughter greeting
Demetrius's yawning and the lovers' embrace, so that Helena's 'Mine own...' was 'still music
among those jarring discords' (Stratford *Herald*, 22 April). In Calthrop's staging, 'after
Theseus and his train had gone off in this scene the fairy influence was resumed and the
stage was again enveloped in twilight gradually deepening to complete darkness with the
lovers silhouetted against it making one of the most striking stage effects I have ever seen.
The traditional kiss at "why, then" was omitted' (Crosse, *Diary* VIII, pp. 97, 99). In Guthrie's
1937 version, the lovers 'were still dazed and did not know how to pair off. This was a
mistake I think' (Crosse, *Diary* XVII, p. 53). For Brook 'the stage is bare, the silence austere,
when the young lovers open their eyes and huddle together with a strange new apprehen-

sion of the world: "Are you sure that we are awake?"' (*Listener*, 17 June 1971). Barton's
lovers, 'instead of behaving like giggly aristos at a deb's ball, are visibly shaken by their
experience' (*Guardian*, 9 May 1977). Bryden had 'four of the fairies steal out of the darkness
to plant a kiss on the newly reconciled lovers' (*Guardian* in *LTR* 1982). The *Guardian* complained of Alexander's lovers, 'if the lovers are meant to be enriched by their night in the
enchanted forest, why do they emerge looking so unaffected?' (10 July 1986). Caird's lovers
shared a look before they began to discuss their experience, but still began to exit in the
wrong couples. Lepage's 'bewildered lovers finally reunited, walk hand in hand towards the
back of the stage, where day dawns and they can at last cleanse themselves of the mud of
their dark desires in showers conveniently plumbed into the forest' (*Daily Telegraph*, 13 July
1992), substituting water for light as the symbolic purifier. Noble's lovers had a last look
back in amazement as they left the forest.

197–211   Colman, Reynolds, Vestris, Kean, Saker, Benson and Daly all played Bottom's speech before
the arrival of Theseus and Hippolyta, partly to prevent two scenes with Bottom being adja-
cent. Bottom's awakening is traditionally one of the play's big moments and is usually very
lightly cut: Bowdler objected to 205–7 (which Hall was to cut), presumably on the grounds
of their blasphemous mangling of the Bible; Tree removed 197, 203–5 and 209–11.

    When Phelps awoke he was preoccupied and his tone was that of 'a man who had lived
with spirits and not yet perfectly returned into the flesh' (Morley, in Rowell, *Dramatic
Criticism*, p. 105). Frank Matthews, in Kean's production, 'expresses very humorously a hazy
condition of the perceptive faculties' (*Times*, 12 February 1859). Benson's Bottom awoke to
what sounds remarkably like an bird symphony: the fairies disappeared at the first ray of
sunlight, Bottom stirred in his sleep, a bird sang alone, Bottom delivered his soliloquy while
property men with birdcalls created the effect of birds in different parts of the woods
answering one another until there was 'a full quire welcoming the dayspring' (Moyr Smith,
Dream, p. xv). George Weir who played the part in many of Benson's productions was
notable for remaining stolid even on waking until he found a wisp of hay in his pouch which
sent him offstage slowly and thoughtfully (Trewin, *Benson*, p. 58). Foss informed Rudolph de
Cordova that Bottom 'finding some hay in his pouch' was 'very old' business: 'beginning in
1880, he has seen it done by every Bottom except the actors who have played the part in his
productions, for he disapproves of it very strongly, as the fairies are not able to provide
Bottom with the food or music for which he asks' (de Cordova's letter to an unidentified
publication, dated 9 August 1936, cutting now in HTC). At the end of the speech, Tree's
Bottom 'rolls up part, sighs, puts it in pouch. feels & brings out hay[,] holds it before him,
pulls out some with L. H. drops it, feels for ears & tail, takes hay out with both hands. Goes
off feeling for ears & tail, and looking at hay' (promptbook). Atkins recalled that in Tree's 1911
revival when Bottom called for Quince 'a rabbit appeared and Bottom beat a swift retreat'
(*Autobiography*, p. 73). Dean's Bottom, Wilfrid Walter, 'did not quite give us the wonder and
pathos of his translation' (Agate, *Chronicles*, p. 42), whereas at the Old Vic in 1926, Baliol
Holloway's 'awakening from his "translation" is a marvel of bemused wonderment and

exaltation' (*Star*, partially identified VW cutting) and at Stratford in 1937 his 'expression of wonderment and amazement on emerging from his woodland dream is a marvel of mute eloquence and drollery' (*Star*, 30 March); Richardson, in Harcourt Williams's 1931 production, 'showed that he was still half in a maze, thinking of Titania and the wondrous fairyland he has been in, not of his tail and ears as Weir did' (Crosse, *Diary* XIII, p. 31). For Bridges Adams, Roy Byford's 'comic perplexity' was expressed in his 'widened eye, wrinkled nose, and twitching finger, as he expounds his bottomless dream' (Stratford *Herald*, 8 June 1934); Jay Laurier (at Stratford in 1942) was bewildered as 'rapt, puzzled and not a little frightened, he stood in wide-eyed wonder recalling the ass-head', at which point 'rude comedy tip-toed enquiringly in the direction of rustic tragedy' (*Birmingham Post*, 6 April). John Slater, for Benthall in 1949, found a flower in his ear at 'methought I had', which he threw away at 'what my dream was', presumably an attempt to convey something of the lasting impact of Bottom's translation; he also had 'shuddering and very effective memories of his ass's bray' (*Guardian*, 25 April). Similarly, Devine's Bottom awoke and found 'one of the musk-roses in his hair' with 'a vague consciousness of a miraculous dream' (*ILN*, 3 April 1954). Opinions were divided over Charles Laughton in 1959: 'in his reflections on his dream [he] missed altogether the overtones of wonder, glee and panic awe which should inspire him' according to the *Sunday Times* (7 June), whereas J. C. Trewin found 'nearly all of the night's dream-sense in Laughton's eye' (*Birmingham Post*, 3 June). The *Guardian*'s comment on Douglas Campbell in Langham's production shows how far the waking had become a benchmark for judging Bottoms: 'the famous awakening was done in a simple way, with kindly puzzlement in due measure. What it lacked was that enormity of surmise which makes the scene one of the best in all comedy' (22 December, 1960). As Brook's Bottom rolled out of the bower the fairies made bird noises (promptbook). When Richard Griffiths woke in Barton's production, 'we see him stirred into poetry and picking up all he can remember of the enchantment' for his ballad, which he actually sang in 5.1 (*Times*, 9 May 1977). For Bryden, Derek Newark was 'short on confused wonderment' (*Financial Times*, in *LTR* 1982); Richard Briers, in Branagh's staging, was 'untouched by residual fear and a memory of delight' (*Observer*, 19 August 1990), whereas Spall (for Lepage) 'captures superbly the tantalising elusiveness of dreams' (*Daily Telegraph*, 13 July 1992). Desmond Barrit, for Noble, looked into his trousers at 'methought I had', in fond recollection of his dalliance with Titania.

201 In Barton's version, 'as Richard Griffiths's plump and homely Bottom describes his dream, fairy voices echo through the wood' (*Guardian*, 9 May 1977).

ACT 4, SCENE 2

Enter QUINCE, FLUTE, SNOUT and STARVELING

QUINCE Have you sent to Bottom's house? Is he come home yet?
STARVELING He cannot be heard of. Out of doubt he is transported.
FLUTE If he come not, then the play is marred. It goes not forward.
    Doth it?
QUINCE It is not possible. You have not a man in all Athens able to   5
    discharge Pyramus but he.
FLUTE No, he hath simply the best wit of any handicraft man in Athens.
QUINCE Yea, and the best person, too; and he is a very paramour for
    a sweet voice.
FLUTE You must say 'paragon'. A paramour is (God bless us!) a thing   10
    of naught.   *Enter* SNUG *the joiner*

SNUG Masters, the Duke is coming from the temple, and there is two

0 SD   This scene has usually been played in the same set as 1.2, emphasising the scenic symmetry
      of the play. Reynolds's brief woodland version of the scene led direct into a performance of
      'Pyramus and Thisbe' in which Theseus, who was in the wood hunting with Philostrate, inter-
      vened. Benson placed this scene after Bottom's awakening and before Theseus' arrival in the
      wood, so that the scene switched from Quince's cottage back to the wood, minimising the
      effect of Theseus' entry into the world of the wood. Daly's acting edition printed this scene
      but it appears in neither promptbooks nor programme. Tree staged it on the opening night
      of his 1900 production but then dropped it to save time; in his 1911 revival it was 'just hinted
      at by the appearance of the Clowns who have apparently come back to look for Bottom and
      rush on to greet him in his restored shape as the curtain falls. One rather suspects that this
      innovation hints a doubt of the actor's ability to give the last speech of the scene in a manner
      worthy of a "curtain" in the modern sense' (Crosse, *Diary* V, p. 49). Crosse found Asche's
      'business of the actors giving up their parts ... amusing' (*Diary* IV, p. 38)
8–11   Directors sometimes reassign these lines, presumably because the mistake about 'paramour'
      seems more likely to have been someone other than Quince's. Reynolds allowed Bottom to
      steal Flute's 'paragon' line as he came between Quince and Snug to make a magnificently
      theatrical re-entry into their lives. Benson cut 10–11. Benthall gave 8–9 to Snout and 10–11 to
      Quince; Bridges Adams and Hall both took 'paramour for a sweet voice' from Quince, giving it
      to Flute and Snout respectively; Alexander's Quince got it right but was corrected by Flute.
12–19   Vestris cut Snug's lines, Kean left only 'if our sport had gone forward, we had all been made men'

or three lords and ladies more married. If our sport had gone
forward, we had all been made men.

FLUTE O, sweet bully Bottom! Thus hath he lost sixpence a day during 15
his life: he could not have 'scaped sixpence a day. And the Duke
had not given him sixpence a day for playing Pyramus, I'll be
hanged. He would have deserved it. Sixpence a day in Pyramus,
or nothing. *Enter* BOTTOM

BOTTOM Where are these lads? Where are these hearts? 20
QUINCE Bottom! O most courageous day! O most happy hour!
BOTTOM Masters, I am to discourse wonders – but ask me not what;
for if I tell you, I am not true Athenian. I will tell you everything,
right as it fell out.
QUINCE Let us hear, sweet Bottom. 25
BOTTOM Not a word of me. All that I will tell you is – that the Duke
hath dined. Get your apparel together, good strings to your beards,
new ribbons to your pumps: meet presently at the palace, every man
look o'er his part. For the short and the long is, our play is preferred.
In any case, let Thisbe have clean linen; and let not him that plays 30
the lion pare his nails, for they shall hang out for the lion's claws.
And, most dear actors, eat no onions nor garlic; for we are to utter
sweet breath, and I do not doubt but to hear them say it is a sweet
comedy. No more words. Away! Go, away! *Exeunt*

and Saker cut everything; Langham gave Flute's speech to Quince. At 14, Brook's Starveling tore
cloth, Snug hit the wall and they all wandered aimlessly in disappointment (promptbook) before
breaking into 'the dirge sung by Quince and his crew to the phrase "Sixpence a day!"' (*Punch*, 15
September 1970). Daniels's Quince took off his false moustache at 'hanged' (promptbook).

19–21 Bottom's return in Brook's production 'causes Quince to weep' (*Daily Telegraph*, 14 September
1970). In Daniels's staging, Bottom was heard whistling offstage before he entered. Alexander's
Mechanicals rushed up to Bottom, and Starveling and Snout chaired him.

26 In the Reinhardt film, Bottom decides against telling his tale when a real ass puts its head
through the window before 'not a word of me'.

26–7 Vestris, Kean and Saker cut 'that the Duke hath dined', presumably on naturalistic grounds.

27–8 Vestris, Phelps, Kean and Saker cut from 'good' to 'pumps'.

30–1 Kean cut any reference to the Lion. In Daniels's staging, the running gag that no-one could
remember Snug's name paid off 'with an original punch line on "Let not him that plays the
lion" with a mid-phrase stutter' (*Financial Times*, 16 July 1981).

32–4 Tree gave this to Bottom in 1.1, Vestris cut all of it, Devine cut 'and I do ... comedy'. Brook's
Mechanicals all tried to exit together through one door (promptbook). In Caird's staging,
'no onions' was motivated by Snout's bad breath.

ACT 5, SCENE 1

Enter THESEUS, HIPPOLYTA, PHILOSTRATE, Lords and Attendants

0 SD   Reynolds began with a formal entrance for Theseus and Hippolyta, supposedly after the true performance of 'Pyramus and Thisbe', into 'Theseus' Grand Hall of Audience'. Very little of his scene was Shakespearean: Theseus protests that he would not watch the forthcoming 'Grand Pageant, commemorative of the Triumphs of THESEUS', but for the fact that Hippolyta has prepared it (presumably this is why she could not make the hunt), Egeus expresses some paternal sentiments Shakespeare had neglected to provide and remembers how like her mother Hermia has become, the lovers are called to account and Demetrius reveals he has changed his mind; faced with filial pleas, Egeus relents and Hippolyta's natural expression of surprise allows Theseus to squeeze in some of the 'the lunatic, the lover and the poet' speech and his 4.1 promise that the lovers will marry at the same time as him, before his 'hardy veterans' arrive to a song from Hermia which suggests that the 'pageant' was in part a patriotic tribute to soldiers returning from the Napoleonic wars (*Dream*, pp. 53–7).

Vestris followed Reynolds with her 'Appartment in the Palace of Theseus'; Phelps had 'a columned hall, with a background of closed curtains, the stage being lighted by Greek candelabra' (Moyr Smith, *Dream*, p. xiii). Saker followed the Mendelssohn Wedding March with a 'grand Nuptial Procession and Floral offering' (playbill), while Benson began with 'an altar and its attendant priests and all the pretty pomp and archaeological interest of a procession of "the period"' (*Era*, 22 December 1889). Tree's opening represents the pictorial Athenian tradition well: 'the interior of Theseus' Palace, amidst lofty columns and magnificent capitals, beneath which Theseus and Hippolyta sit in state surrounded by a guard of Amazons clad in tiger-skins whilst the now happy lovers stand near, and at their feet recline maidens in robes of blue or pink or tan silk. The place is lit by lamps held by tall men dressed in brown and gold tunics, whilst gigantic Negroes stand about like statues' (*Era*, 13 January 1900). Barker used a 'very solidly-built' palace set with steps and solid columns against a star spangled backdrop' (Odell, *Betterton to Irving*, II, p. 408), which may have been intended to represent the stability that had descended on the characters after the turmoil of the woods. Wifrid Walter designed 'a truly classical set of the Great Chamber in the Palace of Theseus' for Thorndike and Warburton (VW cutting). Dean's fairies 'actually open the last scene' (Farjeon, *Scene*, p. 42). In 1949 Benthall began with an extra washing plates (an indication that supper was over) and one of Theseus' attendants chasing one of Hippolyta's ladies and forcing her to sit down; presumably this was intended to have thematic resonances (promptbook). In 1951, Guthrie had 'gentlemen

HIPPOLYTA 'Tis strange, my Theseus, that these lovers speak of.
THESEUS More strange than true. I never may believe
These antique fables, nor these fairy toys.
Lovers and madmen have such seething brains,
Such shaping fantasies, that apprehend   5
More than cool reason ever comprehends.
The lunatic, the lover, and the poet
Are of imagination all compact:
One sees more devils than vast hell can hold;
That is the madman. The lover, all as frantic,   10
Sees Helen's beauty in a brow of Egypt.
The poet's eye, in a fine frenzy rolling,
Doth glance from heaven to earth, from earth to heaven;
And as imagination bodies forth
The forms of things unknown, the poet's pen   15
Turns them to shapes, and gives to airy nothing
A local habitation and a name.
Such tricks hath strong imagination

attendants buckling together a colonnade to represent the Palace' (*New Statesman*, 5 January 1952). Other directors have reverted to their 1.1 sets, although increasingly the stage space for 5 has been created by lighting and the stage floor, rather than by an actual built set.

1   Benson began with Theseus' 'Joy gentle friends' before reverting to Theseus and Hippolyta's dialogue, so that the scene went 29–31 (omitting 'your board, your bed'), 1–17, 32–3–5, then carried on from 38. Caird had Theseus and Hippolyta alone for the initial dialogue; during Theseus' first speech he picked a flower and put it in Hippolyta's hair.

2   Theseus perched on a balustrade for Benthall in 1949, with Philostrate clapping his hands and shushing a servant and all the servants freezing until the end of Hippolyta's reply (promptbook). In Lepage's production, it was 'impossible to concentrate on Theseus' thematically vital speech... because behind him the four lovers (still in nightwear of course) are making an eccentric progress, stepping on chairs round the side of the pool, their servant having to race backwards and forwards transferring the end chairs to the front so that they can keep going' (*Independent*, 11 July 1992). Clare Bayley perceptively pointed out that there was a thematic significance to the lovers' actions since 'once civilised' they stayed out of the mud 'using chairs as stepping stones' (*What's On*, 15 July 1992).

4–6   Cut by Vestris, Phelps, Kean, Saker and Daly (5–6 only) but not by later directors.

7ff.   For Guthrie in 1937, Gyles Isham spoke 'the glorious lines... in a tender confidential aside to Hippolyta' (*Evening Standard*, 28 December).

18–27   Cut by Vestris, Phelps (18–22 only), Kean, Saker, Daly, Benson, Tree and Atkins. While the initial part of the cut reduces the amount of Theseus' generalisations, the later part further shortens Hippolyta's already limited role. Hall also cut Hippolyta's response. Coghill

That if it would but apprehend some joy,
It comprehends some bringer of that joy;   20
Or in the night, imagining some fear,
How easy is a bush supposed a bear?
HIPPOLYTA But all the story of the night told over,
And all their minds transfigured so together,
More witnesseth than fancy's images,   25
And grows to something of great constancy;
But howsoever, strange and admirable.

Enter the lovers: LYSANDER, DEMETRIUS, HERMIA *and* HELENA

THESEUS Here come the lovers, full of joy and mirth.
Joy, gentle friends, joy and fresh days of love
Accompany your hearts!
LYSANDER   More than to us   30
Wait in your royal walks, your board, your bed!
THESEUS Come now: what masques, what dances shall we have
To wear away this long age of three hours
Between our after-supper and bedtime?
Where is our usual manager of mirth?   35
What revels are in hand? Is there no play
To ease the anguish of a torturing hour?
Call Philostrate.
PHILOSTRATE   Here, mighty Theseus.

costumed his lovers in Van Dyck velvet here 'to give solemnity to the comedy' (Coghill letter). Caird's Theseus and Hippolyta kissed at 'admirable'; the lovers and other revellers (including a drunken Puck) entered to the Mendelssohn Wedding March and swirls of confetti.

29 Hermia and Egeus embraced here in Caird's production to onstage applause; Lysander also shook hands with Egeus during this speech. Noble's Egeus was not present in this scene.

31 Kean, decorously, changed 'bed' to 'home', Benson omitted both board and bed. In Caird's staging, Lysander's 'bed' overstepped the bound of propriety, as was indicated by the tone of Theseus' 'Come now'.

33-8 Theseus' references to the forthcoming consummation of the marriages, though relatively general, were too frank for nineteenth-century directors: Phelps, Kean, Saker, cut 33-4; Daly and Benson cut 34 and Benson 36-7, Kean and Saker also cut the last sentence of 36-7.

38 Philostrate is almost invisible before the twentieth century, attracting very occasional attention for the quality of his diction, like J. Fritz Russell who had a 'remarkably clear and cultured delivery' in Asche's 1905 production (HTC cutting). He was 'magnificently overbearing' for Barker (*Era*, 11 February 1914) and Malvolian for Harcourt Williams and Hall (*Stage*,

THESEUS Say, what abridgement have you for this evening?
    What masque, what music? How shall we beguile   40
    The lazy time if not with some delight?
PHILOSTRATE [*Giving him a paper.*]
    There is a brief how many sports are ripe.
    Make choice of which your highness will see first.
THESEUS [*Reading.*]
    'The battle with the Centaurs, to be sung
    By an Athenian eunuch to the harp' –   45
    We'll none of that; that have I told my love
    In glory of my kinsman, Hercules.
    [*Reading.*] 'The riot of the tipsy Bacchanals,
    Tearing the Thracian singer in their rage' –
    That is an old device, and it was played   50
    When I from Thebes came last a conqueror.
    [*Reading.*] 'The thrice three Muses mourning for the death
    Of learning, late deceased in beggary' –
    That is some satire keen and critical,
    Not sorting with a nuptial ceremony.   55

5 November 1931; *Scotsman*, 16 July 1962). Unsurprisingly, he has been seen as 'perfectly Civil Service' (Stratford *Herald*, 30 April 1943) and, in Dunlop's modern dress version, as 'the model of a modern ADC' (*Financial Times*, 27 September 1967). Brook's doubling of the role with Puck yielded no great insights and has not become as established as the doubling of mortal and fairy rulers, though Noble repeated it in 1994. Alexander and Caird are among recent directors to lose Philostrate completely; Caird pressed 'Good Egeus' into service here.

40–1   Tree cut this expansion on Theseus' questions; Kean and Saker had cut the last sentence, which perhaps stressed laziness and pleasure too much.

42   In Daniels's staging 'Theseus chooses the Pyramus play from a handsomely printed royal marriage programme' (*Times*, 16 July 1981).

43   Cut by Saker and Tree, anticipating the fact that only 'Pyramus and Thisbe' is actually performed.

44ff.   Bowdler preferred 'songster' to 'eunuch' in 45 and Kean came up with 'Minstrel'. Many directors broadly follow F in giving the titles of the plays to someone other than Theseus. Vestris, Kean and Daniels, following F, used Lysander; Benthall, Devine and Hall gave the titles to Philostrate; Langham used Lysander and Demetrius.

44–55   One or more of the alternative plays has often been removed: Phelps left out the Bacchanals and the Muses, Benson had only 'Pyramus and Thisbe' on the agenda:, Kean, Saker and Daly omitted the Muses. In Reinhardt's film, Puck substituted the Mechanicals' scroll for the one that Philostrate had chosen, thus giving extra point to his subsequent attempts to persuade Theseus against seeing it. Richardson declared that his production had 'virtually no cuts ...

[*Reading.*] 'A tedious brief scene of young Pyramus
And his love Thisbe, very tragical mirth' –
Merry and tragical? Tedious and brief?
That is hot ice and wondrous strange snow!
How shall we find the concord of this discord? 60
PHILOSTRATE A play there is, my lord, some ten words long,
    Which is as 'brief' as I have known a play,
    But by ten words, my lord, it is too long,
    Which makes it 'tedious'. For in all the play
    There is not one word apt, one player fitted. 65
    And 'tragical', my noble lord, it is,
    For Pyramus therein doth kill himself,
    Which when I saw rehearsed, I must confess,
    Made mine eyes water; but more 'merry' tears
    The passion of loud laughter never shed. 70
THESEUS What are they that do play it?
PHILOSTRATE Hard-handed men that work in Athens here,
    Which never laboured in their minds till now;
    And now have toiled their unbreathed memories
    With this same play against your nuptial. 75
THESEUS And we will hear it.
PHILOSTRATE   No, my noble lord,
    It is not for you. I have heard it over,
    And it is nothing, nothing in the world,
    Unless you can find sport in their intents,
    Extremely stretched, and conned with cruel pain, 80
    To do you service.
THESEUS   I will hear that play;

apart from a few lines at the beginning of Act V, where Theseus reads of the alternative
entertainments available, which involves Shakespeare in some contemporary satire of no
great interest to a modern theatre audience' (interview in *Plays and Players*, February 1962).
59   Omitted by Kean and Saker.
60–76   Saker, pedantically, cut 'some ten words long' as well as following Kean in removing 63–6 and
    67–70 which are naturalistically problematic; Kean also cut 73, perhaps finding it offensive to
    the Mechanicals? Benson cut everything, further reducing Philostrate's contribution.
76–81   Kean and Saker removed Philostrate's critical comments in 80 and 81; Daly cut both
    Theseus' and Philostrate's speeches: Benson let Philostrate get as far as his first 'nothing'. In
    Bridges Adams's 1923 staging, Philostrate's 'delivery of the verse impresses upon you that he
    is a State official of high degree, subservient only to mighty Theseus; and with what wealth
    of expression does he invest those few simple words' (Stratford *Herald*, 18 May).

For never anything can be amiss
When simpleness and duty tender it.
Go bring them in; and take your places, ladies.

[*Exit Philostrate*]

HIPPOLYTA I love not to see wretchedness o'ercharged, 85
And duty in his service perishing.
THESEUS Why, gentle sweet, you shall see no such thing.
HIPPOLYTA He says they can do nothing in this kind.
THESEUS The kinder we, to give them thanks for nothing.
Our sport shall be to take what they mistake; 90
And what poor duty cannot do, noble respect
Takes it in might, not merit.
Where I have come, great clerks have purposèd
To greet me with premeditated welcomes,
Where I have seen them shiver and look pale, 95
Make periods in the midst of sentences,
Throttle their practised accent in their fears,
And in conclusion dumbly have broke off,
Not paying me a welcome. Trust me, sweet,
Out of this silence yet I picked a welcome, 100
And in the modesty of fearful duty
I read as much as from the rattling tongue
Of saucy and audacious eloquence.
Love, therefore, and tongue-tied simplicity
In least speak most, to my capacity. 105

Enter PHILOSTRATE

PHILOSTRATE So please your grace, the Prologue is addressed.

84 Phelps cut the first part of the line and Benson the last.
85–105 Phelps, Kean and Saker cut the initial exchanges between Theseus and Hippolyta (85–7); Tree and Atkins cut the whole of this section. Theseus' speech on welcoming speeches has been very heavily cut: Vestris (followed by Daly, Bridges Adams and Langham) excised 93–105: Phelps, Kean and Saker cut from 91, Benson cut 91–103: Benthall cut from 90.
106 According to the *Times*, 17 November 1840, Vestris's 'Pyramus and Thisbe' was performed 'in a theatre constructed after the antique'. Benson played 'Pyramus and Thisbe' on a platform with curtained doorways. In 1911 Tree performed the play 'with Elizabethan accessories "This is a garden" etc.' (Crosse, *Diary* V, p. 56). Barker's onstage audience (which included Helena's father Nedar in the cause of symmetry, though he spoke no lines) was placed on his less well-lit lower stage, sharing the real audience's view of the performance of 'Pyramus and Thisbe'. Harcourt Williams thought that this was Barker's only mistake, since 'the laughter of Theseus and his Court at the absurdities of Pyramus and Thisbe seemed forced and

THESEUS Let him approach.

Flourish of trumpets.

Enter QUINCE *as Prologue*

QUINCE   If we offend, it is with our good will.
                 That you should think, we come not to offend,
                 But with good will. To show our simple skill,   110
                   That is the true beginning of our end.
                 ꞁConsider then, we come but in despite.
                 We do not come as minding to content you,
                 Our true intent is. All for your delight,
                   We are not here. That you should here repent you,   115
                 The actors are at hand; and by their show
                 You shall know all that you are like to know.

THESEUS This fellow doth not stand upon points.

LYSANDER He hath rid his prologue like a rough colt; he knows not
  the stop. A good moral, my lord; it is not enough to speak, but to   120
  speak true.

HIPPOLYTA Indeed, he hath played on this prologue like a child on
  a recorder – a sound, but not in government.

THESEUS His speech was like a tangled chain, nothing impaired, but
  all disordered. Who is next?   125

killed the genuine laughter of the audience' (*Four Years*, p. 190). Crosse, who had welcomed Calthrop's lovers sitting on the stage with their back to the audience in 1923, thought that it was a mistake in Williams's own production for Theseus and the other spectators to sit at the back 'instead of at the side as usual' (*Diary* VIII, p. 101; XII, p. 50). In Guthrie's 1951 staging the stage audience adopted another strategy: 'the grouped courtiers cannot sit still for a minute: every thirty seconds they pick up their stools and chatteringly rearrange themselves' (*New Statesman*, 5 January 1952).

108   Quince was introduced by a 'cacophonous trumpet' in Calthrop's production (Crosse, *Diary* VIII, p. 101). Randle Ayrton in Bridges Adams's 1926 staging stammered the prologue 'with his rose wreath askew' (*Birmingham Gazette*, 14 April). Guthrie had a 'screen behind which we saw the actors making up and so on' in 1937 (Crosse, *Diary* XVI, p. 138). Bryden's fairies 'enter Theseus' court bearing lanterns which they set down to define a three-sided acting area' (*Guardian*, in *LTR* 1982).

119–25 Kean cut Lysander and Hippolyta, Benson Hippolyta and Theseus, Tree and Atkins cut everything, Devine cut Lysander, Langham cut the exchange between Hippolyta and Theseus except for Theseus' question.

125   The Mechanicals' costumes for 'Pyramus and Thisbe' in most productions remain 'classical' (Cliff Weir played Bottom 'in the high Roman manner with helm and toga' at Stratford in

Enter with a Trumpeter before them [BOTTOM *as*] *Pyramus,* [FLUTE *as*]
Thisbe, [SNOUT *as*] *Wall,* [STARVELING *as*] *Moonshine and* [SNUG *as*]
Lion.

QUINCE (*as Prologue*)
          Gentles, perchance you wonder at this show,
          But wonder on, till truth make all things plain.
          This man is Pyramus, if you would know;
            This beauteous lady Thisbe is, certain.
          This man with lime and rough-cast doth present   130

1944, *Birmingham Post*, 11 May), often the only vestige of the Athenian staging tradition. However, Alexander's performed 'in tights and berets complete with ploddingly illustrative mime and the nauseous habit of applauding their audience' (*Listener*, 17 July 1986). Branagh's Quince had 'a big shot director's outfit of jodphurs, jackboots, beret and mega-phone' and was noteworthy for 'his cringing obeisances before the courtiers and the pecu-liar, white-glove hand motions with which he ushers in and out his hapless cast' (*Independent*, 15 August 1990), presumably parodying the Polish director Tadeusz Kantor. Traditionally, as in Asche's staging which owed much to Benson's, the Mechanicals here were 'acted rather for the laughter due to the absolutely comic than to the humour of the apparently sober yet absurd efforts' (*Sketch*, 6 December 1905), so the performance of 'Pyramus and Thisbe' was the site of very elaborate comic business with technical mishaps, wandering accents, prompting, ad-libbing and uncertain falsettos. Because this elaboration of business was so commonplace, its partial absence in Devine's 1954 staging was the more striking: 'Bottom and Quince have no trouble with a sticking sword. Quince does not paint the blood on "Thisbe's" mantle', but the new business with 'Quince's scroll that will not stay open, Bottom's turban that untwists itself unkindly at the wrong moment, and a nice bit of semi-throttling in the final Bergomask' (*ILN*, 3 April 1954) is typical. Barton's 'Pyramus and Thisbe' was 'all the funnier for being presented with deadly seriousness: lute and wind machine accompany the action, Quince permanently frets over mispronunciation' (*Guardian*, 9 May 1977). Daniels's play scene was 'a mixture of pantomime (Pyramus in harlequin tights and Thisbe as the "Dame"), music-hall (a piano commentary), and morris-dance (with Bottom, of course, wearing the horse's head)' (Warren, 'Interpretations', p. 147). In Branagh's production, where the Theseus/Oberon, Hippolyta/Titania doubles went for little, the *Independent* objected that 'Richard Briers's Bottom shows no twinge of déja vu when he meets Hippolyta in Act Five' (15 August 1990). Noble's staging of 'Pyramus and Thisbe was unusual for Daniel Evans's 'radiantly feminine Flute' and for Desmond Barrit's Bottom, 'a sincere and gifted amateur whose Pyramus is so good it makes the supercilious watchers cry' (Irving Wardle, *Independent on Sunday*, 7 August 1994).

126–50   Vestris and Kean (who extended the cut to 152) removed the descriptive Prologue.

> Wall, that vile wall which did these lovers sunder;
> And through Wall's chink, poor souls, they are content
>   To whisper – at the which let no man wonder.
> This man with lanthorn, dog, and bush of thorn,
>   Presenteth Moonshine; for, if you will know,   135
> By moonshine did these lovers think no scorn
>   To meet at Ninus' tomb, there, there to woo.
> This grisly beast, which Lion hight by name,
> The trusty Thisbe, coming first by night,
> Did scare away, or rather did affright;   140
> And as she fled, her mantle she did fall,
>   Which Lion vile with bloody mouth did stain.
> Anon comes Pyramus, sweet youth and tall,
>   And finds his trusty Thisbe's mantle slain;
> Whereat with blade, with bloody, blameful blade,   145
>   He bravely broached his boiling bloody breast;
> And Thisbe, tarrying in mulberry shade,
>   His dagger drew, and died. For all the rest,
> Let Lion, Moonshine, Wall, and lovers twain
> At large discourse, while here they do remain.   150
>   *Exeunt Quince, Bottom, Flute, Snug and Starveling*

THESEUS I wonder if the lion be to speak?
DEMETRIUS No wonder, my lord; one lion may, when many asses do.
SNOUT (*as Wall*)
> In this same interlude it doth befall
> That I, one Snout by name, present a wall;
> And such a wall as I would have you think   155

---

130 Bryden's Snout 'totters around on brick cothurni' as a 'deadpan Wall, bricks hanging from him like clothes on a washing line' (*Guardian, Financial Times*, in *LTR* 1982).

134 Alexander's 'experimental' Mechanicals went in for 'Brechtian touches such as a halter representing Starveling's dog' (*Guardian*, 10 July 1986).

140 at 'affright' Daniels's Snug turned his claws up and everyone was scared (promptbook).

150 Langham's onstage audience applauded at the end of the Prologue (promptbook).

151-2 Vestris, who had cut the preceeding Prologue, placed these lines after 210; Kean and Devine cut them. In Alexander's production, the Mechanicals' staging, influenced by Kantor and Marcel Marceau, included mime, owl hoots, humming, choric moaning and wind noises.

153 Vestris's 'dressing of Wall and Moonshine was too fine for the occasion' according to the *Athenaeum* (21 November 1840).

154 Theseus shushed the onstage audience in Langham's production (promptbook).

155-60 Saker cut 155-6 and 159-60. The lines are expendable since they duplicate information given elsewhere in the speech, but the comic element here lies precisely in their lumbering redundancy.

That had in it a crannied hole or chink,
Through which the lovers, Pyramus and Thisbe,
Did whisper often, very secretly.
This loam, this rough-cast, and this stone doth show
That I am that same wall; the truth is so. 160
And this the cranny is, right and sinister,
Through which the fearful lovers are to whisper.
THESEUS Would you desire lime and hair to speak better?
DEMETRIUS It is the wittiest partition that ever I heard discourse, my
lord. 165

Enter BOTTOM *as* PYRAMUS

THESEUS Pyramus draws near the wall; silence!
BOTTOM (*as Pyramus*)
O grim-looked night, O night with hue so black,
O night which ever art when day is not!
O night, O night, alack, alack, alack,
I fear my Thisbe's promise is forgot! 170
And thou, O wall, O sweet, O lovely wall,
That stand'st between her father's ground and mine,
Thou wall, O wall, O sweet and lovely wall,
Show me thy chink, to blink through with mine eyne.
[*Wall parts his fingers.*]

163   Cut by Kean and Saker, presumably on grounds of obscurity.

167   At Stratford in 1942, 'instead of the self-confident ranter of tradition, Mr [Jay] Laurier gave us a bungling amateur who, having taken it for granted that he would be "all right on the night" is suddenly smitten by stage-fright into immobility and tongue-tied dependence on the prompter' (*Daily Telegraph*, 6 April). David Troughton, for Caird, and Timothy Spall, for Lepage, both imitated Laurence Olivier in performing Pyramus.

168   Daly's Pyramus was engulfed in darkness when his visor fell 'much to his annoyance' at 'when day is not!' (promptbook).

171–4   Kean cut 171–3 and got rid off 'eyne' by substituting 'O sweet and lovely wall' for everything after 'chink' in 174.

174   Kean's Pyramus bowed to Wall before asking see the chink and peeped through Wall's uplifted fingers; Daly's Wall was uncertain which hand to use for his chink and was also admonished by Quince, at Bottom's prompting, for keeping his hands too high (promptbooks). For Benthall in 1957, Frankie Howerd got 'his nose caught in the chink in the wall' (*Evening Standard*, 24 December).

174–8   In Caird's staging, Bottom got Wall's finger in his eye at 'eyne' and one up his nose at 'this', taking him for a walk during his speech and beating him up at 'deceiving me'.

> Thanks, courteous wall; Jove shield thee well for this!   175
>   But what see I? No Thisbe do I see.
> O wicked wall, through whom I see no bliss,
>   Cursed be thy stones for thus deceiving me!

THESEUS The wall, methinks, being sensible, should curse again.

BOTTOM No, in truth sir, he should not. 'Deceiving me' is Thisbe's   180
cue. She is to enter now, and I am to spy her through the wall.
You shall see it will fall pat as I told you. Yonder she comes.

Enter FLUTE *as* THISBE

FLUTE (*as Thisbe*)
> O wall, full often hast thou heard my moans,
>   For parting my fair Pyramus and me.
> My cherry lips have often kissed thy stones,   185
>   Thy stones with lime and hair knit up in thee.

BOTTOM (*as Pyramus*)
> I see a voice; now will I to the chink,
>   To spy and I can hear my Thisbe's face.
> Thisbe!

FLUTE (*as Thisbe*)
>   My love! Thou art my love, I think?

BOTTOM (*as Pyramus*)
> Think what thou wilt, I am thy lover's grace,   190
>   And like Limander am I trusty still.

FLUTE (*as Thisbe*)
>   And I like Helen, till the Fates me kill.

179 Daly's Bottom pushed Wall back to prevent him speaking at the end of this line (prompt-book). Frankie Howerd, in Benthall's 1957 production was 'caught between the royal mockers on one hand and his feckless colleagues on the other', sending out 'alternate barrages of apology and threat, ingratiation and malevolence, with a wild frustrated gusto' (*Observer*, 29 December). Caird's Thisbe kept trying to make her entrance during Bottom's chat with Theseus.

182 For Harcourt Williams, Richard Ainley's 'accidental exhibition of a pair of red braces when dressed as the female Thisbe in the Interlude met with uproarious success' (*Four Years*, p. 55).

183 Bridges Adams's Flute found it difficult to maintain his falsetto.

184–6 Kean cut 184 and 186, making a couplet; Saker and Daly cut 185–6, which removes any possibility of an indecorous double entrendre on 'stones' as 'testicles'. Given Kean's usual, almost pathological, sensitivity to decorum, his failure to cut 185 is surprising.

191–4 Cut by Phelps, Kean and Saker, a pity in view of the opportunities for byplay on the names

BOTTOM (*as Pyramus*)
  Not Shafalus to Procrus was so true.
FLUTE (*as Thisbe*)
  As Shafalus to Procrus, I to you.
BOTTOM (*as Pyramus*)
  O, kiss me through the hole of this vile wall!   195
FLUTE (*as Thisbe*)
  I kiss the wall's hole, not your lips at all.
BOTTOM (*as Pyramus*)
  Wilt thou at Ninny's tomb meet me straightway?
FLUTE (*as Thisbe*)
  Tide life, tide death, I come without delay.
        [*Exeunt Bottom and Flute in different directions*]
SNOUT (*as Wall*)
  Thus have I, Wall, my part dischargèd so;
  And being done, thus Wall away doth go.   *Exit*   200
THESEUS Now is the mural down between the two neighbours.
DEMETRIUS No remedy, my lord, when walls are so wilful to hear
  without warning.
HIPPOLYTA This is the silliest stuff that ever I heard.

Limander/Lysander, Helen/Helena, which Guthrie picked up in 1951 (Sprague and Trewin, *Shakespeare's Plays*, p. 68).
196 Kean and Daly removed the indelicate 'hole'.
198 In Brook's production, 'the audience are not invited to join with the nobility in sneering at these crude performers. The play is a meeting between friends. At Pyramus's line "I come without delay" all the lovers join in the song' (*Times*, 28 August 1970).
200 There was a long pause before Caird's Wall finally exited.
201–3 Cut by Phelps, Kean, Saker, Daly, Tree, Bridges Adams, Atkins, Benthall, Devine, Hall, Langham; Benson cut only Demetrius. Possibly the uncertainty about the correct form of 201, one of the few textual cruxes in the play, contributed to the decision to cut, but the courtiers' interventions have traditionally been seen as unwelcome interruptions of the fun. Shrimpton thought Bryden was actually attempting to make sense of the crux with his staging here: 'a few moments after Wall, heavily laden with loose bricks, had staggered off, a loud crash came from the wings. An officious Philostrate bustled out to inspect the damage and returned, covered in dust, to point Theseus' line' ('Shakespeare', *SS* 37, p. 170).
204 'In one heartbreaking moment [in Caird's staging], Ms Higgins vents herself of some smartly witty disparagement of the mechanicals' acting skills. From where she is sitting she does not realise that poor Quince is still on stage and is listening to her, frozen in humble distress' (*Independent*, 13 April 1989).

THESEUS The best in this kind are but shadows; and the worst are no   205
    worse, if imagination amend them.
HIPPOLYTA It must be your imagination then, and not theirs.
THESEUS If we imagine no worse of them than they of themselves, they
    may pass for excellent men. Here come two noble beasts in, a man
    and a lion.   210

       Enter [Snug as] Lion and [Starveling as] Moonshine.

SNUG (*as Lion*)
    You ladies, you whose gentle hearts do fear
      The smallest monstrous mouse that creeps on floor,
    May now, perchance, both quake and tremble here,
      When Lion rough in wildest rage doth roar.
    Then know that I as Snug the joiner am   215
    A lion fell, nor else no lion's dam;
    For if I should as lion come in strife
    Into this place, 'twere pity on my life.
THESEUS A very gentle beast, and of a good conscience.

205–9 Tree cut from 205, Benthall after 'shadows', Devine from 208, each as far as 'men'. Kirwan's
'Royal pair and their guests should not look so bored by what had been prepared for their
delight' (Stratford *Herald*, 24 April 1914). Daniels's Victorian staging had 'occasional felici-
tous touches, such as the moment when Theseus carelessly steps halfway across the
mechanicals' footlights for "the best in this kind are but shadows"' (*TLS*, 31 July 1981).

211 Snug's lion head was practical by the time of Kean's production (promptbook). For Brook,
'Snug's lion mask is a box, obviously made by the joiner himself in the likeness of a legless
wash-stand with wooden whiskers' (*Observer*, 13 June 1971). Caird's Snug had a crib which
he consulted several times, needing to be prompted word by word, even on his name and
occupation. Branagh's Snug was 'unable to resist, during the interlude, distributing his
business card among the Athenian nobility' (*Independent*, 15 August 1990). In Noble's
production, Snug's lion's headdress appeared to be made from large wood shavings, an
appropriate touch in view of his trade.

19–46 The courtiers' reactions to the Lion and to Moonshine's attempts to play his part have often
been heavily cut. The fox/goose quibbles and the 'horns' are theatrically obscure and consequently tend to be unfunny. In this context, Hesketh Pearson's note that his 'chief duty' as an
extra in Tree's production was 'to greet the idiotic remarks of Theseus with shouts of laughter
that would scarcely have been justified had they been as witty as the best of Voltaire's'
(*Beerbohm Tree*, p. 207) indicates one way in which directors have tried to encourage their
audiences to appreciate the jokes. While little of this sequence survives in Vestris, Phelps,
Kean, Saker, Benson, Daly, Tree, Atkins, Benthall, Bridges Adams, Devine, Hall, Langham, the
detailed pattern varies: everyone lets Theseus' initial comment stand and most nineteenth-

DEMETRIUS The very best at a beast, my lord, that e'er I saw.   220
LYSANDER This lion is a very fox for his valour.
THESEUS True; and a goose for his discretion.
DEMETRIUS Not so, my lord; for his valour cannot carry his discretion;
and the fox carries the goose.
THESEUS His discretion, I am sure, cannot carry his valour; for the   225
goose carries not the fox. It is well: leave it to his discretion, and
let us listen to the moon.
STARVELING (*as Moonshine*)
This lanthorn doth the hornèd moon present –
DEMETRIUS He should have worn the horns on his head.
THESEUS He is no crescent, and his horns are invisible within the   230
circumference.
STARVELING (*as Moonshine*)
This lanthorn doth the hornèd moon present;
Myself the man i'th'moon do seem to be –
THESEUS This is the greatest error of all the rest; the man should be
put into the lantern. How is it else the man i'th'moon?   235
DEMETRIUS He dares not come there, for the candle; for you see it is
already in snuff.
HIPPOLYTA I am aweary of this moon. Would he would change!
THESEUS It appears by his small light of discretion that he is in the
wane; but yet in courtesy, in all reason, we must stay the time.   240
LYSANDER Proceed, Moon.

century directors (and some twentieth-century ones) then move on to Starveling, sometimes
preserving 'let us listen to the moon', before cutting many of the comments on the moon.
For example, Vestris, Daly, Benson and Bridges Adams kept Demetrius' and Lysander's
responses to Lion, but even twentieth-century directors such as Devine, Hall and Langham
lost them. Daly cut from 228–231, Benson and Tree cut 229–31, Kean and Saker the first part
of 234. While 240 can be regarded as thematically important, it seldom made an appearance before the 1950s. Benson and Hall cut Demetrius' final quibbles, Tree left the last
sentence.

227   Daly's Bottom had to wake Moonshine before this speech (promptbook).

228   In Guthrie's 1951 staging, 'the old, whitehaired man playing Moon is perched on a ladder and
keeps tumbling off all over the courtiers' (*New Statesman*, 5 January 1952).

238–40   In Brook's production, when Hippolyta 'expresses boredom with the actors in a little joke
[238] Theseus reproves her by capping her joke and adds [240]. The Amazon queen is silent, as
if recognising his moral superiority. When she speaks again it is to praise the Moon. From the
slightest of hints, a relationship has been fleshed out' (*Daily Telegraph*, 14 September 1970).

241   Kean gave this to Theseus; Langham gave it to the whole onstage audience, an accurate

STARVELING All that I have to say is to tell you that the lanthorn is the moon, I the man i'th'moon, this thorn bush my thorn bush, and this dog my dog.

DEMETRIUS Why, all these should be in the lantern, for all these are in the moon. But silence: here comes Thisbe.   245

Enter [FLUTE *as*] THISBE

FLUTE (*as Thisbe*)
      This is old Ninny's tomb. Where is my love?

SNUG (*as Lion*) O!

         Lion roars. Thisbe runs off [*dropping her mantle*]

DEMETRIUS Well roared, Lion!

THESEUS Well run, Thisbe!   250

HIPPOLYTA Well shone, Moon! Truly, the moon shines with a good grace.

THESEUS Well moused, Lion!

DEMETRIUS And then came Pyramus –

LYSANDER And so the lion vanished.   255

         [*Lion worries Thisbe's mantle, and exit*]

Enter BOTTOM *as* PYRAMUS

reflection of their interventionist approach to the performance of 'Pyramus and Thisbe' (promptbook).

244 Kean's Moonshine had a real dog, a 'clever little Scotch terrier' who 'barked pleasantly at the lion' (*Press*, 12 February 1859); Ray Llewellyn's real dog at Birmingham Town Hall in 1973 caused havoc among the members of the City of Birmingham Symphony Orchestra on stage to play Mendelssohn's music; Lepage in 1992 also used a real dog.

247 Devine provided his Mechanicals with 'an agreeable little tombstone' inscribed '*Hic jacet Ninus*' (*ILN*, 3 April 1954); Quince was still correcting Flute's pronunciation of Ninus here in Langham's production (promptbook); Brook's Lion went berserk, throwing cushions and startling the court, except Theseus, to their feet. Theseus handed Thisbe's cloak to Lion (promptbook). Caird's Quince gave up on the promptbook here and started drinking. For Branagh, Gerard Horan's 'bearded hard-man Thisbe ... outroars the lion' (*Independent on Sunday*, 19 August 1990).

248 Alexander had Snug on Snout's shoulders to make the lion. For Caird, Thisbe's mantle would not come off at first, then Lion ran amuck among the onstage audience.

249 In Tree's staging, 'the audience roared with laughter at Bottom's scornful discomfort at the applause accorded to Snug's lion' (*Era*, 13 January 1900).

251–2 Benson and Tree allowed Hippolyta only the first sentence.

54–5 Cut by Benson. Here Alexander's Quince took off the sheet which covered Snug and Snout as Lion and threw it down as Thisbe's mantle.

BOTTOM (*as Pyramus*)
    Sweet moon, I thank thee for thy sunny beams;
      I thank thee, moon, for shining now so bright;
    For by thy gracious, golden, glittering gleams
      I trust to take of truest Thisbe sight.
            But stay – O spite! 260
            But mark, poor Knight,
        What dreadful dole is here?
          Eyes, do you see?
          How can it be?
        O dainty duck, O dear! 265
          Thy mantle good –
        What, stained with blood?
       Approach, ye Furies fell!
         O Fates, come, come,
         Cut thread and thrum, 270
      Quail, crush, conclude, and quell.
THESEUS This passion, and the death of a dear friend, would go near
    to make a man look sad.
HIPPOLYTA Beshrew my heart, but I pity the man.
BOTTOM (*as Pyramus*)
    O wherefore, Nature, didst thou lions frame, 275
      Since lion vile hath here deflowered my dear?
    Which is – no, no – which was the fairest dame
      That lived, that loved, that liked, that looked with cheer.
        Come tears, confound!
        Out sword, and wound 280

256 Caird's Bottom made a very elaborate entrance, miming a creaky gate in a mimed wall, killing a fly with his sword, and a bat; he also imitated Olivier's Richard III in his moon speech.

263 Bottom took his eyes out in Caird's production.

266 In Caird's staging the missing mantle was thrown onstage.

269-71 Cut by Benson. Alexander's Quince conducted his team's choric moaning to a stop on 'quell'.

272-4 Cut by Kean, Saker, Benson and Atkins, allowing the performance of 'Pyramus and Thisbe' to proceed unchecked; Phelps cut Theseus' lines, Langham cut Hippolyta's response.

276 Kean's Thisbe was 'destroyed', not 'deflowered'. Caird's Bottom did a 'take' at Hippolyta here.

279 Caird's Bottom showed his 'real' tears to the audience here.

280 Pyramus' sword often proves recalcitrant: at Stratford in 1938, Jay Laurier grabbed a halberd from an attendant 'to stab himself when he found the dagger would not do its work'

The pap of Pyramus,
  Ay, that left pap,
  Where heart doth hop:
Thus die I, thus, thus, thus! [*Stabs himself.*]
  Now am I dead,   285
  Now am I fled;
My soul is in the sky.
  Tongue, lose thy light;
  Moon, take thy flight;

                                          [*Exit Starveling*]
Now die, die, die, die, die. [*He dies.*]   290

DEMETRIUS No die, but an ace for him; for he is but one.

LYSANDER Less than an ace, man; for he is dead, he is nothing.

THESEUS With the help of a surgeon he might yet recover, and yet prove
  an ass.

HIPPOLYTA How chance Moonshine is gone before Thisbe comes back   295
  and finds her lover?

THESEUS She will find him by starlight.

(*Evening News and Time*, 16 May 1938); at Stratford in 1944, Cliff Weir's 'final despatch was made with the most untrusty sword that ever bent to comic imbruement' (*Birmingham Post*, 11 May).

281–3   Cut by Phelps; Kean had 'The heart of Pyramus' to deal with the indecorous 'pap'.

289   Langham had Bottom repeat the line in order to get his deaf Starveling to exit (promptbook).

290   Daly's Bottom had a very elaborate death: 'about to fall back – recovers – falls forward – hurts himself[.] Spreads cloak, lays down helmet gently reclines – but hits his head. Leans on elbow, kisses farewell to Theseus' (promptbook). Hall's 1959 Bottom, Charles Laughton, was 'like a great fat whale expiring on a seashore' who died 'six times over but won't lie down' (*Star*, 3 June). In contrast, Hall's 1962 Bottom, Paul Hardwick, 'really is something of an actor when it comes to the interlude and in particular to Pyramus's death agony' (*Times*, 18 April). Richard Griffiths in Barton's production appears to have been the first Bottom to actually carry out his 4.1 promise to sing a Ballad of Bottom's Dream: 'playing the dying Pyramus he flops down absurdly rearranging his costume, and then proceeds to sing a beautiful death song to his own lyre accompaniment' (*Times*, 9 May 1977). In the same production, Michael Billington detected a moment of genius summing up 'the interpenetration of the mortal and immortal world and the discovery of a universal concord' in a 'thin, silvery woodland chord [which] resounds in sympathetic magic' at Pyramus' death (*Guardian*, 9 May).

91–305   Directors have generally cut this section heavily: Benson removed all of it, moving straight from Pyramus' death to Thisbe's entrance, but most cuts fall in the sections 291–4 and 298–305. Vestris, Kean, Saker, Atkins, Benthall, Devine and Langham cut all of 291–4; Phelps

Enter [FLUTE *as*] THISBE

Here she comes and her passion ends the play.

HIPPOLYTA Methinks she should not use a long one for such a
Pyramus; I hope she will be brief.   300

DEMETRIUS A mote will turn the balance, which Pyramus, which
Thisbe is the better: he for a man, God warrant us; she for a woman,
God bless us.

LYSANDER She hath spied him already, with those sweet eyes.

DEMETRIUS And thus she means, videlicet –   305

FLUTE (*as Thisbe*)

    Asleep, my love?
    What, dead, my dove?
O Pyramus, arise.
    Speak, speak! Quite dumb?
    Dead, dead? A tomb   310
Must cover thy sweet eyes.
    These lily lips,
    This cherry nose,
These yellow cowslip cheeks
    Are gone, are gone.   315
    Lovers, make moan;
His eyes were green as leeks.

(who played Bottom), Daly, Bridges Adams and Hall 291–2, which has the virtue of keeping
Theseus' reference to the ass, which Tree omitted. At 'prove an ass', Phelps as Pyramus
raised his head 'and coolly places his sword away from him then lies again' and Laughton
sat up and did a 'take' (promptbooks); Alexander also gave Bottom a 'take' at 'ass'. In
Noble's staging 'there's a lovely moment when his Theseus, after the death of Pyramus,
winkingly remarks to his future bride that the character might yet recover and "prove an
ass", which instantly sets up all kind of retrospective echoes' (Michael Billington, *Guardian*,
5 August 1994). Devine started to cut again with the end of 298; Kean, Saker, Tree, Atkins,
Hall and Langham followed suit at 299 and cut to the end of 305, although Kean, Langham
and Hall kept 'I hope she will be brief', and Hall also kept 304. Caird's Thisbe reacted bash-
fully to 'sweet eyes'. Daly, Benthall and Bridges Adams cut Demetrius' last two speeches.

306   In Caird's production, 'with his girlish palpitations between hope and dread, Graham
Turner's dozy Thisbe recalls Amanda Bellamy's unhinged Hermia when she awakes from
her nightmare' (*Independent*, 13 April 1989).

310   Between the two 'deads' in Daly's production, Thisbe raised Pyramus' head and let it fall to
the noise of a hammer off (promptbook).

312–17 Neither Kean nor Tree permitted Thisbe's colour confusions to stand.

> O sisters three,
> Come, come to me
> With hands as pale as milk;   320
> Lay them in gore,
> Since you have shore
> With shears his thread of silk.
> Tongue, not a word!
> Come, trusty sword,   325
> Come blade, my breast imbrue! [*Stabs herself.*]
> And farewell, friends.
> Thus Thisbe ends –
> Adieu, adieu, adieu! [*Dies.*]

THESEUS Moonshine and Lion are left to bury the dead.   330

325 Edward Sharpham's *The Fleire* (1607) has a reference to an Elizabethan staging of this line,
     'like Thisbe in the play, 'a has almost killed himself with the scabbard' (Munro, *Shakspere
     Allusion Book*, I, p. 174), which anticipates the order of difficulty subsequent Thisbes have
     had in dispatching themselves.

326 In Langham's production, 'court and players rise in agonised unison to prevent Thisbe from
     "imbruing" herself with the sword she has borrowed from Demetrius' (*Birmingham Post*,
     21 December 1960); Langham's Quince was called upon to prompt for the last time after
     Thisbe stabbed herself (promptbook). Caird's Thisbe said 'She stabs herself', still speaking
     her part 'cues and all'.

329 Daly had Quince throw down his manuscript and exit, disgusted, at the end of the perfor-
     mance (promptbook); Tree's real audience 'roared with laughter at ... the egoistical way in
     which he [Bottom] pushed Flute up the steps to prevent him sharing in the honours of a
     recall' (*Era*, 13 January 1900); Dunlop's Quince raised 'a feeble cry of "Author" after the
     play' (*Times*, 27 September 1967).

330–40 These exchanges are often changed as part of the general reduction in the amount of com-
     ment on 'Pyramus and Thisbe' and if the production does not include a 'Bergomask'. Vestris
     cut everything after 'discharged'; Phelps cut after 'excuse' in 336; Kean (who substituted
     'antic') and Saker (and Langham) cut the references to the Bergomask in 334 and 339–40;
     Kean and Saker, prudish to the last, also cut 'in Thisbe's garter'; Daly cut Demetrius' line and
     Bottom's response to it, ending with Theseus' 'blamed'; Tree cut everything, although 'a fine
     tragedy and very notably discharged' were recycled; Atkins cut from 'Marry' to 'discharged'.
     Reinhardt had a seventh mechanical ready to play the Epilogue in the 1935 film. In Brook's
     production 'As David Waller's Bottom announces "The wall is down that parted our [sic]
     fathers", it is suggested that the actors' art (as much as the fairies') has brought the feuding
     fathers and lovers of the earlier scenes together – *their* rough magic has brought unity to
     the court' (*Plays and Players*, August 1971). In Caird's staging, Quince was too drunk to
     have spoken the Epilogue, motivating a big 'or' from Bottom.

DEMETRIUS Ay, and Wall, too.

BOTTOM [*Starting up, as Flute does also.*] No, I assure you, the wall is down that parted their fathers. Will it please you to see the epilogue, or to hear a Bergomask dance between two of our company?

THESEUS No epilogue, I pray you; for your play needs no excuse. Never 335 excuse; for when the players are all dead, there need none to be blamed. Marry, if he that writ it had played Pyramus and hanged himself in Thisbe's garter, it would have been a fine tragedy: and so it is, truly, and very notably discharged. But come, your Bergomask; let your epilogue alone. 340

[*The company return; two of them dance, then exeunt Bottom, Flute and their fellows.*]

The iron tongue of midnight hath told twelve.

339 Alexander's Bottom was given a purse here.

340 When performed, the Bergomask has usually been an occasion of wildly exuberant humour: in Bridges Adams's 1923 staging, it had 'the unprecedented honour of an encore' (SCL cutting); in Andrew Leigh's Old Vic production it was 'something between a Scottish sword-dance and a burlesque Charleston' (VW cutting); Devine's was 'a rarely comic conception, full of flying arms, precariously held balances and rhythms maintained at all costs, even to slapping hands, in the confusion, with someone behind one's back' (*Leamington Courier*, 26 March 1954). Bryden's was 'pure Wilson, Keppel and Betty sand-dance complete with fezzes, tashes and rolled-up trousers' (*Guardian*, in *LTR* 1982). On several occasions directors have imitated masque practices: in Guthrie's 1937 staging it was 'a little startling to see Theseus and Hippolyta joining hands with the mechanics in their rowdy Bergomask' (Farjeon, *Scene*, p. 47); in Alexander's Bergomask Bottom and Hippolyta danced together and there was a 'take' between Theseus and Hippolyta at 'fairy time'. Caird's Bergomask began with Mendelssohn's music as a morris dance between the Mechanicals but modulated into a general dance with modern music as well as Mendelssohn; Bottom and Hippolyta danced hand in hand but broke when Theseus saw them at ''tis almost fairy time'. Noble's 'Hippolyta finally rewards Bottom with a garland, in fleeting recollection of their woodland nuptials' (Irving Wardle, *Independent on Sunday*, 7 August 1994).

341ff. Daly had midnight tolling throughout a truncated and bowdlerised version of Theseus' speech ('The iron tongue of midnight telleth twelve. / Lovers now list, 'tis almost fairy time. / Sweet friends, / A fortnight hold we this solemnity / In nightly revels and new jollity') culminating in a 'sharp gong' which was presumably both the last stroke of midnight and the cue for the final fairy scene, since all the lights were suddenly extinguished (promptbook). Daly then played Puck's 401–6 before reverting to 369–96 (with internal cuts) to end the play. As the mortals left in Bridges Adams's production, Lysander and Hermia were reconciled with

> Lovers, to bed; 'tis almost fairy time.
> I fear we shall outsleep the coming morn
> As much as we this night have overwatched.
> This palpable-gross play hath well beguiled   345
> The heavy gait of night. Sweet friends, to bed.
> A fortnight hold we this solemnity
> In nightly revels and new jollity.

> *Exeunt*

Egeus: she knelt and Egeus placed his hand on her shoulder and then shook hands with Lysander; in 1949 Benthall had Hermia and Lysander kiss Egeus to indicate their reconciliation (promptbooks).

345–6   Cut by Phelps. Kean's and Saker's lovers, decorous as ever, went 'away' rather than 'to bed'.

348   In Vestris's production Puck rose through the stage and the scene glided away to reveal 'the interior of the palace, with fairies crowded in every part, gliding along galleries, ascending and descending steps, soaring in the air with blue and yellow torches, which produce a curious light' (*Times*, 17 November 1840). For Phelps, when the court party left, 'servants came in and put out the lights, and simultaneously the curtains opened. The fluted columns of the hall were partly "made out" and covered by waxed linen: inside the columns were lengths of gas jets, kept turned down till the curtains opened and the moonlight streamed into the hall: then the gas within the columns was turned up, and the columns appeared as if illuminated by the moonlight. The opening of the curtains disclosed a terraced garden over-looking Athens. down the steps and along the terraces trouped Oberon and Titania with their fairy train, all carrying "glimmering lights." The fairy song and dance were given, and the curtain fell on the moonlighted palace of Theseus, with the slumbering city behind, on the picturesque groups of the fairies arranged on the terraces behind, and on the graceful figures of Oberon, Titania and Puck in front' (Moyr Smith, *Dream*, pp. xiii–xiv). Kean attempted something similar to Vestris, but 'from the want of stage breadth, these galleries are merely painted, and filled with painted figures, the evolutions of the fairies being confined to the stage itself, which, to make the most of all available space, is arranged into platforms of different heights' *(Illustrated Times*, 25 October 1856). Tree's arrangement was similar to Phelps's: 'the columns glow with supernatural sheen, the elves gradually disperse through the corridors, and as their songs sink into silence, the light dies out by degrees, and the curtains descend on a darkened and empty stage' (*Era*, 13 January 1900). Basil Dean carried on with this approach in 1924: 'the white marble walls and columns of the palace were to become transparent as Titania, Oberon and attendant fairies, grouped in a kind of ghostly frieze, were raised on our largest hydraulic lift at the back. Their appearance at the top of the great steps was timed to coincide with the opening bars of the music for the final Fokine ballet' (Dean, *Seven Ages*, p. 242). Crosse thought that Atkins was wrong in 1949 to have a scene after the mortals' last exit when 'the curtains at the back were drawn aside to show the

Enter PUCK [*carrying a broom*]

PUCK   Now the hungry lion roars,
             And the wolf behowls the moon,   350
        Whilst the heavy ploughman snores,
             All with weary task foredone.
        Now the wasted brands do glow,
             Whilst the screech-owl, screeching loud,
        Puts the wretch that lies in woe   355
             In remembrance of a shroud.
        Now it is the time of night
             That the graves, all gaping wide,
        Every one lets forth his sprite
             In the church-way paths to glide.   360
        And we fairies, that do run
             By the triple Hecate's team
        From the presence of the sun,
             Following darkness like a dream,
        Now are frolic; not a mouse   365
        Shall disturb this hallowed house.
        I am sent with broom before
        To sweep the dust behind the door.

wood' (*Diary* XX, p. 17); Coghill, similarly, flew the palace, replacing it with the forest 'as if Nature were following the lovers into their home for a return visit' (Coghill letter) and Alexander tried something similar in his staging: 'the walls of the Athenian palace finally parting to reveal the fairies looking in from the crepuscular wood' (*Guardian*, 10 July 1986).

349   Brook's mortals reverted to being fairies simply by doffing their cloaks but Alexander's Hippolyta at Stratford (but not in the Barbican transfer) had to break from her place as Hippolyta in order to resume her identity as Titania.

349–68   Vestris and Kean cut the gloomy 353–60; Saker and Daly removed everything; Benson started with a version of 365 ('Fairies frolic ...'). Tree sometimes omitted the lines at mat-inées, presumably on the grounds of inappropriateness for a juvenile audience and for the time of day.

368   At the end of Puck's speech, Kean had the back of the scene sink to discover Oberon, Titania and the fairies grouped all over the stage with lighted lanterns which they waved as they tripped up and down during the choruses. In his 1937 pastiche production Guthrie had flying fairies with lighted tapers. Coghill's fairies also carried lighted candles and 'gave a sort of miraculous hush' (Coghill letter). Hall had a similar effect as the fairies appeared to give their blessing: 'tapers are lit from the last flickers of a log fire and as they [the fairies] flit up and down the stairs and along the galleries chanting their moving verses, the play's magnetism is again fully captured' (*Morning Advertiser*, 6 June 1959).

Enter [OBERON *and* TITANIA,] *the King and Queen of Fairies, with all their train.*

OBERON Through the house give glimmering light
     By the dead and drowsy fire;   370
     Every elf and fairy sprite
      Hop as light as bird from briar,
     And this ditty after me
     Sing, and dance it trippingly.
TITANIA First rehearse your song by rote,   375
     To each word a warbling note;
     Hand in hand with fairy grace
     Will we sing and bless this place.
       Song [*and dance*].
OBERON Now until the break of day
     Through this house each fairy stray.   380
     To the best bride-bed will we,
     Which by us shall blessèd be;
     And the issue there create
     Ever shall be fortunate.
     So shall all the couples three   385
     Ever true in loving be,
     And the blots of nature's hand
     Shall not in their issue stand.
     Never mole, harelip, nor scar,
     Nor mark prodigious, such as are   390
     Despisèd in nativity,
     Shall upon their children be.

369–78 Daly gave Oberon's speech to Titania and cut hers. Caird's fairies arrived noisily like an ill-disciplined school choir and gave an excruciating rendition of 'Philomel', thus motivating Titania's speech which she accompanied by giving out song sheets; Oberon's speech had Mendelssohn under it and then the fairies sang 'Philomel' properly and Puck took his ear plugs out.

373–4 Cut by Phelps.

378 Barker, followed by Coghill, believed that the promised song was missing and inserted 'Roses, their sharp spines being gone' from *Two Noble Kinsmen* here.

79–400 Oberon's blessing was problematic in the nineteenth century on grounds of decorum. While Bowdler objected particularly to 383–4, Vestris left 393–4 and 399–400, Kean and Saker cut all of the speech, Daly kept 385–6, reversed the order of 393–4, and kept 395–6, Benson cut all the references to nature's blots (387–92) and gave 393ff. to Titania, Tree cut 381–92. Langham cut 389–92. Hall had glitter dust sprinkled during the final blessing.

    With this field-dew consecrate,
    Every fairy take his gait,
    And each several chamber bless   395
    Through this palace with sweet peace;
    And the owner of it blessed
    Ever shall in safety rest.
    Trip away, make no stay;
    Meet me all by break of day.   400
              Exeunt [all but Puck]

PUCK [*To the audience*]
    If we shadows have offended,
    Think but this, and all is mended:
    That you have but slumbered here
    While these visions did appear;
    And this weak and idle theme,   405
    No more yielding but a dream,
    Gentles, do not reprehend;
    If you pardon, we will mend.
    And, as I am an honest Puck,
    If we have unearnèd luck   410
    Now to 'scape the serpent's tongue
    We will make amends ere long,
    Else the Puck a liar call.
    So, good night unto you all.
    Give me your hands, if we be friends,   415
    And Robin shall restore amends.   [*Exit*]

400 In Atkins's 1944 Stratford production 'the fairy haunted palace melts into the starlit woods' (Stratford *Herald*, 12 May). Brook's staging 'closes on a note of calm social harmony. "Meet we all by break of day".' (*Times*, 28 August 1970)

401–16 Vestris cut 409–12, while Kean cut 405–6, 409–12 and 415–16, ending with Oberon's glimmering light speech (369–74) and 'Trip away …' (399–400). Saker started at 'Gentles'. Benson cut the whole of the Epilogue, though his production ended with Puck floating over the heads of Oberon and Titania. In Asche's 1905 production, Puck spoke part of the Epilogue 'in the midst of the gloom that veils the pillars of Theseus' palace as the curtain falls' (HTC cutting). In 1919 Bridges Adams restored the Epilogue 'spoken by Puck outside the fallen curtain' (Stratford *Herald*, 14 August). Bridges Adams's curtain call supported the idea of Bottom as protagonist since it was arranged so that he appeared last for a solo call (promptbook). In 1954 Benthall had a 'sudden and surprising Peter Pan flying exit of Oberon and Titania on wires and behind the gauze at the last curtain' (*Birmingham Post*, 1 September). Brook's Puck spoke the Epilogue with the house lights up and the cast, taking their cue from 'Give me your hands…', shook hands with members of the audience as they made their exits through the auditorium, adding a final dimension to the unity between audience and action that had been created by the production.

BIBLIOGRAPHY

PROMPTBOOKS AND RELATED MATERIAL
Alexander, Bill. Promptbook, now in the SCL.
Atkins, Robert. Promptbook, now in the SCL.
Barker, Harley Granville. Promptbook, now in the HTC.
Benson, F. R. Promptbook, now in the SCL.
Benthall, Michael. 1949 promptbook, now in the SCL.
Bridges Adams, W. Promptbook, now in the SCL.
Brook, Peter. Promptbooks, now in the SCL.
Bunn, Alfred. 1833 promptbook, now at the University of Michigan.
Caird, John. Promptbook, now in the SCL.
Daniels, Ron. Promptbook, now in the SCL.
Daly, Augustin. Promptbooks, now in the FSL.
Devine, George. Promptbook, now in the SCL.
Garrick, David, and George Colman. 1763 promptbook and related notes,
    now in the FSL.
A Fairy Tale, 1777 promptbook, now in the FSL.
Hall, Peter. Promptbooks, now in the SCL.
Holloway, Baliol. Promptbook, now in the SCL.
Iden Payne, Ben. Promptbook, now in the SCL.
Kean, Charles. Promptbooks and related documents, now in the FSL and
    the HTC.
Leigh, Andrew. Promptbook, now in the SCL.
Martin Browne, E. Promptbook, now in the SCL.
Phelps, Samuel. Promptbook, now in the FSL.
Reynolds, Frederic. Preparation copy of 1763 *Dream*, now in the FSL.
    1816 promptbook, now in the FSL.
Tree, Herbert Beerbohm. Promptbooks and related papers, now at Bristol
    University and in the FSL.

Full bibliographical accounts of promptbooks up to 1960 are given in
Charles H. Shattuck, *The Shakespeare Promptbooks*, Urbana, Ill., 1965, and
'The Shakespeare Promptbooks: first supplement', *TN*, 24, 1969, pp. 5–17.

EDITIONS OF *A MIDSUMMER NIGHT'S DREAM*
AND RELATED WORKS

(Place of publication is London unless otherwise indicated)

Bowdler, Thomas, ed. *The Family Shakspeare*, 6th edn, London, 1831.

Browne, H. B., ed. *A Midsummer Night's Dream*, 1922.

The Fairies. An Opera, 1755.

The Fairy Queen: an Opera, 1692.

A Fairy Tale. In Two Acts. Taken from Shakespeare, 1763.

Guthrie, Tyrone, intro. *A Midsummer Night's Dream*, 1954.

Johnson, Charles. *Love in a Forest*, 1723.

Lampe, J. F. *Pyramus and Thisbe: A Mock Opera*, 1745.

Leveridge, Richard. *The Comic Masque of Pyramus and Thisbe*, 1716.

The Merry Conceited Humours of Bottom the Weaver, 1661.

A Midsummer Night's Dream. Written by Shakespeare: with Alterations and Additions and Several New Songs, 1763.

A Midsummer Night's Dream. A Comedy by Shakespeare, Bell's edn, 1764.

A Midsummer Night's Dream. Written by Shakespeare: with Alterations, Additions and New Songs; as it is performed at the Theatre-Royal, Covent Garden, 1816. [adapted by Frederic Reynolds]

A Midsummer Night's Dream: A Comedy in Five Acts, by William Shakspere. As revived at ... Covent Garden, November 16th, 1840, Pattie's edn [?1840].

Shakespeare's Play of A Midsummer Night's Dream, Arranged for Representation at the Princess's Theatre. ... by Charles Kean, [?1856].

William Shakespeare's Midsummer Night's Dream, ...arranged for representation by Edward Saker, Liverpool, 1880.

The Comedy of A Midsummer Night's Dream written by William Shakespeare and arranged for representation at Daly's Theatre, New York, 1888.

Shakespeare's Comedy of A Midsummer Night's Dream, with a producer's preface by Granville Barker, 1914.

Peter Brook's Production of William Shakespeare's A Midsummer Night's Dream, New York, 1974.

Moyr Smith, J., illus. *A Midsummer Night's Dream, by William Shakespeare*, 1892.

Quiller-Couch, A., and J. Dover Wilson, eds. *A Midsummer Night's Dream*, 1924.

OTHER WORKS

(Place of publication is London unless otherwise indicated)

Agate, James. *Brief Chronicles*, 1943.

Allen, Shirley. *Samuel Phelps and Sadler's Wells Theatre*, Middletown, Conn., 1971.

Amarsinghe, U. *Dryden and Pope in the Early Nineteenth Century*, 1962.

Asche, Oscar. *Oscar Asche by Himself*, [1929].

Avery, Emmet L., et al. *The London Stage, 1660–1800*, Carbondale, Ill., 5 pts in 11 vols., 1960-8.

Atkins, Robert. *An Unfinished Autobiography*, ed. George Rowell, 1994.

Baldwin, T. W. *The Organisation and Personnel of the Shakespearean Company*, Princeton, N.J., 1927.

Bate, Jonathan. *Shakespearean Constitutions*, Oxford, 1989.

Baynton, Henry. Letters in the author's collection.

Beauman, Sally. *The Royal Shakespeare Company*, 1982.

Benson, Constance. *Mainly Players*, 1926.

Benson, F. R. *My Memoirs*, 1930.

Bloom, Harold, ed. *William Shakespeare's 'A Midsummer Night's Dream'*, Modern Critical Interpretations, New York, 1987.

Booth, Michael R. *Victorian Spectacular Theatre, 1850–1910*, 1981.

Briggs, Katharine. *The Anatomy of Puck*, 1959.
   The Fairies in Tradition and Literature, 1967.
   A Dictionary of Fairies, 1976.

Brown, John Russell. *Free Shakespeare*, 1974.

Byrne, M. St Clare. 'Fifty years of Shakespearian production: 1898–1948', *SS* 2, 1949, 1–20.

Calderwood, James L. *A Midsummer Night's Dream*, Harvester New Critical Introductions to Shakespeare, 1992.

Coghill, Nevill. Letter to the author from Nevill Coghill, dated 9 September 1977.

Cole, J. W. *The Life and Theatrical Times of Charles Kean F.S.A.*, 2 vols., 1859.

Cook, Dutton. *Nights at the Play*, 1883.

Crosse, Gordon. *Fifty Years of Shakespearean Playgoing*, 1940.
   Shakespearean Playgoing 1890–1952. 1953.
   MS *Diary*, 21 vols., in the BSL.

Davis, Tracy C. *Actresses as Working Women*, 1991.

Dean, Basil. *Seven Ages*, 1970.

Dean, Winton. 'Shakespeare in the opera house', *SS* 18, 1965, 75–93.

Dickins, Richard. *Forty Years of Shakespeare on the English Stage* [1908].

Dobson, Michael. *The Making of the National Poet*, 1992.

Downes, John. *Roscius Anglicanus*, 1708.

Dymkowski, Christine. *Harley Granville Barker – A Preface to Modern Shakespeare*, Washington, D.C.,1986.

Elsom, John, ed. *Is Shakespeare Still Our Contemporary?*, 1989.

Evans, G. Blakemore. *Shakespearean Prompt-Books of the Seventeenth Century*, Charlottesville, N.C., vol. I, pt i, 1960; vol. III, pt i, 1964.

Farjeon, Herbert. *The Shakespearean Scene*, [1949?].

Farquharson Sharp, R. *A Short History of the English Stage*, 1909.

Felheim, Marvin. *The Theater of Augustin Daly*, Cambridge, Mass., 1956.

Fitgerald, Percy. *Shakespearean Representation*, 1908.

Fontane, Theodor. *Aus England*, Stuttgart, 1860.

Foss, George R. *What the Author Meant*, 1932.

Grady, Hugh. *The Modernist Shakespeare*, Oxford, 1991.

Granville-Barker, Harley. *Prefaces to Shakespeare*, vol. VI, 1974.

Greene, Robert. *James IV*, ed. N. Sanders, 1970.

Griffiths, Trevor R. '*A Midsummer Night's Dream* and *The Tempest* on the London stage, 1789–1914', PhD, University of Warwick, 1974.

'A neglected pioneer production: Madame Vestris' *A Midsummer Night's Dream* at Covent Garden, 1840', *SQ*, 30, 1979, 386–96.

'Tradition and innovation in Harley Granville Barker's *A Midsummer Night's Dream*, *TN*, 30, 1976, 78–87.

Gurr, Andrew. *The Shakespearean Stage*, 3rd edn, 1992.

Guthrie, Tyrone. *A Life in the Theatre*, 1959.

Habicht, Werner, 'How German is Shakespeare in Germany?', *SS* 37, 1984, 155–62.

Halliday, F. E. *Shakespeare and his Critics*, 1949.

Hamburger, Maik, 'New concepts of staging "A Midsummer Night's Dream"', *SS*, 40, 1987, 51–61.

Hartnoll, Phyllis, ed. *Shakespeare in Music*, 1964.

Hattaway, Michael. *Elizabethan Popular Theatre*, 1982.

Hayman, Ronald. *Gielgud*, 1971.

Hoffman, D. S. 'Some Shakespearian music, 1660–1900', *SS* 18, 1965, 94–101.

Holland, Peter. 'Shakespeare performances in England, 1990–1', *SS* 45, 1992, 115–44.

Holloway, Stanley. *Wiv a Little Bit o' Luck*, 1967.

Hughes, Alan. 'The Lyceum staff: a Victorian theatrical organisation', *TN*, 27, 1974, 11–17.

Jacobs, Margaret, and John Warren, eds. *Max Reinhardt: the Oxford Symposium*, Oxford, 1986.

Jonson, Ben. *Oberon*, in vol. VII of C. H. Herford, P. and E. Simpson, eds., *Ben Jonson*, Oxford, 1941.

Jorgens, Jack J. *Shakespeare on Film*, Bloomington, Ind, 1977.

'Studies in the criticism and stage history of *A Midsummer Night's Dream*',

PhD, New York University, 1970.

Kennedy, Denis. *Granville Barker and the Dream of Theatre*, 1985.

Kott, Jan. *Shakespeare Our Contemporary*, 1965.

'Bottom and the boys', *New Theatre Quarterly*, 36, November 1993, 307–15.

Latham, M. W. *The Elizabethan Fairies*, New York, 1930.

Lee, Sidney. *Shakespeare and the Modern Stage*, 1906.

Leiter, Samuel L., ed. *Shakespeare Around the Globe*, New York, 1986.

Lloyds, Frederick. *Practical Guide to Scene Painting*, [1875?].

Lyly, John. *Endymion* in *The Complete Works of John Lyly*, ed. R. W. Bond, 3 vols., Oxford, 1902.

Maas, Jeremy. *Victorian Painters*, 1969.

Manvell, Roger. *Shakespeare and the Film*, 1971.

Mazer, Cary M. *Shakespeare Refashioned*, Ann Arbor, Mich.,1981.

Merchant, W. Moelwyn. 'Classical costume in Shakespearian productions', *SS*, 10, 1957, 71–6.

Shakespeare and the Artist, 1959.

Mullin, Michael, *Theatre at Stratford-upon-Avon*, 2 vols., 1980.

Munro, J. *The Shakspere Allusion Book*, 2 vols., 1932.

Odell, G. C. *Shakespeare from Betterton to Irving*, 2 vols., New York, 1920.

'*A Midsummer Night's Dream* on the New York stage', in Brander Matthews and A. H. Thorndike, eds., *Shaksperian Studies*, New York, 1916, pp. 127–9.

Orgel, Stephen, and Roy Strong. *Inigo Jones: The Theatre of the Stuart Court*, 2 vols., Berkeley, Calif., 1973.

Pearson, Hesketh, *Beerbohm Tree*, 1956.

Pearce, C. E. *Madame Vestris and her Times*, 1923.

Pepys, Samuel. *The Diary of Samuel Pepys*, ed. Robert Latham and William Matthews, 11 vols., 1970–82.

Phelps, W. May, and John Forbes-Robertson. *The Life and Life Work of Samuel Phelps*, 1886.

Phillpotts, Beatrice. *Fairy Paintings*, 1978.

Planché, J. R. *Recollections and Reflections*, rev. edn, 1901.

Poel, William, *Shakespeare in the Theatre*, 1913.

Price, Antony W., ed. *Shakespeare's 'A Midsummer Night's Dream'*, Casebook Series, 1983.

Reynolds, Frederic. *The Life and Times of Frederic Reynolds, written by himself*, 2 vols., 1826.

Ringler, W. A., Jr 'The number of actors in Shakespeare's early plays', in G. E. Bentley, ed. *The Seventeenth-Century Stage*, Chicago, 1968, pp. 110–34.

Roberts, Peter. *The Old Vic Story*, 1976.

Robinson, Henry Crabb. *The London Theatre, 1811–1866*, ed. Eluned Brown, 1966.

Rosenfeld, Sybil. *A Short History of Scene Design in Great Britain*, Oxford, 1973.

Rothwell, Kenneth S., and Annabelle Henkin Melzer. *Shakespeare on Screen*, 1990.

Rowell, George, ed. *Victorian Dramatic Criticism*, 1971.

Savage, Roger. 'The Shakespeare–Purcell *Fairy Queen*', *Early Music*, October 1973, 201–21.

Selbourne, David. *The Making of A Midsummer Night's Dream*, 1982.

Scouten, Arthur, H. 'The increase of popularity in Shakespeare's plays in the eighteenth century', *SQ*, 7, 1956, 189–202.

Shakespeare, William. *The Merry Wives of Windsor*, ed. H. J. Oliver, 1971.

Shaw, George Bernard. *Shaw on Shakespeare*, ed. Edwin Wilson, 1962.

Our Theatre in the Nineties, 3 vols., 1932.

Shrimpton, Nicholas. 'Shakespeare performances in London, Manchester, and Stratford-upon-Avon, 1985–6', *SS* 40, 1987, 169–83.

'Shakespeare performances in Stratford-upon-Avon and London, 1982–3', *SS* 37, 1984, 169–83.

Speaight, Robert. *William Poel and the Elizabethan Revival*, 1954.

Shakespeare on the Stage, 1973.

Sprague, A. C., and J. C. Trewin. *Shakespeare's Plays Today*, 1970.

Stone, G. W., Jr. '*A Midsummer Night's Dream* in the hands of Garrick and Colman', *PMLA* 14, 1939, 467–82.

Styan, J. L. *The Shakespeare Revolution*, 1977.

Thomas, Keith. *Religion and the Decline of Magic*, 1971.

Thomson, Peter. *Shakespeare's Theatre*, 1983.

Tree, Herbert Beerbohm. *Thoughts and After-Thoughts*, 1913.

Trewin, J. C., *Benson and the Bensonians*, 1960.

Shakespeare on the English Stage, 1900–1964, 1964.

Warren, Roger. 'Interpretations of Shakespearian comedy, 1981'-*SS* 35, 1982, 141–52.

Wearing, J. P. *The London Stage, 1890–* , Metuchen, N.J., 1976 etc. (in progress).

Westrup, J. A. *Purcell*, 1937.

White, G. W. 'Early theatrical performances of Purcell's operas', *TN*, 13, 1958, 43–65.

Williams, Gary J. '"The concord of this discord": music in the stage history of *A Midsummer Night's Dream*', *Yale/Theatre*, IV, 1973, pp. 40–60.

'Madame Vestris' *A Midsummer Night's Dream* and the web of Victorian tradition', *Theatre Survey*, 18, 1977, 1–22.

'*A Midsummer Night's Dream*: the English and American popular traditions and Harley Granville Barker's "world arbitrarily made"', *Theatre Studies*, 23, 1976/7.

Williams, E. Harcourt. *Old Vic Saga*, 1949.

Four Years at the Old Vic, 1935.

Williams, Simon. *Shakespeare on the German Stage 1586–1914*, Cambridge, 1990.

Winter, William. *Old Shrines and Ivy*, New York, 1892.

Wolfit, Donald. *First Interval*, 1954.

Young, David P. *Something of Great Constancy*, 1966.

Zimmerman, Franklin. *Henry Purcell*, 1963.

APPENDIX

MUSIC IN THE PRODUCTIONS

date	company/adapter/director	music
pre 1600	Chamberlain's Men	?
1662	King's	?
1692	*The Fairy Queen*	Purcell
1716	*Pyramus and Thisbe*	Leveridge
1745	*Pyramus and Thisbe*	Lampe
1755	*The Fairies* (Garrick/Smith)	J.C. Smith
1763	Colman/Garrick	Smith, etc
1763	*A Fairy Tale* (Colman)	Smith, etc
1816	Frederic Reynolds	Arne, Batishill, Bishop (also arr.), Cooke, Handel, Smith, Stevens
1833	Reynolds, ed. Alfred Bunn	Arne, Bishop, Cooke, Handel, Mendelssohn overture, Smith, Stevens
1840	Madame Vestris	comp. and sel. T. Cooke, Mendelssohn overture
1853–61	Samuel Phelps	Mendelssohn, arr. Montgomery
1856–9	Charles Kean	'A portion of the music hitherto introduced', Mendelssohn; dir. J. L. Hatton
1870	John Ryder (Phelps as Bottom)	Mendelssohn; dir. Schoening
1875	Phelps	Mendelssohn, Bishop etc; dir. Meyer Lutz
1880	Edward Saker	H. Bishop, J. Cooke, C. Horn, Mendelssohn, John Ross, Stevens, Werner
1889–1916	F. R. Benson	Balling, Cooke, Horn, Mendelssohn (+*Bees Wedding, Spring Song*), C. Wilson

date	company/adapter/director	music
1895	Augustin Daly	Mendelssohn, 'various English composers' sel. and arr. Widmer
1900, 11	Herbert Beerbohm Tree	Mendelssohn
1905	Oscar Asche	Cooke, Horn, Mendelssohn (+*Bees Wedding, Spring Song*), Wilson
1914	Granville Barker	folk tunes, arr. Cecil Sharp
1914	Patrick Kirwan	Elizabethan
1914–18	Ben Greet	Mendelssohn, (+*Spring Song*), Shields ('O Happy fair')
1918	George Foss	Mendelssohn
1919, 23, 24, 26, 28, 30, 31	Bridges Adams	Mendelssohn
1921	Bridges Adams	Purcell
1932	Bridges Adams	'representative'
1920	Russell Thorndike, Charles Warburton	Mendelssohn
1920	J. B. Fagan	John Greenwood
1921, 23, 24	Robert Atkins	Mendelssohn
1923	Donald Calthrop	Rupert Lee (1771 harpsichord)
1924	Basil Dean	Mendelssohn
1926	Andrew Leigh	Mendelssohn
1929, 31	Harcourt Williams	folk tunes, arr. Cecil Sharp
1935	Max Reinhardt	Mendelssohn
1937	E. Martin Browne	Elizabethan
1937–8	Tyrone Guthrie	Mendelssohn
1938	Andrew Leigh	Anthony Bernard
1941	Donald Wolfit	Mendelssohn
1942	Ben Iden Payne	Mendelssohn
1942	Robert Atkins	Mendelssohn
1943	Baliol Holloway	Mendelssohn
1944	Robert Atkins	Mendelssohn

date	company/adapter/director	music
1945	Nevill Coghill	Leslie Bridgewater
1949	Michael Benthall	Mendelssohn
1949	Robert Atkins	Mendelssohn
1954	George Devine	Roberto Gerhard
1954	Michael Benthall	Mendelssohn
1957	Michael Benthall	Mendelssohn
1959, 62–3	Peter Hall	Raymond Leppard
1960	Michael Langham	Thea Musgrave
1962	Tony Richardson	John Addison
1967	Frank Dunlop	John Dankworth
1970–3	Peter Brook	Richard Peaslee, Mendelssohn
1977	John Barton	Guy Woolfenden
1981–2	Ron Daniels	Stephen Oliver
1982	Bill Bryden	John Tams
1986–7	Bill Alexander	Jeremy Sams
1989–90	John Caird	Ilona Sekacz, Mendelssohn
1990	Kenneth Branagh	Patrick Doyle
1992	Robert Lepage	Adrian Lee, Peter Salem
1994	Adrian Noble	Ilona Sekacz

INDEX